SHAKESPEARE

Born in Manchester in 1917, Anthony Burgess was educated at the Xaverian College in the city and at Manchester
University, of which he held a doctorate. He served in the
army from 1940 to 1956, and as a colonial education officer in Malaya and Borneo from 1954 to 1960, in which
year, as he put it, 'his brief but irreversible unemployability
having been decreed by a medical death sentence, he
decided to try to live by writing'. His output comprises over
fifty books. He was a Visiting Fellow of Princeton University and a Distinguished Professor of City College, New
York. He was created a Commandeur des Arts et des Lettres
by the French President and a Commandeur de Merite
Culturel by Prince Rainier of Monaco. Anthony Burgess
died in 1993.

BY ANTHONY BURGESS

Anthony Burgess

SHAKESPEARE

VINTAGE

Published by Vintage 1996

2 4 6 8 10 9 7 5 3 1

First published in Great Britain by
Jonathan Cape Ltd, 1970

Vintage
Random House, 20 Vauxhall Bridge Road,
London SW1V 2SA

Random House Australia (Pty) Limited
20 Alfred Street, Milsons Point, Sydney
New South Wales 2061, Australia

Random House New Zealand Limited
18 Poland Road, Glenfield,
Auckland 10, New Zealand

Random House South Africa (Pty) Limited
PO Box 2263, Rosebank 2121, South Africa

Random House UK Limited Reg. No. 954009

A CIP catalogue record for this book
is available from the British Library

ISBN 0 09 959911 2

Papers used by Random House UK Ltd are natural, recy-
clable products made from wood grown in sustainable
forests. The manufacturing processes conform to the
environmental regulations of the country of origin

Printed and bound in Great Britain by
Cox & Wyman, Reading, Berkshire

Alla mia cara moglie

...O meraviglioso mondo nuovo
Che hai di questa gente...
LA TEMPESTA

Contents

Foreword

This is not a book about Shakespeare's plays and poems. It is yet another attempt—the *n*th—to set down the main facts about the life and society from which the poems and plays arose. If I discuss the content or technique of what Shakespeare and other men wrote, it is not with a view to providing literary history or literary criticism; it is because the people in this book are mostly professional writers, and what they attempted in their art often relates closely to what they did with their lives. But it is the lives that come first, and especially one particular life. I know that, as the materials available for a Shakespeare biography are very scanty, it is customary to make up the weight with what Dr. Johnson would have termed encomiastic rhapsodies, but we are all tired of being asked to admire Shakespeare's way with vowels or run-on lines or to thrill at the modernity of his philosophy or the profundity of his knowledge of the human heart. Genuine criticism is a different thing, but that has become very highly specialized, and there is certainly no room for it in a book of this kind.

What I claim here is the right of every Shakespeare-lover who has ever lived to paint his own portrait of the man. One is short of the right paints and brushes and knows one is going to end up with a botched and inadequate picture, but here I have real pictures to help me out. Or, put it another way, my task is to help the pictures.

I have already written two imaginative works on Shakespeare— a novel composed somewhat hurriedly to celebrate in 1964 the quatercentenary of his birth, and a script for a more than epic-length Hollywood film of his life. There is a great deal of verifiable fact in both these works, but there is also a great deal of guesswork, as well as some invention that has no basis even in probability. This present book contains conjecture—duly and timidly signaled by phrases like "It well may be that..." or "Conceivably, about this time...," but it eschews invention. There is, however, a chapter which attempts to reconstruct the first performance of *Hamlet*, and here I have silenced the little cracked fanfares of caution. Instead of saying that the actor Rice was probably, or possibly, a Welshman, I have asserted that he was, and even assigned parts like Fluellen and Sir Hugh Evans to him. The reader will recognize the fiction writer at work and, I hope, will make due allowances. All other assertions, in other chapters, can be accepted as true.

I once wrote an article in which I said that, given the choice between two discoveries—that of an unknown play by Shakespeare and that of one of Will's laundry lists—we would all plump for the dirty washing every time. That Shakespeare persists in presenting so shadowy a figure, when his friend Ben Jonson is as clear as a bell and somewhat louder, is one of our reasons for pursuing him. Every biographer longs for some new gesture of reality—a fingernail torn on May 7, 1598, or a bad cold during King James I's first command performance—but the gestures never materialize. We have Shakespeare's unlocked heart in the Sonnets, but these only prove that he fell in love and out of it, which happens to everybody. What we want are letters and doctors' prescriptions and the minutiae of daily life which build up to a character. It is maddening that Shakespeare gives us nothing when Ben is only too ready to accost us with his mountain belly and his rocky face. It is only among the unsound gossips in both past and present Warwickshire that we learn of Will's having no head for drink and his doses of clap. But gossip denotes concern, even love, and it is encouraging to see Shakespeare sometimes emerging today as a living folk-spirit in lavatory graffiti and pub jokes. Unfortunately, this book has no place for such things. It is, with all its faults, all too sound.

Shakespeare

Prologue

Queen Elizabeth I came to the throne of England in 1558, at the age of twenty-five—some six years before the birth of the man whom we regard as her greatest subject. She was the daughter of Henry VIII and Anne Boleyn. Henry's determination to marry that young woman had been the cause of a royal divorce and the establishment of a national Protestant church in England. To English and foreign Catholics, Elizabeth had no claim to the throne: she was a bastard. Nevertheless, the King of Spain himself—soon to be the great enemy—supported her claim: the alternative to Protestant Elizabeth was Catholic Mary, Queen of the Scots, and Mary was married to the Dauphin of France. The rivalry between the two great Catholic powers, France and Spain, kept Protestant England afloat until the death of the Dauphin. When Spain was thus free to subdue England, in the name of the Catholic Counter-Reformation, England was too strong to be subdued, but the struggle to prove this was stiff and lengthy.

The England of the young Elizabeth was poor in money, in ships, and in armed men. It was too poor to defend itself from enemies without, and the enemies within—chiefly those who thought her Protestantism had gone too far, and those who thought it had not gone far enough—were not easily kept under: the apparatus of true despotism, with a large bureaucracy and a secret police, was too costly for a whole revenue of only half a million pounds. If Elizabeth was to prevail—to keep peace within and keep invaders out—it could only be by the exercise of such personal endowments as cunning, charm, apparent pliability, real strength. She had the mind of a man and the arts of a woman.

She was an intellectual, a linguist, theologian, musician, poet, a great lover of plays, pageants, hunting and dancing. She was too clever to marry: she used her spinsterhood (termed virginity) as a bait and as a weapon. She had inherited her father's stubbornness and patriotism but not his capacity for blind and tyrannous rages. She had inherited her mother's allure and coquetry but not her foolishness and indiscretion. She kept her head and she would keep her head. This applied also to her heart. The Queen of Scots would lose one and then the other. Elizabeth died in her bed—almost forty-five years after her accession. She was lucky in her chief ministers—men like Sir William Cecil and Sir Francis Walsingham, and they were lucky in her.

She liked her own way but she had no love of the techniques of despotism. "I thank God," she told her Parliament, "I am endued with such qualities that if I were turned out of the realm in my petticoat, I were able to live in any place in Christendom." Prizing her own individuality, she prized individualism in others—so long as it could be turned to promoting the welfare of the state. In her reign, England became a great maritime power. This was because there were men whose skill at sea was sharpened by personal acquisitiveness. There was untold wealth waiting for the brave and curious in the new worlds that were opening up. Fire such acquisitiveness with patriotism and a liking for the Cranmer prayer book, and you could get a naval force that would mop up any number of invincible armadas.

England had once been on the very edge of the world. Now, with America discovered and even colonized, England was in the middle of it. The islanders' sense of their new importance, as well as the discovery of their new strength, promoted a zest and an energy and a love of life that had hardly been known before. There was even a pride in their language, that remote and once disregarded dialect, and an urge to make a literature that would match modern Italy's or even approach that of ancient Rome. The language itself was in the melting pot—not fixed and elegant and controlled by academics, but coarsely rich and ready for any adventures that would make it richer. English was a sort of Golden Hind.

The times were propitious for the birth of a great English poet.

I

Home

~~~~~~

The plays of Shakespeare have much to say against the evils of social ambition, but they are merely plays, entertainments for a couple of idle hours; they are not considered and sober testimonies of their author's convictions. For one of the few things we certainly know about the character of this glover, playwright, poet, actor, gentleman, is that he was socially ambitious. We may take that as an inherited quality, for his father was socially ambitious too. John Shakespeare was the son of Richard Shakespeare, a yeoman farmer of Snitterfield, which is a village a few miles to the northeast of Stratford-upon-Avon in Warwickshire. John was not content to plow the land for small profit, nor to live out his days among horny yokels. He turned himself into a tradesman and rose to the dignity of alderman of a fair borough.

Stratford, even in the middle of the sixteenth century, was all of that. A town of about fifteen hundred inhabitants, it sat in a fine wooded valley and was surrounded by crops and cattle. *Emporium non inelegans* was the summing-up of a contemporary gazetteer—a market town not lacking in grace, charm, and beauty. It was no backwater; it lay no more than a hundred miles from London and it had good communications with the historic towns of the Midlands—Worcester, Warwick, Banbury, Oxford. Its architecture was distinguished. Holy Trinity Church and the chapel of the Guild of the Holy Cross dated from the thirteenth century. The Avon was spanned by a not inelegant bridge, built in 1490 by Sir Hugh Clopton. Sir Hugh Clopton was a perpetual reminder that there were greater ambitions than those that a John Shakespeare might fulfill, for that pontifex had left Stratford to become lord mayor of London. Not even William Shakespeare became that, but his ambitions were not civic. It was enough for him to be able to buy Sir Hugh's house in Stratford and act his last part there—that of a retired private gentleman.

John Shakespeare's ambitions were decent enough in the field of what a yeoman's son might reasonably attain—prosperous small-town tradesman, respected small-town burgess; but he had an ambition in a different sphere, and this was mystical and concerned with blood. He wanted the Shakespeare name to carry an aura not only of present achievement but of past glory. The name was, and is, a very satisfactory one: it connotes aggression, libido, and no fantastication of the spelling—Shogspar, Choxper, or whatever else the scrivener's ingenuity could contrive—can totally mask the image of some remote warlike progenitor. But John knew that the name was not an aristocratic one. When, in the 1570s, he first made application for a coat of arms, which meant confirmation in the rank of Gentleman, he conjured some vague great ancestor honored by Henry VII. The conjuration did not achieve any sharpness of definition, for the application was, for reasons we can deal with later, speedily withdrawn. But when, in 1596, a new application was made, its confidence owing much to William's achievement (in money more than in art), the main claim of blood was a vicarious one. It was hoped that Garter King-of-Arms would be moved by John's having married "the daughter and heir of Arden, a gentleman of worship." As we know, the arms were granted, and we may assume that the grounds were Shakespeare achievement more than Arden blood. Still, when the grant was confirmed in 1599, there was an official addition: "We have lykewise uppon an other escutcheone impaled the same with the Auncyent Arms of the said Arden of Wellingcote."

Wellingcote was really Wilmcote, three miles northwest of Stratford. The locals, including William Shakespeare himself, called it Wincot, and as Wincot it appears in the introduction to *The Taming of the Shrew*. The daughter and heir of Arden was Mary, and the Shakespeares had, up to the time of John's striking out, been tenants of the Ardens. There is something

satisfyingly romantic about a yeoman's son wooing and winning
the daughter of the aristocratic landlord. But the Ardens were,
in their circumstances if not in their blood, not all that
aristocratic. Robert Arden, farmer of Wilmcote and owner of
the Snitterfield farm where Richard Shakespeare was tenant,
was comfortable, but he had to work for his comfort. He was in
the position of the runt of the litter, what the French call the
cadet. The real glories and wealth of the Ardens lay elsewhere—
in, for instance, the mansion called Park Hall near Birming-
ham. Still, a younger son could take pride in belonging to a
family that had been vigorous before the Conquest and had lost
few of its possessions to the Conqueror. The Ardens had been
called Turchill in the days when England was an Anglo-Saxon
kingdom; when an Anglo-Saxon name became a badge of the
conquered, they took the name of the great Midland forest. It is
not this forest that appears in *As You Like It*; the Forest of Arden
there is Shakespeare's own exotic invention, but it is a creation
to which he gives—with pride, one presumes—his mother's
family name. And in this forest which is also a dukedom he
carefully plants a William.

Mary was the eighth daughter of Robert Arden. When he
died in 1556, her portion was surprisingly large—six pounds
odd and a sixty-acre farm called Asbies. This, to the man she
married, must have seemed a useful piece of potential collat-
eral, its cash value more important than its cultivability. He was
glad, when hard times came in 1578, to mortgage it for forty
pounds. But in 1557, the probable year of their marriage, there
was only the exhilaration of a new life. The yeoman's son was
an independent tradesman, the aristocrat's daughter a tradesman's wife, and they had their own house and shop in a
bustling, not inelegant, country town. In a sense, they were
very Elizabethan in their willingness to break away from the old
inherited agrarian pattern, but Mary was probably the more
conservative of the two. The family house and estate were only
a few miles away, there were undoubted contacts with the
greater Ardens, who might even call at the shop-house in
Henley Street to break a journey from Park Hall to London via
Oxford. In religion, the Ardens tended to the ancient Catholic

loyalty, while John Shakespeare, as a tradesman, probably favored the strict Brownist or Puritan faith that was eventually to flourish in the Midlands and turn England into a holy republic. We have no evidence of strong piety on either John's or Mary's side, and this lukewarmness, along with social ambition and fiery (or ardent) family pride, seems to have been passed on to the eldest son.

John Shakespeare's trade was that of glover. There must also have been a penumbra of cognate trades around this central one: he was surely interested, commercially, in other products of the calf than its skin. He may have bought calves on the hoof and sold the flesh before cutting the tranks. There is certainly a tradition that turns him into a butcher and has young William recapitulating the evolution of drama from bloody sacrifice by making him kill the calves to the accompaniment of highflown speeches, as though he were Brutus and the little brutes all Caesars. Remember *Hamlet*:

> POLONIUS: I did enact Julius Caesar; I was kill'd i' the Capitol; Brutus kill'd me.
>
> HAMLET: It was a brute part of him to kill so capital a calf there.

This is all fancy, and we believe what we wish, so long as we do not assume the Shakespeare house to be sweetly lavender-smelling. It may not have been a shambles, but William must have been born into certain characteristic stinks. As for the trade of glover, we must not imagine John Shakespeare's entering on it with amateur's lightness, like a man of today opening a tobacconist's shop. He had to be a member of the Craft of Glovers, Whitetawers (dressers of white leather) and Collar-makers, and this entailed the prior serving of a seven-year apprenticeship. Stratford records show that he was already selling gloves in Henley Street in 1552, so that his marriage to Mary Arden comes presumably in a period of certainty, people buying Shakespeare gloves and the future bright. John was good at clothing five fingers, as his son was to be good at clothing five feet.

In the civic sphere, John Shakespeare began to do well as soon as he achieved the settled gravity of marriage. A bachelor father of the community is an uncleanly idea: a borough councilor needs a wife to take to mayoral banquets and to serve wine and kickshawses when brother dignitaries call at the house to play politics ("If we can get enough votes together we can have *him* thrown out as well as his proposal"). In 1557 John was elected to the Common Council and made borough ale-taster —a job for a sober man. He was constable in 1558, affeeror in 1559 (an affeeror assessed amercements; amercements were mulcts or penalties imposed by a local court; these were of a discretionary kind, unfixed by statute). Then 1562 saw him appointed chamberlain and—this was quite without prece- dent—he held the office for four years. The chamberlain's duties were highly responsible ones: they entailed keeping the borough accounts, paying relief money when catastrophes like plague hit the town (this happened in 1564, the year of William's birth), doling out the meager fees of visiting troupes of actors. Thus it was John who gave nine shillings to the Queen's Players and twelve pence (it sounds more put like that) to the Earl of Worcester's Men when they came to entertain Stratford. I need not stress the relevance of this aspect of the office to our main subject. The young William knew about players—how they were organized and what they did. In 1568 John was made bailiff, and it was by virtue of this appointment that he might justly claim to be a gentleman and seek his coat of arms.

The claim, as we know, was made, but it was withdrawn. In 1577, after twenty years of service and high office, John ceased to attend the meetings of the Council. Something had gone wrong. In 1578 he was one of six aldermen who failed to contribute to the cost of a constabulary—four men with bills, three men with pikes, and one man with a bow and arrow. He stopped paying the statutory aldermanic subscription of four- pence a week for poor relief. He was in debt. In 1579 his wife's estate Asbies had to be mortgaged. It is conceivable that John Shakespeare had been neglecting his shop for the sake of his civic duty, which was also his civic glory. In 1586, reasonably enough, he was stripped of the one because he had not fulfilled the other: "Mr. Shaxpere dothe not come to the Halles when they be warned nor hathe not done of longe tyme." Farewell the aldermanic fur.

There was other trouble. In 1580 he was summoned before the Queen's Bench in Westminster, along with 140 other men of the region, to provide sureties that he would maintain the Queen's peace. He did not go, and he was fined twenty pounds. He was at the same time fined another twenty pounds in respect of a man in the same position for whom he had stood surety. John Shakespeare had not been breaking the peace in any spectacular way. He had probably been acting sullen and had been keeping away from church as well as from "the Halles." And it was breaking the law, or the peace, not to go to the services of the Church of England. We must not think of him, much as we would like to, as talking loudly in his cups of the superiority of the Puritan God over the Angelic one; recusancy could be a negative thing. Three years later, recusancy of a more positive kind flashed out from the family of Mary Shakespeare. An Arden had his head cut off for being involved in a Catholic conspiracy, and the head was stuck for men to see and kites to eat on London Bridge. There was, well known to the Shakespeares, a man very ready to harry both the flanks of heresy—Catholic and Puritan indifferently. This was Archbishop Whitgift of Canterbury, elevated from the diocese of Worcester to be the official scourge for England's God and a great bore. John Shakespeare failed in his modest ambitions and knew penal fear. Things only came right again in the final years of the century, when William had made money and restored the family honor.

William was the Shakespeares' third child, but the first to live beyond infancy. Joan was born in 1558. There is no record of her death, but we must assume she was already dead in 1569, when another Joan was born. This new Joan was to demonstrate that there was nothing essentially feeble about the name. She lived to the age of seventy-seven and, through her marriage to William Hart the hatter, became the sole instrument of transmitting the Shakespeare genes to far posterity. The Harts beat on today with Shakespeare blood in them. John and Mary's second child, Margaret, was born in November 1562 and died the following April. April has always been a cruel month in England, and not just in the ironical sense of *The Waste Land*. The daffodils are there but the winds are bitter and the body weak after the long English winter. Another daughter, Anne, died in her eighth year in April 1579. William himself was to die in April. He also dared the fates by being born in April. That was 1564, in a bad season of plague. Undoubtedly his mother, determined that this third child and first son should survive, bundled him away to Wilmcote and the clean secluded air.

We do not know the exact date of William's birth, but the parish register records that Gulielmus, son of Johannes, was christened on April 26, 1564. The old Catholic custom of christening children as soon as possible after birth had not yet gone: wash original sin off the child's soul and, if he died immediately after, it was some comfort to know he was not languishing in Limbo. As William died on April 23, 1616, it has been found convenient to make that also his birthday. It is St. George's Day and helps to reinforce Shakespeare's function as one of England's chauvinistic glories. The neat symmetry is a kind of harmless magic. As we shall see, it fits in with the forty-sixth Psalm's eternization of the great name Shake-spear by including it, piecemeal, among its other resplendent words. Shakespeare was also once thought to have produced a genetic miracle. His first child was born six months after his marriage and lived and flourished. No delinquent imputation dare be attached to him, the Bard. Ergo, God had speeded up the process of gestation as a mark of special favor.

Because we love the man, or rather his works, this side idolatry, we are all prone to attach magic to the very name. We like to feel, for instance, that the only English pope, Nicholas Breakspear, was drawn by the gods into the right onomastic area for international greatness, but that for him to be called Shakespeare would have been going too far. Adrian IV, with his bull *Laudabiliter*, broke the spears of the Irish. His rimesake is caught in a pose of entirely benevolent aggression. The gods knew what they were doing. As for the baptismal name, we like to think of it as wholly appropriate in its familiar form Will. We would not want to call Milton Jack, but Shakespeare seems to ask for an intimacy of address. This has something to do with a great creative libido, a love of bawdry, and the compound invitation we find in the following sonnet:

> Whoever hath her wish, thou hast thy Will,
> And Will to boot, and Will in overplus;
> More than enough am I that vex thee still,
> To thy sweet will making addition thus.
> Wilt thou, whose will is large and spacious,
> Not once vouchsafe to hide my will in thine?
> Shall will in others seem right gracious,
> And in my will no fair acceptance shine?
> The sea, all water, yet receives rain still,
> And in abundance addeth to his store;
> So thou, being rich in Will, add to thy Will
> One will of mine, to make thy large Will more.
> Let no unkind, no fair beseechers kill;
> Think all but one, and me in that one Will.

There the connotations of the name Will are exploited to the limit—lust, phallus, vagina. The sonnet is wittily lecherous and must have begged to be copied out, learnt by heart, grinned over in taverns and the Inns of Court. And there, walking the London streets, is Will with the large will. Will Shakespeare—the name is a small hymn to male thrust, Him that shaketh his spear and breaketh hymens. From now on we shall say Will, and not William.

With the birth and survival of Will, the male Shakespeare element became assertive. Another son, Gilbert, was born in 1566, and yet another, Richard, in 1574. The last child was Edmund, born in 1580, the child of a year of ill fortune. The total record of longevity, if we leave the second Joan out of the tally, is not impressive. Will was to die at fifty-two, Gilbert at forty-five, and Richard at thirty-eight. Edmund, who became an actor like Will, was to die at twenty-seven. None of these sons left any issue except Will, and Will's own son was to die at eleven. Mary Shakespeare, then, bore a total of eight children, three of whom were lost very early and only one of whom was to reach old age.

We wonder what Will's brothers and sisters were like. We know nothing at all about them: there is not even any record of Edmund's acting career. There is an eighteenth-century tradition that Gilbert went once to London and saw his brother Will act the part of a decrepit old man with a long beard, who had to be carried to a table to eat and, while he ate, somebody sang a song. This is evidently Will as Adam in *As You Like It*. As for Richard, Richard is a mere name.

There is no harm in imposing appearance and character on the brothers and sisters, so long as we regard this as a mere device for solidifying Will's physical background. We are entitled to visualize him as a boy eating, singing, and sleeping in the house on Henley Street, and it is convenient to have him surrounded by something thicker than swatches of ectoplasm with name tags. For my part, I seize on the song in *Love's Labor's Lost* to visualize the sister Joan as a greasy girl who spends much of her time washing pots and pans in cold water. Gilbert I see as dully pious and possibly epileptic, the source of the falling sickness that comes in both *Julius Caesar* and *Othello*. I think of him as a stolid carver of tranks and snipper of gussets, a natural successor to his father in the glover's trade. Of Richard, Stephen Dedalus in the Scylla and Charybdis chapter of James Joyce's *Ulysses* has taught us to think in more sinister terms. Will's wife was Anne. In *Richard III* the villainous eponym seduces an Anne. He is hunchbacked and he limps. In *Hamlet* another brother seduces the widow of a man whose son's name is close enough to the name of Will's own son— Hamnet. Will is believed to have played the father's ghost when the play was performed at the Globe Theatre. The brother's name is Claudius, which means a limper. Richard III and Claudius conjoin in the real brother Richard. He may have been sly and lecherous and, in Will's absence in London, ready to post to incestuous sheets. He may have limped. On the other hand, he may have been an upright well-made young man who loved his eldest brother and respected his sister-in-law. I cannot push Edmund beyond the image of a baby crawling and dribbling among the rushes of the living-room floor. I see nothing of him in the Edmund of *King Lear*.

The parents John and Mary seem, without benefit of novelist's fancy, already solid enough for all practical purposes. Mary talks of her great connections but, when her husband has sunk low, is perhaps too much of a lady to make many wounding comparisons between the respective achievements of the Ardens and the Shakespeares. She has borne many children and seen too many of them die. She has learnt to be a philosophical and prudent housewife, quiet in sorrow, patient under affliction; but she has not learnt to subdue the family pride. John is ebullient but capable of depression and of sullenness. He is a voluble talker and perhaps something of a blusterer and bluffer. From such a combination, with the addition of literary talent, an actor-dramatist might well emerge. It is doubtful if the elder Shakespeares had much time for literature, but we need not assume that either was illiterate. John Shakespeare was known to make his mark with a cross, but that is no proof of illiteracy: many literate Elizabethans seem to have wearied occasionally of signing their names (or perhaps wearied of trying to establish a consistent spelling) and scratched a cross instead. Even today businessmen, to show how busy they are, sign letters with an indecipherable ideogram. Mary might well have gone to school, as many Elizabethan girls did. There may even have been a few books in the house on Henley Street—the Geneva Bible, a prayer book, a manual like Andrew Boorde's *A Breviarie of Health* (useless at best, at worst lethal). But it was Will who was to import the real literature.

That the Shakespeare parents were kind to their children we have no reason to doubt. Samuel Butler, author of the classic study of father-son enmity, *The Way of All Flesh*, points out that in Shakespeare's plays the father and son are always friends. The notion of the rude son striking the father dead is one of the most terrible symptoms of the breakdown of social order that Ulysses, in *Troilus and Cressida*, can conceive. If this seems to imply that the status of the Elizabethan father was godlike, we can take it that this was an easy convention, healthy like all conventions, for conventions do not have to be taken seriously.

The loving paterfamilias of Victorian England was the true, terrible, unpredictable, vindictive Jehovah, weaving numinous clouds under his smoking-cap. One cannot think that there were frightful Freudian repressions bubbling away in the young Shakespeare. Whatever troubles he knew in his father's house were imposed, not immanent. His love of his parents seems proved by certain gifts of his maturity—the pastoral kingdom of *As You Like It* for his mother, and for his father the coat of arms of a gentleman. The two men could toast that in a pot of ale, smiling at each other, brothers in achieved ambition.

2

School

❦❧❦❧❦❧❦❧❦❧❦❧❦❧❦❧❦❧❦❧

Shakespeare biographers of the romantic school have always been ready to give us full-blown portraits of the artist as a young dog. F. J. Furnivall, for instance:

> So our chestnut-haired, fair, brown-eyed, rosy-cheekt boy went to school. . . . Taking the boy to be the father of the man, I see a square-built yet lithe and active fellow, with ruddy cheeks, hazel eyes, a high forehead, and auburn hair, as full of life as an egg is full of meat, impulsive, inquiring, sympathetic; up to any fun and daring; into scrapes, and out of them with a laugh . . .

One reads this uneasily and then wonders what, apart from the *Boy's Own Paper* tone, is really wrong with it. We possess a couple of mature portraits of Shakespeare; we know his coloring and the shape of his face. The high forehead probably came with baldness, and we can see the boy with chestnut locks tumbling over his eyes if we wish. Dr. Caroline Spurgeon, in her *Shakespeare's Imagery*, invites us, on the strength of certain descriptive preoccupations in the plays and poems, to believe that he flushed and whitened easily, and that he was strongly aware of the mechanism of the face's responses to emotional stimuli. He could probably hide little and was bad at the dissimulation needed to escape lawful punishment. We can assume that he was healthy. He had survived the normal hazards of an April birth as well as the free gift of the plague. We cannot doubt the intelligence and quickness and the emotional lability. Being myopic myself, I suspect that Shakespeare was myopic. He sees the minutiae of the natural world, as well as the writing on the human face, with the excessive clarity of one who peers. He was undoubtedly a reader. He probably read while other boys got into scrapes.

Not that, by our standards, there was much to read. Nor was the public education of the times likely to encourage, save in the exceptional, a love of books. Will possibly started his public education early, entering a petty school at the age of seven. He would already know how to read and write English, having worked through the alphabet with a hornbook—"A per se A, B per se B," and so on to "& per se &," which gives us *ampersand*. If you knew the alphabet, you could put English words together: no learning of phonic groups, "i before e except after c," *symmetry* and *cemetery*, *harass* and *embarrass*. The spelling of English then was gloriously impressionistic. It awaited the rough-and-ready rationalization of Civil War journalism, when editors were too rushed to bother with anything except the most economical spellings and ignored the old need to fill out or to "justify" a line of type with supernumerary letters (turning, for instance, *then* to *thenne* or *wit* to *witte* or even *only* to *ondelyche* at the end of a line, so as to secure a uniform right-hand margin). More than that, it awaited the systematization of Dr. Johnson's great Dictionary of 1755. To learne to wrytte doune Ingglisshe wourdes in Chaxper's daie was notte dificulte. Nobody rapped you for orthographical solecisms, for there were none. Anything went, from Queen Elizabeth downwards.

The purpose of the petty school, whose qualification for entry was minimal literacy in English, was to prepare scholars for the hard grind of the grammar school. A grammar school had one purpose only and that was proclaimed in its name—to teach grammar, Latin grammar. No history, geography, music, handicrafts, physical training, biology, chemistry, physics; only Latin grammar. William Lily, first high master of St. Paul's School, dead in 1522, lived on in a *Grammaticis Rudimenta* which was the secular bible of Stratford Grammar School as much as Eton or Westminster. It was to the grind of Lily's Grammar that the young Shakespeare was committed, a dull pedantic gateway to the glories of Rome.

Latin is disappearing from our modern curricula. There are even self-proclaimed students of Roman literature who have never read Ovid or Virgil in the original. But Elizabethan England looked to the Roman Empire as a model of the civic virtues; the heroes of the English were Roman heroes. A Brutus had once been believed to be the founder of Britain, and a textbook of English history could be called, as Layamon's chronicle had been called, simply a Brut. The Romans, though dead, inhabited a higher plane of reality than the English, dead or living. The English language, being alive, moving and untidy, lacked the calm and finished patterns that Lily laid out on his anatomist's slab. Admittedly there had been Geoffrey Chaucer, but his language was quaint and his verses did not seem to scan. To find culture a man had to go to the ancient world. The greatness of the Greeks was acknowledged, but there were not many Greek scholars around, especially in small towns like Stratford. The universities were your proper Greekmongers. Roman culture had absorbed Greek, and you could learn all about Troy and the wanderings of Ulysses from Latin authors. Latin had everything. The learning of Latin did not, as today, require any justification. "Today, boys, we start Latin, and perhaps you'll wonder why we bother, in this day and age, with the tongue of a long-dead nation. Don't yawn, Wetherby." None of that. The Elizabethan Latinists wielded rods of authority. Sometimes, alas, all too literally.

It was generally acknowledged among Elizabethan educationists that children had to have knowledge crammed, and sometimes beaten, into them. There were more than two centuries to go before the romantic view of children, the creation of men like Wordsworth and Rousseau, became current, and children were regarded as repositories of divine wisdom. Wordsworth looked with awe on the aura of prenatal knowledge that glowed about the infant, and he called him the best philosopher. The child was ready equipped with a grasp of eternal truth, and growing up was a process of forgetting, of seeing the divine light fade into the murk of common day. This notion had been long propounded in Plato's dialogue *Phaedo*, where a slave child without education is, with gentle leading or education from

Socrates, shown to be capable of demonstrating advanced geometry. The Elizabethans knew this dialogue, but they did not take it seriously.

Elizabethan parents could be tender, but they could not be sentimental. They were unromantic about children perhaps because children were so expendable: they died off, as Will's sisters did, and had to be replaced. Even the Shakespeares' unwillingness to waste a good name, Joan, may be seen as an aspect of their realism. The sooner children became adults the better, and one could make a start by dressing them like adults: the notion that children should dress like children is a very new one. It was left to the teachers, not the parents, to be impatient that children were so slow in learning to *behave* like adults, and the slowness was seen as an aspect of original sin. It had to be beaten out; the resultant vacuum had to be filled with useful (i.e., useless) adult knowledge, and the need to do this was so urgent that there was no time for play. School was grim. Those bottom-worn benches were no beds of roses, though Lilies lay on the desks.

The schoolboy began at seven in winter and six in summer. After praying to be made good and holy boys, full of Latin, the pupils got down to work till nine, when they were allowed breakfast. More work till eleven, and then a blessed two-hour gap for the main meal of the day. Back to school at one, salt meat and sour ale and dark bread grumbling within, and hard slog till five. Two half-days off a week, forty days vacation a year. The day might have been more tolerable if only the work had been varied, and if only humane and realistic pedagogic techniques had been employed. But education was less leading than feeding. I was once told, and by a Jesuit Latin teacher too, that *educate* came from an *educare* that was cognate with *manducare*, meaning to eat, and had nothing to do with that dictionary *educare* which is close to *educere*, to draw out. This false etymology seems to have been at the root of Elizabethan pedagogics, and the feeding was gross, overfacing, and screamingly monotonous.

One can believe that Will's masters saw Latin poetry, drama, and history less as the delightful end towards which the learning of grammar moved, than as useful material for illustrating the rules. The Romans kindly wrote books so that Master Lily could produce a grammar. Nothing we learn of the chief masters of Stratford Grammar School in Will's time disabuses us of the suspicion that they were, to say the least, uninspired. On the other hand, they do not seem to have been sadists. Walter Roche did not care much for education anyway, and he left the mastership to practice law in Stratford. That was in 1571, when Will was only seven. Simon Hunt followed, a crypto-Catholic who, though inclined to Jesuitry, was weak on discipline. He died in Rome in 1585, a minor pillar of the Counter-Reformation. Thomas Jenkins took over from him in 1575, a Welshman whom Shakespeare apparently eternized as Sir Hugh Evans in *The Merry Wives of Windsor*. Sir Hugh (whose honorific does not denote a knighthood but the possession of a bachelor's degree) is no fearsome lasher: he is likable and comic. He unvoices some of his voiced stops in the manner of all stage Welshmen (seeing through Falstaff's female disguise, for instance, by spotting his "great peard"). Significantly, he examines a boy called William in Latin, and this enables Mistress Quickly to make corny jokes about "poor Jenny's case" and *hanc hoc*, turned to "hang-hog," being Latin for bacon, I warrant you. Very poor schoolboy wit, probably drawn straight from 1575, when Jenkins was new and Will only eleven.

We cannot doubt that Will gained something, perhaps a great deal, from the Latin texts he read at school. He loved Ovid and was probably overjoyed when, towards the end of the century, Francis Meres wrote: "As the soule of *Euphorbus* was thought to live in *Pythagoras*: so the sweete wittie soule of *Ovid* lives in mellifluous and hony-tongued *Shakespeare*." The classical imagery of the plays is frequently drawn from Ovid's *Metamorphoses*, the fifteen books of mythological tales which are loosely linked with the theme of miraculous transformation. Most of the myths of Greece and Rome are here and even, as a *bonne bouche*, the murder and deification of Julius Caesar. The story of Pyramus and Thisbe, which most of us first meet in *A Midsummer Night's Dream* and can therefore never take seriously, is in Book IV, along with Perseus and Andromeda (those

two wall-defying lovers, incidentally, are exotics—from Babylon, not Greece or Rome). In Book X young Will read about
Venus and Adonis, but probably considered making his own
poem about them only when the myth seemed to strike home in
his own personal life—we shall discuss that later. Proserpina,
whom *The Winter's Tale* loads with Warwickshire flowers, comes
in Book V. All the myths that season the poems and plays are
there in the *Metamorphoses*.

It is likely that Will did not wholly rely on the Latin to learn
what Ovid was saying. The *Metamorphoses* were translated by
Arthur Golding and published in the first few years of Will's
life. Ezra Pound says: "Can we... know our Ovid until we find
him in Golding? Is there one of us so good at his Latin, and so
ready in imagination that Golding will not throw upon his mind
shades and glamours inherent in the original text which had for
all that escaped him?" Here is Golding translating Book V:

> While in this garden Proserpine was taking hir pastime,
> In gathering eyther Violets blew, or Lillies white as Lime,
> And while of Maidenly desire she fillde hir Haund and Lap,
> Endeauoring to outgather hir companions there. By hap
> Dis spide her: lovde her; caught her up: and all at once were
> nere.
> So hastie, hote, and swift a thing is Loue as may appeare.

This measure is the old "fourteener"—seven iambic feet to the
line—and Will must have been aware of its comparative crudity.
But English verse had to learn and, if the swelling Renaissance
melody was not yet ready, the narrative sweep was already there:
it was being learnt out of the craft of translation.

This craft of translation had, in the Earl of Surrey's *Certain
Bokes of Virgiles Aeneis*, published (in 1557) before Shakespeare's birth, already produced an experimental metric that was
to transform the whole face of English literature and make
possible Elizabethan drama as we know it.

> They whistled all, with fixèd face attent
> When Prince Aeneas from the royal seat
> Thus gan to speak, O Queene, it is thy will,
> I should renew a woe can not be told:

How that the Grekes did spoile and overthrow
The Phrygian wealth, and wailful realm of Troy,
Those ruthful things that I myself beheld.

This is the first poem in blank verse, a form Surrey devised in order to meet the rhymeless challenge of Virgil's hexameters. It is, or course, profitless to speculate what might have happened to Elizabethan drama (or the Miltonic epic, for that matter) if Surrey had not tried to find a suitable verse-medium for rendering Latin epic poetry. Somebody else might have hit on blank verse, or the drama might have developed in the rhymed couplets that make up so much of *Romeo and Juliet* and *Richard II*. But blank verse was there, waiting, seven years before Shakespeare's birth, and it might not have been there if Englishmen had not esteemed the classics so highly that they wanted to turn them into English poetry. A new literature is often born out of the translating of an old one.

We can assume that other Roman poets as well as Ovid and Virgil came into the Stratford curriculum—Horace, perhaps a little Catullus and Lucretius. For prose, there would be Livy, Caesar, Tacitus (though Tacitus would be dangerous: he broke too many of Master Lily's rules). That mixture of morality and biography which the Elizabethans loved could be obtained from Suetonius's *Twelve Caesars*. Plutarch was a better moralist, and his *Parallel Lives* of twenty-three Romans and Greeks arranged in pairs would provide a fine ethical stiffening for a narrow philological course, but Plutarch wrote in Greek. Will was later (or perhaps even in his schooldays, extramurally) to read Plutarch in North's translation from Amyot's French translation. In his Roman plays he followed North closely. This is proved—to take a notable example—by comparison of North's description of Cleopatra in her barge with Shakespeare's astonishing blank-verse heightening of the plain North *donnée*. We can see Will tearing off his lines with North in front of him as his guide. Here are the prose facts; a little manipulation will turn them into poetry. Cold North to hot south (Egypt as it ought to have been, whether it was or not) with a few magic strokes. Thus North:

... she disdained to set forward otherwise, but to take her barge
in the river of Cydnus, the poop whereof was of gold, the sails of
purple, and the oars of silver, which kept stroke in rowing after
the sound of the music of flutes, hautboys, citherns, viols, and
such other instruments as they played upon in the barge. And
now for the person of herself: she was laid under a pavilion of
cloth of gold of tissue, appareled and attired like the goddess
Venus, commonly drawn in picture: and hard by her, on either
hand of her, pretty fair boys appareled as painters do set forth
god Cupid, with little fans in their hands, with the which they
fanned wind upon her. Her ladies and gentlewomen also, the
fairest of them were appareled like the nymphs Nereids (which
are the mermaids of the waters) and like the Graces, some
steering the helm, others tending the tackle and ropes of the
barge, out of the which there came a wonderful passing sweet
savor of perfumes, that perfumed the wharf's side, pestered with
innumerable multitudes of people. Some of them followed the
barge all alongst the river's side: others also ran out of the city to
see her coming in. So that in the end, there ran such multitudes
of people one after another to see her, that Antonius was left
post alone in the marketplace, in his imperial seat to give
audience...

And Shakespeare:

The barge she sat in, like a burnish'd throne,
Burn'd on the water. The poop was beaten gold;
Purple the sails, and so perfumèd that
The winds were lovesick with them. The oars were silver,
Which to the tune of flutes kept stroke, and made
The water which they beat to follow faster,
As amorous of their strokes. For her own person,
It beggar'd all description. She did lie
In her pavilion, cloth of gold of tissue,
O'er-picturing that Venus where we see
The fancy outwork Nature. On each side her
Stood pretty dimpled boys, like smiling Cupids,
With divers-colored fans, whose wind did seem

To glow the delicate cheeks which they did cool,
And what they undid, did...
Her gentlewomen—like the Nereids,
So many mermaids—tended her i' the eyes
And made their bends adorings. At the helm
A seeming mermaid steers. The silken tackle
Swell with the touches of those flower-soft hands,
That yarely frame the office. From the barge
A strange invisible perfume hits the sense
Of the adjacent wharfs. The city cast
Her people out upon her: and Antony,
Enthron'd i' the marketplace, did sit alone...

The Romans wrote plays, and Plautus and Terence had to be
brought into the Stratford curriculum. Certainly *The Comedy of
Errors* attests Will's close study of the *Menaechmi* of Plautus,
and it is doubtful if, at the penniless start of his career as a
dramatist, he had time to read Plautus to see how to write a
farce about mixing up twins. He read it at school or (another
possibility, as we shall see) taught it in school, and remembered
it well enough to make it the model of an apprentice comedy. It
is conceivable that, under Jenkins, who might have had the
Welsh histrionic gift along with the *hwyl*, the boys of Stratford
Grammar School actually performed the *Menaechmi* or some
other play of Terence or Plautus, to which proud and uncompre-
hending parents were invited, and that Will of the mobile face
strutted the improvised boards in a foreign tongue. If not yet in
himself, certainly in the world outside, Plautus and Terence
were helping to prepare the way for professional drama. Nicholas Udall, headmaster of Eton before being dismissed for some
unspecified grave charge, later headmaster of a more tolerant
Westminster, had died eight years before Will's birth, but not
before producing the first English secular comedy—*Ralph Rois-
ter Doister*. He was, needless to say, soaked in the comic
Romans. Thomas Tusser, author of *A Hundreth Good Pointes
of Husbandrie*, complained of being severely flogged by Udall
"for fault but small or none at all," so that it was possible for a

teacher to be a sadist as well as a jolly thespian. Or perhaps Udall loved the drama of the swishing taws.

There was also the tragedian Seneca to be studied, though it was less as a dramaturge, and a very influential one, that he appealed to Elizabethan educationists than as a moral philosopher. Seneca lived under Caligula, Claudius, and Nero and had good cause to formulate the stoical guide to living, and dying, which appealed so much to the graver sort in Tudor England. He incurred Caligula's hate, was banished from Rome at the instigation of Messalina, and, back in Rome again, committed suicide when the Neronian tyranny was at its blackest. His themes are dignity in adversity, the ultimate inviolability of the just man, the virtues of a kind of Confucian "human-heartedness"; in his writings the Christian and pagan worlds seem to meet. T. S. Eliot sees his stoicism in the whistling-in-the-dark doggedness of Shakespeare's beset tragic heroes. This, and the question of Seneca's formal influence as a composer of chamber tragedies (tragedies for private recitation rather than public acting), we shall have to consider later. Will the schoolboy was probably little exposed to Seneca the dramatist. When the time came to write his own early tragedies, he went to the translators and the imitators. *Gorboduc*, the first notable piece of Senecan tragedy in English, had been acted before the Queen in 1561, three years before Will's birth. The "Tenne Tragedies" were translated in 1581. There was little need for the tragic apprentice to go straight back to the Latin.

If Will read the Romans in translation while still a boy, where did he get the books? There is no problem here. John Bretchgirdle, the local rector, had a fair-sized library and even gave books away to those likely to profit from them. There must have been other bookish men. One doubts, during the penurious period when Will was a schoolboy, whether John Shakespeare was ever able to dole out money for his son to buy books to put on a private shelf in the bedroom he shared with a brother or brothers. But a boy who wants books will always get them somehow. Especially if, for his further education, he is totally reliant on books.

The learning displayed in Shakespeare's plays seems, to some, incompatible with the plain classical fodder purveyed by a rural grammar school. In the nineteenth century the Baconian heresy sprang up, with its contention that only a heavily erudite man, university trained, skilled in the law and the sciences, his eyes and ears schooled by the Grand Tour, could write the works traditionally attributed to a player out of the gross byre or pigsty of Warwickshire. I do not wish to go into the cryptogrammatic detail which makes Baconians see in the word "honorificabili- tudinitatibus" (*Love's Labor's Lost*, Act V, Scene 1) a cipher for "These plays, F. Bacon's offspring, are preserved for the world," though Bacon is welcome, except for the songs at the end, to have one suety comedy. It is enough to note that people exist who spend time (better given to rereading the plays for pleasure) on demolishing Shakespeare's authorship and attributing his works not only to Bacon but to anyone else with a title or a well-attested university education. There have been many can- didates for the post of True Author, from the Earl of Oxford to the first Elizabeth herself. The least implausible attribution is that made to Will's fellow playwright Christopher Marlowe, who is supposed to have shammed dead to escape his enemies and then, from exile, ghosted for Shakespeare. This sort of theory has its own fascination, but it is of a crossword or whodunnit order.

It boils down to this: Shakespeare could not make himself a supreme man of letters without benefit of something better than a free grammar school education. And that he had nothing more than this seems evident. There is no record of his going to the university. He was married in his teens and, besides, where was the money to come from? But it is nonsense to suppose that high art needs high learning. Any peasant can teach himself to write, and write well. Any peasant writer can, by reading the appropriate books and by keeping his senses alert, give the illusion of great knowledge of the world. The plays of Shake- speare, through the trickery of the artist, give the illusion that their creator has traveled widely, practiced all the learned professions, bent his supple knee in courts domestic and for- eign. The brilliant surface suggests an erudition and an experi- ence that need not, in fact, be there: the artist does not have to be a courtier, traveler, or scholar, though it may be his task to create such men out of his imagination. The Baconians and the rest of the heretics are deluded into thinking that a work of art is of the same order as a work of scholarship: this play shows a knowledge of the law, therefore the playwright must have studied the law; that play is set in Upper Mongrelia, therefore the playwright must have traveled thither. There are no Baconians among practicing literary artists, and there never have been: they know too much about the workings of the minds of professional writers.

"A snapper-up of unconsidered trifles"—that is Autolycus in *The Winter's Tale*; it is also Shakespeare and, indeed, any writer of drama or narrative fiction. The writer needs a scrap of psychoanalytical terminology: he does not have to read the whole of Freud; he merely has to filch something from a paperback glossary or a learned man met on a bus. He needs to know something about Madagascar or Cipango, so he asks a sailor who has been there. You may know the fiction-writer by his library, whose contents flatter neither the eye nor the owner's capacity for systematic reading. Instead of phalanges of rich uniform bindings, there are old racing guides, dog-eared astrological almanacs, comic periodicals, secondhand dictionaries, unscholarly history books, notebooks full of odd facts picked up in lying-in hospitals or taxidermist's shops. When Shakespeare achieved a library, if he ever did, we can be sure it was not like Bacon's.

What no amount of academic training can bestow on a potential writer is the gift of words. It can add to his vocabulary, as can a sojourn among Billingsgate porters or beatniks, but it cannot teach the fundamental skill of putting words together in new and surprising patterns which, miraculously, reflect some previously unguessed truth about life. Shakespeare's supreme power in the exploitation of his native tongue sprang from a natural endowment, but it could only be fostered by the use and observation and love of English, a subject not taught in the schools.

He was not unique in loving the toughness and tenderness of a language which the world had yet to take seriously. English was not one of the languages of diplomacy, foreign scholars saw little point in learning it, and there were plenty of home-grown scholars, Bacon among them, who preferred to entrust their deeper thoughts to Latin (Latin, being already dead, could not die). The love of English was not a thing that Shakespeare learned from its literature. Chaucer was there, and he had taught posterity that the future of English lay in one of its dialects—the East Midland English that was spoken in the Court and the universities, the language of government and polite society—but he wrote when that dialect was ready for violent change (unlike those other dialects, Scots and Lancashire among them, which had produced literatures but lacked both metropolitan preferment and an inner dynamo that would keep them on the move). If the schoolboy Will was learning to love English, it was not because great men had written in it but because it was a rich demotic medium in which his thinking lived.

The people of Tudor England, like the modern Irish, were great talkers. One imagines their speech as rapid, bubbling, both earthily exact and carelessly malapropistic. It was perhaps a McLuhanesque medium, itself its own message, and it exhibited the essential function of language—to maintain social contact in the dark. It is doubtful whether man learned to speak in order to convey information or emotion; it was rather that, with the light gone and the comforting visible world with it, he had to convince himself that he was not alone among the possible terrors of the night. Speech, when you come to think of it, is not a very exact medium: it is full of stumblings and apologies for not finding the right word; it has to be helped out with animal grunts and the gestures which, one is convinced, represent man's primal mode of communication. Take speech as a flickering auditory candle, and the mere act of maintaining its light becomes enough. Tales, gossip, riddles, wordplay pass the time in the dark, and out of these—not out of the need to recount facts or state a case—springs literature.

Shakespeare was nourished on the colloquial babble of a country town, but this was not very different from the social noise of London. We have only to read the pamphleteers—

Nashe, Greene, Dekker, and the rest—to see how much men of any station liked to be involved in chatter, brilliant chatter if possible, but essentially the processes of speech, not any possible end-product of those processes. Add odd scraps of learning, strange words invented or out of books, an attempt to maintain structure on the Latin model (not the relentless *and . . . and . . . and . . .* of old country gossips), and you are moving towards something we can call Shakespearean language.

It is strange that the Baconians should associate the dialogue of Shakespeare's plays with deep and subtle learning. A Shakespeare character, especially in the works of the early and middle periods, will prattle on ("prattle" was, in *Richard II*, Shakespeare's own way of designating an actor's speech) until he is counterprattled by another character. There is not much of the laconicism we find, for instance, in Bacon's *Essays*. The content of the dialogue may draw on book-learning, perhaps less with a conviction of its true value than with a commercial eye to what will please the masters of arts in the audience, but it may be unsound on court protocol and matters of foreign travel. There will be a provincial shrewdness, a carefully learnt politeness, a tendency to be proverbial and even parsonical—for the Sunday sermon was an aspect of the total speech continuum. There will be, in fact, an image of what the poet essentially was—a country boy determined to beat the polished metropolitans at their own game, but one frequently too impatient to learn all the lessons thoroughly. But that he learned enough of them is proved by the fact that the Baconian heresy exists at all. Will might, on a visit back from the grave, be pleased by its existence. His business, after all, was pretense.

But the time for business is not yet. The potential poet has to keep his eyes and ears open, absorbing myths domestic and foreign, country lore, local trades, such matter from the bigger world outside Stratford as can be picked up from his nobler relatives and from casual travelers at the inn and in the family shop. And his emotions have to be educated and his sensorium sharpened by love, or something like it.

3
Work, Play

Let us try to visualize Will, his state and his prospects, in that
year of his father's lowest fortunes, 1580. In the cruelest month,
the family gloomily remembered the death of Anne Shakespeare, not yet eight, in the previous year. ("Item for the bell
and pall for Mr Shaxper's dawghter, VIIId," say the chamberlain's accounts. Poor as he had become, that sum would not
break him.) In May 1580, the death of a daughter was balanced
by the birth of a son—Edmund, the last of the brood. It may
well have been a difficult birth; though we do not know
precisely how old Mary Shakespeare was, she must have been
approaching her forties or perhaps already in them. Her difficulties may have been the main reason for John's nonattendance
before the Queen's Bench at Westminster.

Will was now sixteen, well set up physically, with a beard
coming. His jerkin, trunks, and hose were not new, but his
gloves were. His brothers and sister must also have had a look of
shabby gentility: Gilbert was fourteen, Richard six, Joan eleven.
Of the public education of these children there is no record.
There is no record, for that matter, of Will's education either,
but that he went to that free royal-foundation grammar school is
an assumption that few will quarrel with. The evidence in the
plays and poems of a conventional education is very strong. It is
easier to suppose that he gained it at Stratford than at Birming-
ham, Worcester, or Nether Wallop. At sixteen he had probably
left school. What was he do to with the future?

It is likely that he, along with Gilbert, did some glover's
work, though neither officially entered the trade as their father

had done. Nor would their father's depression and disillusion at this time impel him to make his sons follow an example that seemed dismal. Could he, brought low as he was, his civic glories wrenched away, honestly commend his craft and his life to his intelligent eldest son? But, in default of other work, Will must cut tranks and snip gussets and deliver the finished products, the calfskin or kidskin couplets, to the houses of those who had ordered them, taking a farthing or halfpenny gratuity with a wry smile. He probably vaguely knew the future that he wanted, dreaming of it while he acted the role of delivery boy. The important thing was to make the name of Shakespeare respected once more, but how? Nothing through trade. He must already have been disclosing a literary talent, writing odd poems in the living room amid the noise of children and a harassed mother, or in the bedroom when he had it to himself, or, in fine weather, by the river bank. His literary problems would be considerate and depressing, however. What models could he follow? What should he write about?

I assume that his aim was to be a poet and not a prose writer. As with the ancients, prose then was a medium for exposition of the useful or the moral: it was for recipes, homilies, history. It was not art. The name Shakespeare could become honorable through art but not through practice of a mere craft. Prose writing was, admittedly, a craft more distinguished than glove-making, but Sir Philip Sidney had not yet demonstrated how, through wit, melody, and a gently compelling narrative, it could be turned into an art close to that of poetry. If a man wrote a great poem, he could perhaps persuade some big man at Court to accept it, along with a fulsome dedication, and thus secure patronage. What might follow? Gifts of gold, friendship in high places, perhaps even the ultimate admiration of a monarch who did not despise poetry, even wrote it herself. The ambitions of the young Will had to be greater than those of his father but, in his adolescence, they could sustain their daring only by presenting themselves as dreams.

I do not think that, at sixteen, he saw many prospects in the art of the drama. Actors were a kind of masterless men who evaded the charge of vagabondage and sturdy beggardom only by sheltering under the nominal patronage of some noble lord. Will would probably have less against that than against the poetic quality of such plays as had been performed in the Guildhall at Stratford. Christopher Marlowe was to startle the playgoing world in 1587 with his *Tamburlaine*—an astonishing poetic achievement which, even today, has power to shock and overwhelm with its sophisticated brutality and its lyrical fire— but 1587 was seven years off. The drama that the young Shakespeare saw in his hometown could not have seemed very promising.

Yet I feel that the first extended piece of verse writing that Will achieved was probably dramatic. He needed to stretch his wing, and, even in his adolescence, may have considered, or even started, the writing of a narrative poem on some theme from Ovid's *Metamorphoses*. But the technical difficulties would have been enormous. It would be far easier to attempt something loose and perhaps comic. Why not try an adaptation of a play by Plautus or Terence? Why not write it in the blank verse which, though the medium of the as yet despised professional stage, still possessed the dignity of its original purpose—to convey something of the unrhymed flow of Virgil's hexameters? What was good enough for the Earl of Surrey was good enough for William Shakespeare.

I do not think that the motive for writing an adaptation of a Roman comedy came pure and unbidden. I think we have to relate it to one of the commonest conjectures as to what Will was doing for a living between leaving school and going to London to become an actor. The *Brief Lives* of John Aubrey, written in the Restoration period, have a great deal that is totally unreliable to say about Shakespeare's brief life, but they have this observation: "Though as Ben: Johnson sayes of him, that he had but little Latine and lesse Greek, He understood Latine pretty well: for he had been in his younger yeares a Schoolmaster in the Countrey." He adds in the margin that he obtained this information from "Mr. Beeston." This Mr. Beeston was the son of the Christopher Beeston who, we know, was a fellow actor of Shakespeare's. The information may be false, like so much of Aubrey's, but there is a chance that it may be right. It is at least reasonable to assume that a boy as intelligent as Will, and with a love of poetry sufficient to sweeten the learning of the mechanics that would lead him to Ovid, might be very useful as an usher in a grammar school. Or even, as some suppose, a tutor in Gloucestershire. The references to Berkeley Castle in *Richard II* seem to imply a firsthand knowledge of the Severn country, and certain of the names mentioned by Shallow in *Henry IV* Part Two derive from that region. Will may have spent quite some time there. It is hard to see what he could have been doing except teaching.

As a tutor rather than as a grammar-school usher, perpetually supervised by his headmaster, he would have been better able to try a particular teaching experiment. This experiment would consist in acting a play of Plautus not in Latin but in English. If, as is believed by some, he was tutor to the sons of the Earl of Berkeley, the Earl would have taken kindly to such an experiment, since he was a noted patron of drama and protector of the troupe of players that bore his name. Let us imagine that Will starts to translate the *Menaechmi* of Plautus into English. Like other creative artists, he becomes bored with following another man, word by word, and ends with a translation that is, though close to the original in theme, characters, general movement, yet very different in its deployment of words—a translation so free as to develop into an original work. There is a type of creative mind that finds sheer faithful copying—the translator's virtue—harder than fresh creation, and I consider that Shakespeare had this type of mind. Starting to write the *Menaechmi* in English, he ends up with *The Comedy of Errors*.

Let us compare the two plays. In Shakespeare's there is enmity between Syracuse and Ephesus, and any Syracusan found in Ephesus is killed unless he can pay a thousand marks. Aegeon, an aged Syracusan merchant, has been arrested in Ephesus, but he is given the opportunity of telling the duke why he is so imprudent as to be there. He had twin sons, both called Antipholus, and each had a twin slave with the identical name Dromio. In a shipwreck, Aegeon, along with one twin and slave, became separated from the other twin and slave. He has been looking for them ever since, and this has brought him, in the normal course of travel, to Ephesus. The duke is impressed by this story, and he gives Aegeon till evening to find the ransom he has not got. Now Antipholus (I or II) has been living in Ephesus with Dromio I or II, and may now be called Antipholus of Ephesus. Antipholus (II or I) has arrived in Ephesus that very morning with Dromio II or I, looking for his brother and mother. We may call him Antipholus of Syracuse. Comic mix-ups ensue because the two Antipholuses are identical in appearance and so are the two Dromios. Finally Antipholus of Ephesus is locked up as a madman, and Antipholus of Syracuse enters a convent to get away from his twin's jealous wife.

Aegeon, still ransomless, is taken off to execution. But Antipholus of Ephesus asks for mercy and so does Antipholus of Syracuse. The twins, and their slaves, are now at last seen together, and everything is explained. The abbess of the convent where Antipholus of Syracuse sought refuge turns out to be Aegeon's lost wife Aemilia. Touched by the multiple reunion, the duke lets Aegeon go free and all ends happily.

Plautus's play is more easily summarized. A Syracuse merchant has identical twins. One, Menaechmus, is stolen at the age of seven. His brother, Sosicles, changes his name to Menaechmus in memory of his missing brother. When he is grown up, Sosicles (or Menaechmus II) goes to look for his brother and finally comes to Epidamnus where, by chance, that brother is living. Menaechmus II is involved in confusions with the mistress, wife, and father-in-law of Menaechmus I, and he is adjudged insane. But it is Menaechmus I whom they attempt to commit to an asylum. There is the inevitable confrontation, clearing-up, joy in reunion.

Shakespeare's play is far more complicated than the Plautus original, and I do not pretend that his first draft was much like the version that we have (first acted, incidentally, at the latest in 1594). Nor do I suggest that he necessarily wrote the first draft while still little more than a schoolboy, though the blank verse, in its desperate blankness, suggests the clever sixth-former more than the aspiring poet:

DUKE: Again, if any Syracusian born

Comes to the bay of Ephesus—he dies,
His goods confiscate to the Duke's dispose,
Unless a thousand marks be levied,
To quit the penalty and to ransom him.
Thy substance, valued at the highest rate,
Cannot amount unto a hundred marks;
Therefore by law thou art condemn'd to die.
AEGEON: Yet this my comfort: when your words are done,
My woes end likewise with the evening sun.

The so-called "hidden years" take us into his early twenties, and he could have been a schoolmaster or tutor up to the day of his departure (probably in 1587) from Stratford. All I propose is that *The Comedy of Errors*, in one form or another, be accepted as a work that had its origins less in professional dramaturgy than in amateur pedagogy, and that it was the first work of any length that Shakespeare completed. It is the link, I believe, between his marking time in Stratford and his making a name as *Johannes Factotum* in London. It was, I think, the play—though it might have been no more than a single act in draft—that he handed to a troupe of players as an earnest of what, given the chance, he could do.

Before we leave *The Comedy of Errors*, I would say that its possibilities were best realized in a Hollywood musical called *The Boys from Syracuse*, with songs by Rodgers and Hart. This version kept Shakespeare's plot but threw out his dialogue. The double twins were convincing, for camera trickery worked on them: they are, of necessity, never convincing on the stage. The errors were genuinely comic. If Will had seen it, he would hardly have regretted the loss of that long-winded creaking dialogue. The laughs were laughs of situation, and they were nearly all his.

The evidence of the works that Shakespeare wrote as a professional has been taken, by the naive and the various kinds of Baconian, as indicating that he followed other careers than that of teaching in that long period of silence. There are books about Shakespeare the sailor; there is even Duff Cooper's study of Sergeant Shakespeare, the hard-bitten fighter of the Low

Countries. There is a great deal about Shakespeare the lawyer's clerk, and the image of a young man with a beard and receding hair, scratching away at conveyances in dusty chambers, has assumed the status almost of a portrait from the life. The fact is that, though Shakespeare shows himself the Autolycus of most professions and trades, he exhibits, in the legal department, more authority than is proper to a mere snapper-up of unconsidered trifles. Admittedly, he was a buyer of property and had the countryman's shrewd eye for sharp practice, but the flow of legal jargon in both the plays and the sonnets sounds as though it comes from the lawyer's, not the client's, side of the desk. Take, for instance, the graveyard scene in *Hamlet*, where there is a quite irrelevant cadenza full of quiddits and quillets, statutes, recognizances, double vouchers, recoveries, as well as a kind of enharmonic chord which modulates from one known trade to another:

HAMLET: Is not parchment made of sheepskins?
HORATIO: Ay, my lord, and of calfskins too.
HAMLET: They are sheep and calves which seek our assurance in that.

There would probably have been little difficulty in Will's finding a place in a Stratford lawyer's office, or with the town clerk. And the clerking does not necessarily cancel out the schoolmastering: he may have tired of one (or even been dismissed from one) and taken to the other. But these two trades, or semiprofessions, are the likeliest candidates for the gainful occupations which Will had to undertake while (the pupils translating an unseen, the double vouchers put aside for a moment) he tried to turn himself into a poet.

Life was not all work. If we envisage Tudor Stratford as a dull and unsavory place, where the only excitements were provided by christenings, weddings, and funerals, the arraignment of citizens for leaving dunghills outside their houses (this had happened to John Shakespeare once), long sermons, takings in adultery, nonattendance at church (John Shakespeare again), witch-baiting, the torture of animals, hunting by the gentry, gross and bloody football, the reported appearance of ghosts and fairies and the Puck or Robin Goodfellow (an apotropaic nickname, to show how much he was feared), fairs, itinerant balladmongers' visits, seasonal ceremonies, cows lowing in labor, the felling of bobby-calves, the sticking of swine, flies in summer, frozen pumps in winter, plague, dysentery, the failure of crops, fornication, Jack-in-the-green, drunkenness, threats of damnation from religious fanatics, skittles, poaching, the young beating up the old, harvest home, the rethatching of roofs, fires raging through dry timber structures, ways foul after rainfall, trees down in storms, coarse jokes, toothache, the scurvy of a bad winter diet, then we shall not be far wrong. But there were other things.

There were the visits of the players, for instance, and the borough-subsidized performances in the Guildhall—the Earl of Worcester's Men in 1569, 1575, 1576, 1581, 1582, and 1584; the Queen's Men in 1569 and 1587 (probably, as I shall show later, a momentous visit); Leicester's in 1573 and 1576 and 1587; Warwick's in 1575; Strange's (as Derby's) in 1579; Berkeley's in 1581, 1582, and 1583—need one go on? There was singing, also dancing. There was the Lord of Misrule, the worship of Robin Hood (a spirit of the greenwood, like that original Amloth who became Hamlet), also the ceremony of Mayday, much condemned by such Puritans as Philip Stubbes, who, in his *The Anatomie of Abuses* (1583), says:

... their chiefest jewel they bring from thence is their May-pole, which they bring home with great veneration, as thus. They have twenty or forty yoke of oxen, every ox having a sweet nose-gay of flowers placed on the tip of his horns: and these oxen draw home this May-pole (this stinking idol, rather) which is covered all over with flowers and herbs, bound round about with strings from the top to the bottom, and sometime painted with variable colors, with two or three hundred men, women and children following it with great devotion. And thus being reared up with handkerchiefs and flags streaming on the top, they straw the ground about, bind green boughs about it, set up summerhalls, bowers, and arbors hard by it; and then they fall to banquet and feast, to leap and dance about it, as the heathen people did at the dedication of their idols, whereof this is a perfect pattern, or rather the thing itself.

What has passed down to us as an anemically pretty children's frippery was then, as Stubbes realized only too well, a pagan glorification of the ithyphallus, with *al fresco* fornication galore. There was a good deal of lust about in Stratford, as in other Tudor towns and villages, and some of this lust was not secretive but periodically exalted as an aspect of that whole life-process—the breeding of animals, the burgeoning of the earth—in which an agricultural society was so desperately involved. Young men and girls lost their virginities early in those days, and we cannot think that Will was an exception.

4

Marriage

The Victorians worshiped the Bard as a Christian philosopher and a moral guide (after, that is, Thomas Bowdler had bowdlerized all the indecencies out of the works and turned them into the "Family Shakespeare"). Even now there are some who treat April 23 as a saint's day and piously celebrate the uplift of plays and poems they have never read. The equating of high morality and high art is a tradition in the Anglo-Saxon world, as also in Germany: the greater the artist the more exquisite his moral sensibility. This, of course, is nonsense. It is very pleasing, in the faces of the lovers of Will the Moral Artist, to be able to record that Will fornicated before his marriage, and that there is statistical proof of this. On November 28, 1582, two Warwickshire farmers stood surety for the legality of a marriage between a certain William Shagspere (there is a nice low touch in that spelling) and a certain Anne Hathwey. It is all there in the Bishop of Worcester's register. In the register of Stratford Parish Church we read that, on May 26, 1583, a girl child, daughter to William Shakespeare, was christened Susanna. The child was born six months after the wedding.

It is held by some scholars, especially those who want no feet of clay on their moral idol, that the betrothal must have taken place in the preceding August, and that the consummation of a betrothal had much the same status, even in ecclesiastical custom, as the consummation of a marriage. I do not believe this, and I do not think Shakespeare believed it either. In *The Tempest* he makes Prospero promise the choicest disasters, including "barren hate, sour-eyed disdain, and discord," if

Ferdinand breaks the virgin-knot of Miranda before the "sanctimonious ceremonies" of marriage are performed. He is very strong indeed on this, and we can take it that he was voicing the law and approved custom of the time. William Shakespeare copulated with Anne Hathaway (to give the usual form of her name) at least three months before he married her, or she married him, and there was probably no talk of betrothal. It was wanton fornication, doubtless perpetrated in a ryefield in high summer, and well remembered in *As You Like It*:

Between the acres of the rye,
With a hey, and a ho, and a hey nonino,
These pretty country folk would lie,
In spring time, etc.

About the marriage that, we presume, followed because of Anne's pregnancy and the urgency of two Warwickshire farmers who stood surety for its legality, there is a certain mystery. On the day before this standing surety, which is very well documented, a marriage license was issued between a certain William Shaxpere and a certain Anne Whateley of Temple Grafton. This is clearly recorded in the Worcester episcopal register. Few doubt that this Shaxpere was Anne Hathaway's Shagspere, but some have doubted whether there was such a person as Anne Whateley and, knowing the orthographical fantasies of Tudor scriveners, have affirmed that "Whateley" was a somewhat extreme version of "Hathaway." But Anne Hathaway came from Shottery, not Temple Grafton, and no amount of ingenuity can turn the one place into the other, geographically or orthographically. Both places lie west of Stratford, but if Shottery is going to be absorbed by some bigger unit, then this would be Stratford rather than Temple Grafton. Indeed, this has long happened, Shottery now being a mere suburb of Stratford. Temple Grafton stands aloof from the absorption, with Binton and Dodwell and Drayton set as a triple barrier.

It is reasonable to believe that Will wished to marry a girl named Anne Whateley. The name is common enough in the Midlands and is even attached to a four-star hotel in Horse Fair, Banbury. Her father may have been a friend of John Shakespeare's, he may have sold kidskin cheap, there are various reasons why the Shakespeares and the Whateleys, or their nubile children, might become friendly. Sent on skin-buying errands to Temple Grafton, Will could have fallen for a comely daughter, sweet as May and shy as a fawn. He was eighteen and highly susceptible. Knowing something about girls, he would know that this was the real thing. Something, perhaps, quite different from what he felt about Mistress Hathaway of Shottery.

But why, attempting to marry Anne Whateley, had he put himself in the position of having to marry the other Anne? I suggest that, to use the crude but convenient properties of the old women's-magazine morality stories, he was exercised by love for the one and lust for the other. I find it convenient to imagine that he knew Anne Hathaway carnally, for the first time, in the spring of 1582, perhaps in the casual transports of the ceremonies of the May. He must have known her socially somewhat earlier, but the gap between their ages was, until he began to approach manhood, too great to admit of a sexual rapprochement. There were eight years between them: at the time of their marriage, Anne was twenty-six and Will eighteen. Her father, dead in 1581, had been a farmer in Shottery, and the house now known as Anne Hathaway's Cottage is properly Hewland Farm. Richard Hathaway's will charged his son and heir, Bartholomew, to move into the farm and direct it on behalf of the widow. The widow was Richard's second wife, not Anne's own mother, and Anne must have felt herself to be living in a house full of mere near-kin, as there were three half-brothers and, three months after Bartholomew's taking over, a sister-in-law (Bartholomew had now the means of marrying) who saw herself probably as mistress of the farm, with Richard Hathaway's widow as dowager. Anne had no real status, though she must have had work to do—looking after the dairy, probably. At twenty-six, already past the normal marrying age, she must have started looking around fairly desperately for a husband, and there may have been pointed remarks over the supper table about her prolonged spinsterhood.

One way of finding a husband was to become impregnated by a man who, having done the indecent thing, would then proceed, perhaps with threats in his ears or a gun in his back, to do the decent. Will's poem *Venus and Adonis* is about the wooing by an aging goddess of a beautiful young man who is not yet ready for love. He likes to hunt instead: to his creator there must have been a small verbal joy in the opposed ideas contained in the one word *venery*. Venus is eloquent, wanton, very persistent, but the silly pouting boy rejects her proffered treasures. He goes off after wild boar, and a wild boar, with wild justice, gores him to death. Venus weeps, partly with self-pity: that lovely mangled body is now beyond her seduction. But Will-Adonis was quite certainly given to venery of the nonhunting kind, and Venus-Anne would not have to spend much eloquence on him. And, though he tried to marry someone else, she prevailed without need for eloquence. As Stephen Dedalus puts it, whoever hath her Will, Anne hath a way.

I consider that the lovely boy that Will probably was—auburn hair, melting eyes, ready tongue, tags of Latin poetry—did not, having tasted Anne's body in the spring, go eagerly back to Shottery through the early summer to taste it again. Perhaps Anne had already said something about the advantages of love in an indentured bed, away from cowpats and the prickling of stubble in a field, and the word *marriage* frightened Will as much as it will frighten any young man. But, with the irony of things, he fell in love with a younger Anne and himself began to talk about marriage. This Anne was chaste, not wanton and forward, and there was probably no nonsense in her family about allowing consummation of the betrothal. Sanctimonious ceremony or nothing. Will, wooing her near-Platonically through the long summer of 1582, felt his own will, or libido, pricking hard. Rather than force this dainty flower, an unthinkable act, he found himself, perhaps to his own surprise, back in Shottery, Adonis hunting out Venus. There was a bout of lust in the August fields, a cathartic measure really (so his casuistic mind might argue), a means of maintaining his pure love for the other Anne until her, and his, parents gave their hymeneal blessing. From this August encounter Anne Hathaway grew pregnant.

Two centuries were to pass before the blessings of Dr. Condom descended on English manhood; fornication was a chancy thing. But country copulatives had their rough contraceptive lore, including the sin of Onan, and the lecheries of May did not necessarily bear fruit in the new year. But Will was unlucky or careless or overwrought that August day.

The two Warwickshire farmers who stood surety at Worcester on November 28, 1582, were Messrs. Fulk Sandells and John Richardson, perhaps friends of the dead Richard Hathaway and posthumously loyal in their concern about his daughter. I should imagine that they confronted Will when it became evident that Anne was pregnant, told him to play the man and do right. Will, perhaps reasonably, though unchivalrously, might have answered that, if she had been so free with him, she had probably been equally free with others. The two men would not like this, and they might raise brawny yeomen's fists in threat. When November came, Will might see a shotgun wedding in the offing and hence urge on the Whateleys and on his own family the need for himself and the virginal Anne to marry at once. Why at once? Well, from December 2 to January 2 there could be no wedding without a special license that cost dear—something to do with the church's attitude to Advent—and from January 27 to April 7 there was a similar mad ecclesiastical veto. Let expense be spared, then, and the marriage take place before Advent begins. Thou arguest well, boy; see about the license. Hence that entry in the Worcester register on November 27.

It was at this point that Sandells and Richardson rushed in with their incredible payment of forty pounds—a great deal of money in those days, almost enough to buy New Place, the finest house in Stratford—in order to indemnify the Bishop of Worcester and his myrmidons should any suit arise out of the grant of a special license for the marriage of this man Shagspere and an Anne who was coyly and falsely set down as "maiden." The payment represented a warranty that nothing should prevent the marriage from being valid under law: there was no previous marriage on the part of either partner, there was no prohibitive consanguinity. The special license meant only two readings of the banns, not the three normally required. Anne, through brawny and powerful friends, is demonstrating that she hath a way.

The other Anne, along with the parents on both sides, must have found out about this. Will had gotten a girl (well, hardly a girl) in the family way and had been trying to evade the penalty. Will gave in, with bitter resignation, and was led to the slaughter, or the marriage bed. The role of honorable Christian gentleman was being forced upon him. This, anyway, is a persuasive reading of the documented facts, but no Shakespeare-lover is necessarily bound to accept it. It is just possible that the William Shakespeare who is entered in the episcopal register on November 27, 1582, is not the man who was to write plays. The Warwickshire Shakespeares have died out, but there may have been plenty of them around in Tudor times. Our Shakespeare is certainly the Shagspere of the following day's entry. It is a coincidence soothing to those who wish Will's career to begin, as it was to end, in bourgeois decency. But I, along with others, such as Frank Harris, may be forgiven for believing that Will entered on a forced marriage with a woman he did not really love, and the lovelessness of the marriage was one of his reasons for leaving Stratford and seeking a new life in London.

When Will and Anne set up house together, it could not have been anywhere but in the home of his parents on Henley Street. John Shakespeare had, in his prosperous days, bought a messuage or so, but these had been sold when misfortune struck. Anne brought a very small dowry—six pounds, thirteen shillings, and fourpence, "to be paid unto her at the day of her marriage," as her father's will puts it. The newly married couple could not afford a house of their own, and Sandells and Richardson had already shot their bolt so far as generosity to Anne was concerned. It is possible that John Shakespeare's property on Henley Street was not limited to the house now exhibited as the birthplace, and that he also owned the house next door. But one cannot dispel the image of Anne and Will as having no place of their own except a bedroom (Gilbert now made to share with Richard and Edmund), with no more marital furniture than a double bed for, as the Elizabethans would coarsely put it, the galloping of four bare legs (there be some that say five). Anne herself may have imported this bed from Shottery—her father and stepmother's nuptial couch, no longer needed in widowhood; the dowager Mistress Hathaway could take over the single bed of her stepdaughter. Perhaps this was the second-best bed specifically bequeathed to Will's own widow. However little he was prepared to leave to Anne (she was able to claim her widow's dower by common law), he could hardly deny her entitlement to her own father's double bed. But this, of course, is mere supposition.

After the preliminary fencing of mutual distrust and jealousy ("my son little more than a baby, and thou somewhat overripe in thy years"), Mary Shakespeare may well have been pleased to have a mature daughter-in-law about the house, one skilled in kitchen economy and brisk with a broom, especially as, since the birth of Edmund, she may have been tired and aware of growing old. There were five helpless males to look after, and Joan, however willing, was only thirteen. Here was an Anne Shakespeare to replace the one lost, and she was only a couple of years older than that long-dead proto-Joan would have been, had she but lived. Anne may have found comfort in the cosseting of a mother-in-law experienced in the glories and agonies of obstetrics. How Anne and her husband got on together we can only guess. Will may have kept his roving eye and yearned for the younger flesh he saw around in Stratford. If, as I think, *The Comedy of Errors* was conceived and drafted between 1582 and 1587, then one may be excused if one seeks a privy significance in the shrewishness of Adriana. She, suspecting her husband of infidelity, tells the Abbess that she taunted him with it enough:

> In bed, he slept not for my urging it;
> At board, he fed not for my urging it;
> Alone, it was the subject of my theme;
> In company, I often glancèd it;
> Still did I tell him it was vile and bad.

The Abbess rebukes her gravely:

And thereof came it that the man was mad.
The venom clamors of a jealous woman
Poisons more deadly than a mad dog's tooth.
It seems his sleeps were hinder'd by thy railing,
And thereof comes it that his head is light.
Thou say'st his meat was sauc'd with thy upbraidings:
Unquiet meals make ill digestions;
Thereof the raging fire of fever bred;
And what's a fever but a fit of madness?
Thou say'st his sports were hinder'd by thy brawls.
Sweet recreation barr'd, what doth ensue
But moody and dull melancholy,
Kinsman to grim and comfortless despair,
And at her heels a huge infectious troop
Of pale distemperatures and foes to life?
In food, in sport, and life-preserving rest,
To be disturb'd would mad or man or beast.
The consequence is, then, thy jealous fits
Have scar'd thy husband from the use of wits.

This is eloquent enough to suggest genuine conviction, but Will may have been (a) thinking of someone else's wife or (b) inhabiting the temporary world of pure dramatic imagination.

Yet wives have a tendency to nag, even the best of them, and I feel that Anne reserved her viraginian acts for the circumstances of her new life more than for Will's suspected infidelities. When was she to have a house of her own? When was Will going to remove her from the smell of tannin and a wretchedly small bedroom and a communal dining room and give her what, as a wife who was no mere chit of a girl, was her domestic entitlement? Only when he obtained a decent situation, but when was that to be? There was no future in the classroom, since he had no degree, and no prospect of advancement in law, again since he had no degree. He was trying to write poetry, but what good would come of that? Her father had at least run a prosperous farm and bequeathed her a dowry. What was he, Will? Neither a farmer nor a full member of a craft. What would he have to leave to his children?

Children. That, of course, was another problem; most immediately a problem of space. Susanna was, as we have seen,
christened on May 26, 1583. On Candlemas Day, February 2,
1585, there came the baptism of twins—Hamnet and Judith. To
the large enough complement of the original Shakespeare household there was now an addition of four. There had better not be
any more children. Judith, heroine of the Apocrypha, cut off
the head of Holofernes. Holofernes was a name sometimes
jocularly given to the male member. Let the arrival of Judith
Shakespeare signal an end to begetting. The absence of further
birth records shows that it did.

I propose to indulge myself in an onomastic fancy that the
hardheaded reader is welcome to ignore. I am tempted to think
that the names of Shakespeare's children were not chosen
arbitrarily or sentimentally, though the evidence suggests otherwise. Hamnet and Judith were, we are told, named for Master
and Mistress Sadler, who were neighbors of the Shakespeares.
Susanna is just a good, rather Puritanical, biblical name. But
Susanna also stands as a symbol of purity assailed by the lust of
elders. In later years, when Susanna Shakespeare became Susanna Hall, wife of a respected local doctor, she repudiated a
charge of adultery and saw her accuser excommunicated. In
babyhood her name was ironical: she was the product of lust,
not love, and there was one lustful elder involved, Anne
Hathaway. When Will chose the name Holofernes for the
pedantic pedagogue of *Love's Labor's Lost*, he took it from the
pedantic tutor of Gargantua in Rabelais. Gargantua is mentioned in *As You Like It*; Shakespeare knew his Rabelais (further
proof comes in Dr. Hotson's discussion of the provenance of the
"Vapians" in *Twelfth Night*). Had Rogers, town clerk of Stratford, been teaching Will French as a language necessary for the
law, and had he been using Rabelais as a text? Did Will,
remembering that he had been a sort of Holofernes himself,
start thinking of the first Holofernes and the woman associated
with him? He had now a child whose name began with an S,
and another whose name was to begin with a J, and, with
Stratford perhaps deluged by the late January or early February
rains, he might see himself as a sort of Noah, the names of

whose children began respectively with an S and a J and, finally, an H. He could not have a Shem and a Japhet, but he could have a Ham, or rather a little Ham. Hamnet was the common diminutive, and frequently found in those days both as a first name and as a patronymic. A Kate Hamnet had, during Will's boyhood, drowned herself in the Avon—some said for love. Ophelia, maddened by the death of a father she loved, was also to drown herself. Hamlet and Hamnet were interchangeable. The provincial English mouth found the consonant group *mn* difficult to pronounce and preferred to say *chimley* for *chimney*, often interposing the buffer of a *b* between the nasal and the lateral. We still hear *chimbley*. Young Hamnet Shakespeare probably heard "Hamblet!" when he was wanted for supper or bed. The whole of this paragraph is very unsound.

Will had a long time to go before transmuting his own son into a mad Danish prince, but it is possible that, during his five years of married life on Henley Street, he was working on another myth—that of Venus and Adonis, taken from Ovid's *Metamorphoses*. The myth had come home to him; it had personal application. The physical immediacy of the poem, with its exactly rendered countryside and its all too credible talking goddess, is what raises it above other Elizabethan treatments of classical legend, those chill exercises in poeticizing. The language of *Venus and Adonis* is brilliant but full of conceits and quibbles (Dr. Johnson said that a quibble was to Shakespeare the fatal Cleopatra for whom the world was well lost), and it is in spite of the diction, rather than because of it, that the reality of snails, hunted hares, snorting stallions, and the pleas of lust come through.

Venus and Adonis is set in the countryside of Warwickshire. That "dew-bedabbled wretch," the hunted hare, is "poor Wat," a beast of rural England. Film the poem for some arty television series, and you will not need to take your camera team to the land of moly and asphodel. Venus is an English beauty of strong lust but very good family. Adonis is the spoilt son of some local magnate. Because of the personal associations of the poem, we can somehow never doubt that Anne was blonde, strapping, and, in her mature way, not ill-looking. But we must not push the autobiographical element too far. Will has very little sympathy for the younger hunter: he is always on the side of the hunted. Venus, though she talks too much, is one of the most seductive characters in all fiction. I suggest only that Will was drawn to this above all other myths of the *Metamorphoses* because it touched his own life in the most general way—mature woman seeking to seduce mere boy. If, after his marriage, he began to write a narrative poem of some length, then this, in one form or another, was the poem he began to write.

Both *Venus and Adonis* and *The Comedy of Errors* have a property in common, and that is a somewhat cold, and even coarse, attitude to sex. The sex is, so to speak, pure, uncontaminated love. Here is Venus talking to Adonis:

"Fondling," she saith, "since I have hemm'd thee here
Within the circuit of this ivory pale,
I'll be a park, and thou shalt be my deer;
Feed where thou wilt, on mountain on in dale;
    Graze on my lips; and if those hills be dry,
    Stray lower, where the pleasant fountains lie.

"Within this limit is relief enough,
Sweet bottom-grass, and high delightful plain,
Round rising hillocks, brakes obscure and rough,
To shelter thee from tempest and from rain;
    Then be my deer, since I am such a park;
    No dog shall rouse thee, though a thousand bark."

The topography is ingenious, a little too much so for hot passion. In *The Comedy of Errors*, topography becomes world geography. Dromio of Syracuse sustains an extended metaphor in very poor taste. The woman who wants him is, he says, spherical, like a globe. At once, as in a poem by John Donne, the globe has to be painted with countries. "In what part of her body stands Ireland?" asks Antipholus of Syracuse, and Dromio replies: "Marry, sir, in her buttocks; I found it out by the bogs." And where are the Netherlands (Holland or Hole-land)? "O, sir, I did not look so low." Marriage has not made Will capable of that rapturous spiritualizing of the female body which springs from true love. The Platonic sonneteers, "who have no mistress but their muse," go too far one way; Will, with his schoolboy's snigger, goes too far the other.

Marriages cannot be maintained by sex alone. Drawn to Anne by physical desire only, Will may have known transports of disgust (he certainly knew them in later life, as witness the sonnet beginning "The expense of spirit in a waste of shame"). The fear of adding to a family already too large to support comfortably may have pleaded a continence impossible of fulfilment. He had to get away from Anne, at least for a time. This is a possible reason for his leaving Stratford, along with her nagging him about his lack of ambition. Driven to exasperation in the hot summer of 1587, he may have replied to the effect that he could only achieve the prosperity he sought as much as she be by getting out of Stratford. Well, get out then. I will, I will.

A more melodramatic reason for his self-exile has been put forward, though now generally rejected. This relates to Will's alleged poaching forays on the estate of Sir Thomas Lucy at Charlecote. Charlecote is a good four miles out of Stratford, a long walk there, a longer walk back, no matter how many in the poaching company, with a trussed deer to lug. But, contrary to traditional belief, Charlecote had not at that time been legally emparked, so deer-slayers were not legally poaching. It is cinematically thrilling to think of a poaching Will being caught and whipped by Sir Thomas's keepers, or even by Sir Thomas himself, answering back pertly, being thrown into jail, being sprung by his luckier confederates, making a fast getaway south, but we have no evidence; we lack even the thin prop of possibility. Will probably left Stratford on impulse, but the impulse was backed by long brooding. There was perhaps the bitterness of seeing young Richard Field, another Stratfordian, going to London as a printer's apprentice and then, on his master's premature death, marrying the widow and controlling an efficient and prosperous business (Field was to print *Venus and Adonis*). There was perhaps a blazing row with Anne and a dramatic exit apt for blank verse and a clinching heroic couplet.

But, going off into the night, or day, did he know that he was about to become an actor and play-maker?

However poor most of the plays and performances he had seen in the Guildhall, he must have been fired by the brilliance of at least one player. This player was Edward Alleyn, the first of the great professionals, two years younger that Will and already a star of the Earl of Worcester's Men, that troupe which, as we know, paid six visits to Stratford while Will, boy and man, was living there. Alleyn was to become the superb interpreter of Marlowe's tragic heroes; Will himself was to write for him; he was to end prosperous, respected, Dr. John Donne's son-in-law, owner of the Manor of Dulwich, founder of Dulwich College of God's Gift. As a young man he must already have been showing massive potentialities. Will, seeing him, might have had a sudden flashing glimpse of the latent glory of a poet's theatre. Certainly he would be unable to despise the actor's craft after seeing Alleyn. He might, trained in the rhetorical thrust and counterthrust of marital arguments, observe the seeds of an actor's gift within himself. An actor could not yet be a gentleman but, prophetically, he may have seen that it was only a question of waiting. Perhaps from Alleyn there already glowed the lineaments of a lord of the manor.

In the summer of 1587, the Queen's Men paid a second visit to Stratford, probably performing a play called *The Seven Deadly Sins*. The chief comic men of this company were Dick Tarleton and Will Kemp. Kemp's career was just beginning: he was to achieve his greatest success as a fellow player of Shakespeare's. Tarleton's career was near its end. In the following year he was to die of poverty and a wrecked liver. He had joined the Queen's Men in 1583 and had achieved a great reputation as a witty improviser and a resourceful knockabout comedian. He was sometimes too witty, over-pert in the wrong company, and, in 1587, he had incurred the Queen's displeasure through an impudent mock on his first patron, the Earl of Leicester. In that last Stratford summer of his youth, Will would see a brilliant clown with sad eyes and a decaying body. It may have been to him that he made a stammering or confident application to be considered as a member of the company. Thou art too old, laddie, to be a prentice in the craft. Canst mend plays? Will might then show what he had done: an act in draft of *The Comedy of Errors*, a stanza or so of his Venus and Adonis poem. Thou hast a fair hand. Canst copy fast? And he is well enough set up, is he not? Let us see how he makes an entrance.

Sometime like that. Back from the inn where the players lodged to Henley Street, to bundle up his few clothes, beg a little money from his father, be sprayed by tearful farewells. And then to cease to be Will of Stratford. The role of Sweet Master Shakespeare awaited him in a bigger town—filthy, gorgeous, mean, murderous, but the only place where a member of his new breed, without land, without craft, could hope to make money and a name.

5

London

❦❧❦❧❦❧❦❧❦❧❦❧❦❧❦❧

This is the moment for the traditional florid cadenza to mark Will's first glimpse of London. Very well, then. The city to which he emigrated was nothing like today's ludicrous megalopolis. It was an overgrown village not yet too anxious to expand west. Piccadilly, named for Pickadilly Hall, where dwelt a family grown fat on the manufacture of pickardils or ruffs, was a secluded place of country estates. The city of London meant roughly what we mean today by the City of London—a crammed commercial huddle that smells the river. The Thames was everybody's thoroughfare. The Londoners of Chaucer's time had had difficulty in bridging it; the Elizabethans had achieved only London Bridge. You crossed normally by boat taxi, the boatmen calling "Eastward-ho" and "Westward-ho." There was commerce on the river, but also gilded barges, sometimes with royalty in them. Chained to the banks there were sometimes criminals who had to abide the washing of three tides. The river had to look on other emblems of the brutality of the age—the severed heads on Temple Bar and on London Bridge itself.

The streets were narrow, cobbled, slippery with the slime of refuse. Houses were crammed together, and there were a lot of furtive alleys. Chamberpots, or jordans, were emptied out of windows. There was no drainage. Fleet ditch stank to make a man throw up his gorge. But the city had its natural cleansers— the kites, graceful birds that made their nests of rags and refuse in the forks of trees. They scavenged, eating anything with relish. One of Will's first surprising sights may have been their tearing at a freshly severed head on the spikes by the law courts. And, countering the bad man-made odors, the smells of the countryside floated in. There were rosy milkmaids in the early morning streets, and sellers of newly gathered cresses.

It was a city of loud noises—hooves and raw coach-wheels on the cobbles, the yells of traders, the brawling of apprentices, scuffles to keep the wall and not be thrown into the oozy kennel. Even normal conversation must have been loud, since everybody was, by our standards, tipsy. Nobody drank water, and tea had not yet come in. Ale was the standard tipple, and it was strong. Ale for breakfast was a good means of starting the day in euphoria or truculence. Ale for dinner refocillated the wasted tissues of the morning. Ale for supper ensured a heavy snoring repose. The better sort drank wine, which promoted good fellowship and led to swordfights. It was not what we could call a sober city.

People sang readily, perhaps because of their malted euphoria. You bought ballads in the streets, and there was a large public repertoire of popular songs. The gap between music as pastime and music as uplift, a distressing feature of our own times, did not then exist, and doctors of music, like Byrd and Weelkes and Wilbye and the saturnine genius called John Bull, were ready to compose fantasies on "The Carman's Whistle" or "John Come Kiss Me Now." As for the educated classes, it was assumed that an ability to bear a part in a madrigal was one of the unremarkable marks of a lady or gentleman. Sight-reading (for which British musicians even today are famous among Continental conductors) was no rarer a gift in music than in the field of words, and some of the madrigals they sang are, for us, not easy to read at sight. There were plenty of skilled players on the lute (or guitar) and the recorder. The keyboard instrument of the day was the virginals—perhaps so-called because it was considered fitting for young girls: the name became very appropriate when the Virgin Queen herself was known to excel at it, or them. (The Elizabethan term was plural—a pair of virginals.) Among the louder instruments were cornetts (trumpet-sounding cylinders of ivory or wood, holed like recorders) and sackbuts—our own trombones. The Elizabethans were mad for sweet and strong concords.

Will would hear music coming from open summer windows, from barbershops (where a boy would sing to a lute over the scraping and clipping) and, of course, from taverns. In this musical London he would have to learn how to write lyrics not just good enough for a play, but good enough for remembering when the play was over. He would have to be Lorenz Hart as well as William Shakespeare. That his musical knowledge became considerable seems evident from the musical references in the plays. Thus, Lady Macbeth's admonition to her husband —"Screw your courage to the sticking-place"—is directly drawn from the act of tuning a lute. *Romeo and Juliet* is full of technical musical punning. The expertise of actors, in their singing and dancing aspects, had to be very considerable, since the gentler and nobler audiences were expert themselves. Music was close both to words and physical movement. The Queen herself was one of the great dancers of the age.

It is difficult for us to match his love of art with the known relish for brutality. When we recoil from the brutality of Shakespeare's own plays, as early as *Titus Andronicus* and as late as *King Lear*, we have made the mistake of assuming that Will is one of us and that he had unaccountably lapsed into the cruelty of a period that is his only by accident. But it is only by accident that Will is "for all time"; he is essentially one of them—the pre-Freudian relishers of anything that could quicken the blood and fire the libido. And the brutality was, in a way incomprehensible to us, capable of being reconciled with the aesthetic instinct. Thus the hangman who officiated at Tyburn had to be more than a butcher. It required huge skill to cut out the heart of the hanged victim and show it to him before his eyes finally closed. And the quartering of the still steaming corpse had to be effected with the swift economy of the true artist.

Walking through London one walked literally through death and pain—the kites pecking out eyeballs, the screams of the whores whipped at the Bridewell. In *King Lear*, Will was to gouge out eyes, but he was also to inveigh against the whore-whipper as the hypocrite who lusted hotly for the stripped flesh he lashed. He saw what lay behind the sadism of his age, but he did not expend ink on reformist pamphlets. He accepted. He accepted the baiting of the bears Sackerson and Harry Hunks on the Bankside, within hearing of the theatre where he worked, and of the tearing to pieces by dogs of a terrified ape. He accepted the "hangman's hands"—and when Macbeth sees his own as those, he is not thinking of the manipulator of a rope: he is thinking of the fresh blood and the clotted entrails on fists that have plunged into the open belly of the victim. Will accepted what it was not his mission to change: he was a playwright, a recorder of life. And he accepted the bestowals of a God who must have seemed as cruel as men—the diseased bodies of beggars, the periodic visitations of the plague.

London, with all its horrors, had glories enough to make it seem the most desirable place in the world. It was a true capital, not a provincial backwater of Europe. The great river flowed into Europe's rivers, and Europe's rivers flowed back. It was the capital not only of Protestant England but of Protestant Christendom. When, in 1587, Will from Warwickshire arrived, he met the full hogo of an issue that Stratford knew only in stray whiffs from a distance: could the reformed churches of the Germanic-speaking countries survive? It was a religious issue that was also a political issue, for, with the death of Protestantism, there would follow the deaths of the nations that had come to self-realization through Protestantism, with a vernacular Bible and, as in England, a secular head of a national church. The forces of the Counter-Reformation, which meant chiefly Spain, were powerful and had still to show the full extent of their power. England was weak, but she was united under a brilliant leader. In 1587, Queen Elizabeth was fifty-three years old and she had been ruling for twenty-eight years. Aging by the standards of those times, she was nevertheless spare and healthy in body and sane and vigorous in mind. This was more than could be said of the great counselors who had helped guide her hands in earlier years: Cecil and Walsingham were decrepit, Leicester growing puffy and self-indulgent. But Elizabeth was still the cleverest and trickiest monarch in Europe, and Europe knew it.

Long past an age to bear children, she could no longer

employ her once tantalizing spinsterhood in the great game of dynastic alliances. (Ben Jonson, talking to Drummond of Hawthornden, doubted if the Queen had ever been really marriageable: "She hath a membrana which rendereth her incapable of man.") The succession to the throne had been a problem for a long time, a worry to Protestant Europe as well as Protestant England. But matters were more hopeful in 1587 than they had been for many years. If Will had arrived in the February instead of (to keep to our arbitrary assumption) the summer of that year, he would have been overwhelmed by the clash of bells, flare of bonfires, thunder of guns, drunken noise of rejoicing. On February 8, firm to the last in her Catholic faith, Mary Queen of Scots had been executed, and a great threat to the Protestant Crown had been removed. There was rage in the Scotland which had once followed John Knox in denouncing "our Jezebel mistress," but Mary's son, James VI, looked to his own future. "How fond and inconstant I were if I should prefer my mother to the title let all men judge. My religion ever moved me to hate her course, although my honor constrains me to insist for her life"—those had been his unfilial words a mere year back. But those who had feared that a Catholic would come from Scotland to ascend the English throne had no need to fear longer. The English Catholics had lost the center of their hopes. When some of them looked to Philip of Spain's daughter as a new claimant, they found that too many of their coreligionists turned into Englishmen first, Catholics second. Spain, whether it was the Pope's sword-arm or not, was a foreign power, and it threatened English soil.

The threat was growing closer while Will was settling down in his first London lodgings. There was little panic, but there was a good deal of precautionary activity, meaning the jailing of Catholic laymen and the torturing, hanging, drawing, and quartering of Jesuit equivocators. The exiled English Catholics of Rome and Douai were doing their home-based brethren little good with their vituperation against a Queen they termed not merely an heresiarch but an incestuous bastard and a voluptuary given to "unspeakable and incredible variety of lust." Elizabeth, for her part, might be a heretic, but she was not prone to the vilifications of bigotry. She would have been better content with an English church organized on the lines of Hooker's *Ecclesiastical Polity*, with room for most kinds of Christian believers. The intolerance that soured the lives of Catholics, free-thinkers, and actors alike was no emanation from the Crown. There was a new type of fanatic growing up, and he was well represented among the city fathers and in the Privy Council itself. Quiet patriotic Catholics could better have been absorbed into the fabric of Elizabeth's Christianity than the new militant Protestants with loud voices. But the issue was simple to minds less subtle than the Queen's: Catholicism meant Spain, and Spain was the enemy.

Spain's threat to invade did not reach fulfilment till 1588. That was a year in which Will was to learn what English patriotism was, and how useful a property it could be in the popular drama. In 1587 it was recognized that war was coming, and the Queen and her counselors knew, if her subjects did not, how little England could afford it. Money was short. It could no longer come from monastic plunder or brutal expropriation; it was not obtained by the Continental system of a crown debt to wealthy subjects; it was mostly borrowed at high interest in Antwerp, with the City of London (meaning the individual merchants who thus mortgaged their goods) standing as guarantor. There were other things than war to spend the money on: there was, for instance, the great showpiece of the Royal Court, a wonder to foreigners, an advertisement for English culture, wit, beauty, and gallantry, as well as the illusion of affluence. Its brilliance had to be sustained, and noblemen who squandered their patrimonies could not go in rags: they must seek help from the royal purse. But the real drain on limited resources was due to the need to keep Continental Protestantism alive and hopeful. Philip II's power in the Netherlands had to be broken, the French Huguenots helped, Irish rebellions and insurrections in the Catholic North of England put down. A great deal of the military money, to Elizabeth's shame and anger, was pocketed by the captains, who, like Falstaff, let their soldiers starve in half a shirt. She had, in the still current phrase, to thank God for a navy.

Not that British achievements at sea were triumphs of large-scale planning, with briefcase-carrying admirals scurrying about Whitehall. Elizabethan England was technically a highly centralized despotism; in practice, it rejoiced in individual enterprise. Thus, war with Spain, an essentially collective act, was anticipated on a plane of individual harassing. Drake and Hawkins sailed insolently into the home ports of Spain, there to disturb the Armada that was under preparation, and as insolently plundered Spanish possessions. Such piracy was officially disapproved by the Crown; Elizabeth's private judgment was a different matter. Drake, *El Draque*, the Dragon, was a prodigy. He and his fellow pirates had no doubt at all that Spain could be defeated at sea: it was a matter of the streamlined new way confronting the lumbering old. The Spaniards had built a fleet suitable for the calm waters of the Mediterranean but totally inefficient for the wider seas they wished to master. Their mode of naval war belonged to the Middle Ages: a floating fort approached the enemy with grappling irons, fastened herself to her prey, then discharged soldiers to fight a deck battle while the sailors looked on. The English ships were lean and fast. As long ago as Henry VIII, true founder of the navy, they had been fitted with broadside guns. The battles were sailors' battles.

When Will was in London during that marvelous year, he would learn more than the temper of his potential audiences, the popular themes that would appeal; he would, if he were at Tilbury, learn something about the rhetoric proper to princes. Here was Elizabeth reviewing her army:

> I know I have the body of a weak and feeble woman, but I have the heart and stomach of a king, and of a king of England too, and think foul scorn that Parma or Spain, or any prince of Europe should dare to invade the borders of my realm; to which, rather than any dishonor shall grow by me, I myself will take up arms, I myself will be your general, judge, and rewarder of every one of your virtues in the field.

His own Henry V was hardly to do better. The boldness of the words was no empty performance, superb actress though the Queen could be. The news was already through that the

Armada had been defeated: less than half of the great fleet had been able to limp back to Spain; not one English ship had been taken. If now, as the rumor had it, the Duke of Parma was going to invade England, he would meet a rage and defiance unprecedented in the annals of any nation, a patriotic spirit never before so perfectly incarnated in any leader of Europe and, despite the example of Winston Churchill, inheritor of a debased rhetoric, never again. Parma did not invade. The King of Spain prayed all day in the Escurial. The bells clamored through England and the English capital.

Will had come to this English capital at the right time. The trouble with Spain was not yet over, but a small nation had demonstrated how determination, patriotism, and the fire of individual enterprise could break the strength of a great empire. The confidence of the capital, which was the confidence of England, required its articulation in a popular art-form which Will, a man of the people, was best qualified, when he had learned the knacks of the trade, to purvey. Drama was no longer a commodity to beguile the boredom of a country town, the little occasional treat of Stratford's Guildhall. It was an aspect of the great world.

6

Drama

❦❦❦❦❦❦❦❦❦❦❦❦❦❦❦

The term *professional* has two senses. It is predicated of things that are done for money; it also conveys a notion of skill, pride, dedication, perfectionism. Both meanings are applicable to the Elizabethan-Jacobean drama in its greatest phase. Before that, there had been a strictly pecuniary attitude to play-making and play-acting. And this narrow and venal approach had been preceded by centuries of amateurism.

Drama begins as a kind of magic. Ceremonies designed to bring the rain, make the spring come, revive the failing crops are an essential part of primitive life. Once the forces that determine the procession of the seasons and the fertility of the earth are personified into gods, then certain magical dramatic enactments become possible. At the darkest time of the year, when the sun is dying, a people with no scientific knowledge will try to aid the sick fire-god in the heavens by using sympathetic magic. An actor representing darkness fights with an actor tricked out as the sun-god; the sun-god wins, darkness lies dead. What is presented symbolically must now, according to the law of sympathetic magic, be fulfilled in reality. And, of course, the winter passes and the sun revives and it seems that sympathetic magic really works. Sympathetic magic in its lowest form still, even in civilized countries, has its adherents. Frustrated clerks will try to kill tyrannical bosses by sticking pins in their wax images. There is a bond of sympathy between the reality and the picture of the reality. Most of us are unhappy when a framed photograph of someone we love falls from the sideboard.

A more sophisticated kind of primitive drama-magic occurs

when the god, or symbol, of fertility is killed in representation, only to come back to life. The Christmas play that is still sometimes performed in English villages has Saint George killing the Dragon, the Turkish Knight, and the Giant Turpin. A doctor comes in with a "little bottle of alicumpane," brings the dead back to life, and bids them fight again. This obviously has its roots in some old vegetation ceremony. Sometimes a sacrificial element enters, so that the term *tragedy*, which traditionally relates to the downfall and death of some great man for the good of the people (Oedipus, for example), can be traced back to the Greek word *tragos*, which means a goat. The goat has always been an ambivalent animal—symbol of lust and fertility, but also the creature on whose back the sins of the people must be loaded before ritual slaughter or, as the Hebrew scapegoat, driving out to starve in the desert. *Comedy*, while we are on this subject of dramatic categories, derives from *komos*—a country revel honoring the god Dionysus, the wine-god and vegetable-god who suffers, dies, and comes back to life again.

From magic to religion is a short step. But, historically, a long tradition of secular drama came between the ritual beginnings and the taking over by the Christian church of mimesis, or man's innate acting instinct, in the service of ceremony or moral teaching. Greek tragedy had a moral function and also, as Aristotle taught, a psychological one. The fall of a great man showed that the gods distrusted greatness: the flaw of *hubris*, or self-confident contempt for the divine moral order, was incident to great men, and it had to be punished. But the spectacle of the punishment, and the suffering imposed on the tragic hero, aroused pity and terror in the auditor. The strong emotion was purged in the process known as *catharsis*. For civilized men this was a salutary experience, a means of ridding the system of elements which, in a primitive society, were aroused and cathartized by action. The function of the Greek comedians was social in a similar way. The flaws in civilized man were made more apparent than in real life by exaggeration and fantasy. Man is absurd, and the absurd is meant to be laughed at. The laughter is another kind of catharsis: it provides a temporary release from responsibility and the stain of living in a civilized society.

Comedy and tragedy are not opposed poles: they are the two sides of one coin.

The Romans produced original comedy, though both Terence and Plautus acknowledged the influence of the Greek comic realist Menander. Seneca wrote closet-tragedies that owe much to Sophocles and Aeschylus, but there is a new element—the stoic dignity of the tragic hero which is a kind of quiet *hubris,* a sense of human identity which survives in the face of divine punishments. The gods are powerful, but they may not be just. Seneca influenced the popular dramatists of Renaissance Italy, France, and England, but he was, in his own day, a purveyor of texts for aristocratic play-readings: he filled no amphitheatre. The drama that was presented publicly to the jaded subjects of the last emperors was a drama of cruelty, and of obscenity, that our own age, with all its candor or corruptness, cannot touch. For the sexual act was openly presented on the stage, and the true, not enacted, execution of criminals would form part of a plot. The sick tradition of enstaged reality, as opposed to mere stage realism, lasted into the early Christian era, and the church condemned it. If this was drama, the church wanted nothing of the drama.

But, whether it willed it or not, drama was already in the church. The Mass presents the sacrifice of Christ by symbolic but highly dramatic means. There is dialogue, color, climax. As early as the ninth century we find, with little surprise, that the ceremony tolerates old dramatic insertions appropriate to some festival of the church. Easter, for instance, with this:

ANGELS: Whom do you seek in this tomb, O followers of Christ?
WOMEN: We seek Jesus Christ Who was crucified, O Angels.
ANGELS: He is not here: He has risen again as He said He would.
Go proclaim that He has risen from the sepulchre.

There were similar dramatic presentations on Good Friday and at Christmas. There is a thirteenth-century manuscript in France which contains very simple dramatic scenes based on the angelic announcement of Christ's birth, the coming of the Magi, Herod's slaughter of the innocents, as well as the miracles of St. Nicholas, Paul's miraculous conversion, Christ's appearance on the road to Emmaus. The language is Latin; we assume the actors were clerical, not lay.

The Normans introduced sacred drama to England. At first it was closely tied to church ritual; later it detached itself and moved first into the churchyard, later into the streets of the town. Then came secularization, with the laity playing a bigger part in the representation of fragments of the Gospel story, and soon, inevitably, there was a popular tendency to seek in this early drama entertainment as well as instruction. In 1264, Pope Urban IV instituted the feast of Corpus Christi. It was not actually observed until 1311, when a Church Council decreed that it should be celebrated with all due ceremony. In England this came to mean the performance of religious plays by the trade guilds. These are often called mystery plays, and the term *mystery* should be taken to mean less the mysteries of the Christian faith than those of the trades themselves. We no longer use the word in this sense in English, but Italian still has *mestiere* and French *métier*.

The guilds would choose episodes from the Bible for dramatization, and the choice would usually be appropriate to the trade practiced. Thus the Chester guilds had the Last Supper acted by the Bakers, the Passion and Crucifixion of Christ by the Arrowmaker (or Fletchers), Coopers, and Ironmongers, and the Descent into Hell by the Cooks. Each guild had its own decorated cart, called a *pageant*, a sort of portable stage to be dragged through the town, set up at different spots, and, at the end of the long day's acting, dragged back to its shed for another year. The upper part of the pageant was a sort of stage in the round, so that the audience could surround it and see the action from any angle. The plays were presented in strict chronological sequence, starting with the Fall of Lucifer or the Creation of the World, and ending with the Day of Judgment. The total number of plays performed in Chester on Corpus Christi was usually about twenty-four, but Wakefield could have thirty-three, Coventry forty-two, and York fifty-four. The actors and audience needed the long summer daylight of that feast to get through so formidable a schedule.

The performers were all amateurs, but they expected to get

payment out of guild funds. The Coventry Smiths' Guild in 1490 lists a few of the sums expended:

> Imprimis to God, ijs.
> Item to Heroude, iijs. iiijd.
> Item to the devyll and to Judas, xvijd.

The part of Herod was an important one, calling for loud ranting. In the Coventry Nativity Play he announces himself as "he that reigns as king in Judea and Israel" and continues:

> For I am even he that made both heaven and hell,
> And of my mighty power holdeth up this world round.
> Magog and Madroke, both them did I confound,
> And with this bright brand their bones I brake asunder...
> I am the cause of this great light and thunder;
> It is through my fury that they such noise do make.
> My fearful countenance the clouds so doth encumber,
> That often for dread thereof the very earth doth quake.

It seems likely that Shakespeare saw a ranting Herod in some guild presentation, or at least heard from his father about the traditional mode of acting the part. In *Hamlet*, when the prince gives his author's own views on acting technique, there is strong condemnation of those who "tear a passion to tatters, to very rags, to split the ears of the groundlings." Such ham-acting, says ham-hating Hamlet, "out-Herods Herod."

The guild plays are all anonymous and, fitting the anonymity, there is rarely any sense of genuine artistic aim, the careful working at form, or a searching after verbal power. There is realism, and there is humor, but there is little we can imagine pleasing a cultivated audience. Yet the guild dramas had in all nearly three centuries of life, and they disappeared only because the spirit of the English Reformation was hostile to them. But through them the tradition of a popular drama was fixed firmly in the towns of England, and some of the features of the sophisticated theatre of London are not all that remote from the secular attractions of the mystery plays. Tamburlaine and Barabas in Marlowe may be examples of the big modern Machiavelli persona (evil and intrigue and utter Godlessness), but they have a flavor of Herod or Pontius Pilate. The low clowning which Shakespeare expunged, along with Will Kemp, from his later works, has its roots in plays like the Wakefield Second Shepherds' Play, with sheep-stealing Mac, or the Chester Play of the Deluge (performed by the Water-leaders and Drawers of the River Dee), with its comic cross talk between Noah and his wife. But Elizabethan drama could not arise directly out of this demotic tradition. It needed a tradition of secular subjects and professional actors to present them.

The secular subjects make their way into English drama through a new kind of religious or semireligious play—the morality. The morality was not a guild play, and it did not take as its subject a story from the Bible. Instead, it tried to teach a moral lesson through allegory, through presenting moral abstractions as if they were real people. The moralities are mostly dull, ill-made, didactic, totally lacking in both action and character. *Mind, Will and Understanding; Mankind; The Castle of Perseverance*—these and others like them parade their pasteboard personifications—Wisdom, Mischief, Pleasure, Folly, Backbiting, Indignation, Sturdiness, Malice, Revenge, Discord, and so on. We long for genuine conflict and a little humor, more humanity and less morality. But from the extant manuscripts we do learn something of value. We learn, for instance, that *The Castle of Perseverance* was performed by a group of players who traveled from town to town, setting up their scenes as a modern circus sets up its tents and cages, and performing for money. Professional drama, in its primal pecuniary sense, is at last with us. And, if we watch closely, we see that a leavening of low humor is to start work in the form of the Vice (whom Feste in *Twelfth Night* remembers, as well as Prince Hal in *Henry IV*)—a personification of immorality able, at length and through genius, to become Falstaff.

In the last days of the fifteenth century it becomes difficult to distinguish between the morality and the interlude. The main difference seems to lie not in theme and treatment, but in place and occasion of performance. An interlude was, as the name suggests, a short play performed in the middle of something else, perhaps a feast—a sort of incidental entertainment. The audience would probably be somewhat more enlightened than that which flocked to the traveling moralities for lack of something better. In other words, a demotic and an aristocratic development of the same dramatic form are beginning to subsist side by side. The noblemen in their fine houses watch refined moralities performed by players who are a sort of upper servants, wearing their master's livery; the common people, in the innyards or on the village greens, see cruder moralities performed by masterless wanderers who would be glad of the protection of a livery. The two need now to merge.

The aristocratic morality play, the interlude, can often be assigned to an author, and names like Rastell, Medwall, and Bale begin to appear. Bale, in his *Interlude of God's Promises*, goes in overmuch for learned disputation about free will and grace, in the manner of a true Reformation sermon, but his language is well chosen, his play has some shape, and he has already learnt the formal advantage of a division into acts. Medwall wrote *Fulgens and Lucrece*, whose title already suggests an Elizabethan play, and its use of an old Roman story to illustrate a discussion on the nature of true nobility is halfway to Elizabethan practice. But we gain little enjoyment from the Tudor interludes until the deliberately noninstructive trifles of John Heywood, who died when Shakespeare was leaving school. *The Four P's* is nothing but talk—a lying contest between a palmer, a pardoner, a 'pothecary, and a pedlar—but it is talk unstiffened by moral purpose. The *Play of the Weather* is a mere bubble, but it pretends to be nothing more. It is refreshing to find the yeast of pure entertainment working through the heavy didactic dough.

The English drama needs other things before it can become the Elizabethan tradition which Shakespeare was to enter, to modify, and to help enternize. First, it needs a theatre. The physical structure which the Swan, the Rose, the Globe, and the Fortune had in common was derived out of the Elizabethan inn, the innyard proving, to the wandering morality players, to be the most convenient location for a one-day stand. The square yard was enclosed by an upper gallery, on to which the bedchambers opened. Here, then, was space for the casual groundlings, standing-room only, and, above, balcony accommodation for the better sort, the ladies and gentlemen staying at the inn. The stage would be an improvised platform at one end of the innyard, and the fixed gallery above might also be used as an acting area. Play-performances encouraged the sale of wine and ale, and, with the growth of potential audiences, some entrepreneurs were encouraged to take over inns and turn them into permanent theatres. The stage now became a fixed structure—a platform or apron jutting into the auditorium; a roof supported by pillars to keep rain off the players; the upper gallery above the stage an essential element, though once a mere accident, and now called the tarrass; a couple of doors for exits and entrances; a recess behind the apron suitable for intimate scenes and called the study. The innyard origin was visible in outdoor theatres till the end, and the sale of liquid refreshments was a lucrative adjunct to art. When Shakespeare's Globe was burnt down in 1613, an auditor whose breeches were set on fire had the flames doused with bottled ale.

If the theatre derived from the court of an inn, its plays derived from the Inns of Court. The long demotic tradition made its way into the public drama of London, if at all, by very indirect means. The educated amateurs showed the professionals what to do. In 1561, as we know, *Gorboduc*, in the blank verse that the Earl of Surrey had invented, was produced. Its authors were Thomas Norton and Thomas Sackville, and it was performed at the Inner Temple. The story is taken from the *History of the Britons* by Geoffrey of Monmouth, the medieval chronicler, and it tells of the quarrel between Ferrex and Porrex, sons of King Gorboduc and Queen Videna, over the division of the kingdom of Britain. Porrex kills Ferrex, and Queen Videna kills Porrex. The Duke of Albany tried to take the country over, and civil war breaks out. There are horrors enough, as in all Elizabethan tragedy, but Norton and Sackville respect the Senecan tradition, which is to reserve the horror for the language and never show it in the stage action. The Senecan way was also the Athenian way: if a character is raped, mutilated, or murdered, have a messenger announce this; never sicken your refined audience by showing it.

There were, in fact, three ways in which Elizabethan tragic dramatists could write what are called Senecan plays. They could go straight to the Latin texts of Seneca, and try to transmit their spirit through English. This was the way of the amateurs who wrote for the Inns of Court. The second way was to go to the French dramatist Garnier, and accept his watering-down of Senecan language as less offensive than the fierce rhetoric of the Roman himself. This was not a way likely to succeed either in the drawing room or in the popular theatre. Samuel Daniel anticipated Shakespeare by writing a tragedy called *Cleopatra* for the delectation of the intellectuals who grouped themselves about the Earl of Pembroke. It is intolerable, especially if we come to it straight after rereading Shakespeare's *Antony and Cleopatra*, because it lacks savor of language and does not compensate for this with high-flavored action. The third way was that followed by most of the popular dramatists—imitation of the Italian tradition which called itself Senecan but littered the stage with corpses, some headless, others tongueless, yet others limbless. This was the tradition that Shakespeare pushed to its limit in *Titus Andronicus*, where there is rape, murder, mutilation, and, finally, cannibalism.

We can take it that Will, in his first prentice years in London, was learning hard, less from the amateur Senecans than from the Oxford and Cambridge masters of arts who provided sweated material for the professional theatres. What was a hobby to the dramatists of the Inns of Court, whose primary concern was the learning of law and the refinements of courtly living, was a means of earning a living to those graduates who had no vocation for the church or the bench and despised the craft of the teacher. In the days before Elizabeth's father dissolved the monasteries, the cloister and the monastic library had been ready to receive the penniless scholar, but now the penniless scholar was on his own. All that young men of learning like Greene and Nashe and Peele and Kyd could do was to write eyecatching pamphlets and essay the drama (unless, of course, they wished to take up espionage like Marlowe and end up with a dagger in the frontal lobes. But Marlowe had to write plays as well). It was, then, a hard enough life without nongraduates like this man from Stratford stepping in and doing better than his betters. We first meet the name of Shakespeare the dramatist in a sneering parody, in a context of bitterness and jealousy and scorn.

7

Shakescene

Thank God for Philip Henslowe. This was not the view of many who knew him personally, for so to know him meant mainly to owe him money. A typical Elizabethan entrepreneur on a modest scale, he owned a starch works, various brothels, a pawnbroker's shop, and a theatre. Of his birth and origins we know nothing, except that the family must originally have come from Hounslow. Of his death, we know that it came in 1616, the same year as Shakespeare's. His life was spent in making money and being conventionally pious or, some would say, hypocritical. To keep brothels and yet to preface his account books with ejaculations like "Jesus" might strike many who do not know the Elizabethans, or the English for that matter, as, to say the least, inconsistent. But the fact that he kept account books, with whatever religiose trimmings, is why we thank God for him. After all the speculation about Shakespeare's early life, the listening to posthumous gossip, and the piecing together from half-facts, it is a relief to approach a region of theatrical statistics—to know that, for the renovating of the Rose Theatre in 1592, Henslowe bought two dozen turned balusters at 2¼d each, and a further two dozen with a farthing discount, and that the new flag-mast, with a painted rose waving in the breeze, cost 12s.

In the New Year of 1592, when Will Shakespeare was approaching his twenty-eighth birthday, there were three play-houses in London. I have perhaps, through my intimation that the new proud London was a potential audience for Shake-speare, given the impression that the rulers of the city were as eager for playhouses as were the citizens. This is not true. The City Fathers distrusted the playhouses as places where plague might spread, unruly elements assemble, religion be mocked (acting, a kind of lying, was already a vague sin), and the tone of the capital be let down. Moreover, theatres were often a mere aspect of a total entertainment complex—as in Paris (or Paradise) Garden—with bull-baiting, bear-baiting, and ape-baiting to excite, make noise, and generally impair the dignity of a lofty place of trade. So the three theatres of London stood outside the city boundaries, in the aptly called "liberties"—the Theatre and the Curtain, both to the north in Shoreditch, and the Rose in Southwark, south of the Thames, not far from London Bridge.

The Rose, rethatched, replastered, repainted, refurbished at a total cost of £100, was ready in February 1592 to house Lord Strange's Men. This was a distinguished company, often called to play at Court (four times the previous Christmas, twice this Shrovetide), and it was led by the most accomplished actor of the day—Edward Alleyn. On February 19 the troupe opened a busy season with a comedy by Robert Greene—*Friar Bacon and Friar Bungay*. The house was only half full. There followed a number of anonymous plays—*Muly Mulocco, The Spanish Comedy of Don Horatio, Sir John Mandeville*, and *Harry of Cornwall*. There was also a tragedy by Greene—*Orlando Furioso*. None did very well, to Henslowe's undoubted gloom, in terms of takings. But on February 26, a Saturday, there was a packed house for a play by Christopher Marlowe—*The Jew of Malta*. On the following Friday, March 3, a chronicle play was presented which drew the highest takings of the entire season. It was called *Harry the Sixth*, and we know, though the audience did not, that its author was William Shakespeare.

In these bare facts there is a great deal to digest. Shakespeare had joined the best acting company of the day at some time between 1587 and 1592. He had left the Queen's Men, if he had ever belonged to the Queen's Men, along with Will Kemp, who was now chief clown to Lord Strange's. Tarleton was dead, the Queen's Men in decline, the future lay with high rhetorical art rather than with improvisations, caperings, and leerings. If Shakespeare was play-making for Lord Strange's, he was also acting, though probably only as a messenger or fourth gentle-man or fifth murderer. The composition of *Harry the Sixth*, new in March 1592, must have been preceded by hackwork of various kinds—finishing plays started by others, brightening up old stuff with fresh topical references, throwing in new rhetorical monologues to swell the lungs of the star performer. But *Harry the Sixth* showed the Rose audiences that here was a new man who was as good as Marlowe and better than Greene, showed Alleyn that he had a resident playwright who could sound the whole dramatic diapason, showed Henslowe that there was money to be made out of the nongraduate from Stratford.

The skill, craft allied with craftiness, that animates *Harry the Sixth* can best be appreciated if we look briefly at two things—the state of the times and the state of the drama as Shakespeare found it. *Harry the Sixth* is old history, but it is history that is made to seem relevant to the 1590s. It is about the warring factions that disrupt England on the death of Henry V and the accession of the infant king, leading to the outbreak of the Wars of the Roses. It is also about the revolt of France against its English rulers, the crowning of the Dauphin in Rheims Cathedral, the phenomenal military successes of Joan of Arc, or La Pucelle. The hero of the chronicle is Sir John Talbot, who puts Joan's forces to flight but dies when Somerset and York, who distrust each other, fail to give him unified support. Talbot is a great patriot, above the self-seeking of the red-rose and white-rose factions, and his speeches, though they are not above the punning ingenuity which Will could never resist, anticipate the white-hot oratory of a king who, though dead at the beginning of this play, is to be brought back to life later in a play of his own:

How are we park'd and bounded in a pale,
A little herd of England's timorous deer,
Maz'd with a yelping kennel of French curs!
. . . Sell every man his life as dear as mine,
And they shall find dear deer of us, my friends.
God and Saint George, Talbot and England's right,
Prosper our colors in this dangerous fight!

The anti-French feeling was opportune, and it was colored with some of the defiant spirit of 1588. In 1589, with the Armada defeated but the Spaniards ready to make another invasion attempt, if only they could assemble a fleet on the coast of Britanny, the great scene of the religious war had become France, where Henry of Navarre was struggling against the Catholic League to gain the throne. English money and English arms were supporting him, and various expeditions were sent—including one under the command of the young Earl of Essex—though with no decisive result. Whatever the outcome, Catholic France was to a dramatist a fine loaded property, especially with a witch like Joan to burn. Will was learning the box-office value of sex and sadism.

He was also learning how to write great speeches. There was a good deal of useful Senecanism in Thomas Kyd's *The Spanish Tragedy*, with its larger-than-life tragic hero, Hieronimo, one of Alleyn's most successful parts, and its highly memorable lines. Most of the cultivated knew the following by heart:

> What outcries pluck me from my naked bed,
> And chill my throbbing heart with trembling fear,
> Which never danger yet could daunt before?
> Who calls Hieronimo? Speak, here I am.

And this too, where Hieronimo cries out on the murder of his son:

> O eyes, no eyes, but fountains fraught with tears!
> O life, no life, but lively form of death!
> O world, no world, but mass of public wrongs,
> Confus'd and fill'd with murder and misdeeds!

Popular, but Will needed greater sophistication, as well as the fine excess which, with encouragement, he felt himself quali-fied to purvey. The dramatist he could best learn from was Christopher Marlowe.

Marlowe was Shakespeare's own age, but he had started earlier in both poetry and drama and had already achieved a reputation that was not all literary. He had been born in

Canterbury of a shoemaking family, so that his stock was much like Will's, though without the gentle leavening of county blood like the Ardens'. But he had been fortunate enough to get to Cambridge, where, along with other promising undergraduates, he had been drawn into the world of espionage, or so—with not very ample evidence—we like to believe. First, we may suppose that Marlowe, being a good son of Canterbury, had ambitions in the ministry. As often happened, he was approached in his second year at the university by agents of Catholicism. It was urged on him to serve the one true church and pursue his theological studies at the English College in Douai or Rome. Then agents of Her Majesty's Secret Service, under Walsingham, would step in and advise that he go along with the Catholic exhortation, thus gaining information in Rome or Douai of what Catholic subverters were to be sent to England. This would be a patriotic and pious act, though, unfortunately, the Queen's Majesty not granting a very large allowance for this valuable work of spying, it could not be well rewarded.

Marlowe did not join the ministry but, we presume, kept on with some sort of espionage work. In London he got drunk, smoked, indulged in pederasty (he once said that they were fools that liked not boys and tobacco) and, more than anything, blasphemed, saying that Moses was but a juggler, Christ's miracles were naught, and that Christ was, moreover, a sexual pervert himself who indulged in sodomy with the beloved disciple John. Marlowe, strangely or perhaps not, was not dragged into jail for his atheistical talk and his drunken violence (the watch, or constabulary, said they were in fear of him). It is possible that the roaring spitter at things sacred was using this front to hide other activities and that the Privy Council, knowing of these activities, left him alone. And the man who wrote the plays and poems was certainly no mere drink-sodden profligate, waiting for justice or a ruined liver to claim him.

He was a lyric, rather than a dramatic, genius, and the glory of plays like *Tamburlaine* and *Doctor Faustus* lies in the orchestral range of the verbal music, and the manner in which classical properties, mere dust in the hands of the versifiers who have only their learning to commend them, are transmuted into air, fire, and crystal. The lines are given to characters who are full of life but hardly seem human. Tamburlaine, the Scythian shepherd who becomes conqueror of Asia, is a dynamo of ingenious cruelty that makes the Marquis de Sade's creations seem very prosaic and reasonable. Tamburlaine slaughters all the girls of Damascus, uses the Soldan of Turkey as a footstool, then carries him about in a cage till he beats out his brains against the bars, burns the town in which his mistress Zenocrate dies, kills his own sons because of their alleged cowardice, harnesses two kings to his chariot, and shouts:

Holla, ye pamper'd jades of Asia!
What! can ye draw but twenty miles a day,
And have so proud a chariot at your heels,
And such a coachman as great Tamburlaine?

He takes Babylon and, before drowning all the inhabitants in a lake, has the governor pierced with arrows. One performance drew the audience into a session of gratuitous participation, for a child was accidentally shot with an arrow and died. There were not wanting those who said that Marlowe had put that in the script. Cruel as he is, Tamburlaine cannot help being a lyric poet:

Now walk the angels on the walls of heaven,
As sentinels to warn the immortal souls
To entertain divine Zenocrate.

Contemporary God-fearers were not slow to ascribe Tamburlaine's atheistical *Machtpolitik* to his author. And when *Doctor Faustus* appeared, it was assumed that Marlowe was being fancifully autobiographical: he, like the fearless seeker after ultimate truth and pleasure, must have sold his soul to Lucifer. Again, here was a play that spilled into the auditorium. At several performances real devils appeared to assist the enacted Mephistophilis on the stage. An apparition at Dulwich so scared the actors that they spent the night in prayer and fasting, and the next morning the actor who had played Faustus vowed to found a college in that very town and to call it the College of

God's Gift. The actor was Edward Alleyn, and the college still stands.

The poetry of *Doctor Faustus* is very remarkable, and it compensates for weak construction and tedious clowning. Much of the play is evidently the work of hack collaborators, but this is not:

> Was this the face that launch'd a thousand ships
> And burn'd the topless towers of Ilium?
> Sweet Helen, make me immortal with a kiss.
> Her lips suck forth my soul—see, where it flies:
> Come, Helen, come, give me my soul again.

Nor is this, the last choked utterance of Faustus:

> My God, my God, look not so fierce on me:
> Adders and serpents, let me breathe awhile:
> Ugly hell, gape not, come not, Lucifer—
> I'll burn my books . . . ah, Mephistophilis.

Apart from its poetic and dramatic interest, *Doctor Faustus* is worth examining as a Marlovian inconsistency. If Marlowe was a genuine atheist who believed that "hell's a fable," why did he expend such eloquence on demonstrating that hell was real? If, as some say, he was a true man of the Renaissance and an exponent of the unfettered human soul, why does he go to such trouble to justify the ways of God to man, thumping out almost sermonically the limitations of human ambition under the divine law? *Doctor Faustus* could have been written by a practicing Catholic. Perhaps it was: we shall never know the whole truth about Marlowe.

The play that was produced in the 1592 season that saw also *Harry the Sixth* shows other aspects of Marlowe. *The Jew of Malta* is about Barabas, a rich merchant who embodies the capitalist aspect of the Renaissance, as Faustus stands for the spirit of enquiry and Tamburlaine for glory in secular power. His story is prefaced by a speech from "Machiavelli"—not the true author of *Il Principe* but the popular Elizabethan travesty of him. Niccolò Machiavelli was "Old Nick," the Devil himself, the spirit of absolute evil. He is incarnated in characters like the

Duke of Guise in Marlowe's *The Massacre at Paris*, a being who scoffs at religion and will do anything to attain power:

> Set me to scale the high Pyramides
> And thereon set the diadem of France.
> I'll either rend it with my nails to naught,
> Or mount the top with my aspiring wings,
> Although my downfall be the deepest hell.

Hell again. Barabas the Jew meets a very tangible hell onstage. The Knights of Malta take all his wealth in order to pay their ransom to the Turks, much in arrears. Barabas embarks on a long career of revenge. His atrocities are on a smaller scale than Tamburlaine's, but this may be excused since Malta is a smaller place than the whole of Asia. Still, he poisons a whole convent of nuns, contrives that his daughter's two lovers shall kill each other, and finally proposes to slaughter the leaders of the invading Turks and to massacre the Turkish troops in a monastery. He has arranged to drop some of his enemies into a cauldron of boiling oil, but—through a trick of the governor of Malta—it is he who falls in:

> ... Had I but escap'd this stratagem,
> I would have brought confusion on you all,
> Damn'd Christian dogs and Turkish infidels!
> But now begins the extremity of heat
> To pinch me with intolerable pangs:
> Die, life! Fly, soul! tongue, curse thy fill, and die!

This is a very improbable dying speech, but so much in Marlowe, if viewed from the angle of dramatic naturalism, is improbable. It was T. S. Eliot who suggested that Marlowe's horrors are comic ones, that the technique of exaggeration is deliberately in the service of a philosophy that, though it seems to raise man to a heroic level never before seen in literature, really reduces him to the status of a monster with great ingenuity but no soul. And even in descriptive passages where we have a right to the sober notation of fact, the exaggerative faculty (which may be an aspect of the lyric-rhetorical faculty) takes over:

                    I rose,
And looking from a turret, might behold
Young infants swimming in their parents' blood,
Headless carcases piled up in heaps,
Virgins half-dead dragg'd by their golden hair
And with main force flung on a ring of pikes,
Old men with swords thrust through their agèd sides,
Kneeling for mercy to a Greekish lad
Who with steel pole-axes dashed out their brains.

That is Aeneas, recounting the taking of Troy to the heroine of *Dido, Queen of Carthage*. We cannot take the horrors as seriously as she does, for they are too baroque, too coldly organized into an image of excess—those swimming infants (I see them doing a strong overarm); all the virgins blonde; one Greekish lad attending, with a plurality of pole-axes, to several old men. It is horror-comedy.

Shakespeare's art did not develop out of Marlowe's. They were temperamentally too different, and it is to Ben Jonson—as we shall see later—that Marlowe leads, to a kind of satirical comedy which Shakespeare never had any desire to write. But Marlowe was to the apprentice Will a model for the organization of words into swelling speeches, a master of declamation which could modulate easily from the lyrical to the pounding rhetorical, and a great phrasemaker. In one early play, perhaps composed before the *Henry VI* sequence but not recorded among the Rose performances till the end of 1592, Shakespeare tried, as a deliberate task, to push horror to the limit and to create a Machiavellian character that should outbombast any of Marlowe's. This play is *Titus Andronicus*.

A recent revival of this work in London caused some members of the audience to walk out in nausea, and one lady fainted. Shakespeare had digested the unsavory attractions of *The Spanish Tragedy*, in which Hieronimo bites out his tongue on the stage, and he had probably seen executions at Tyburn. If the horror-lovers thought they could take anything, then let them take a scene in which a girl is raped by two brothers on the corpse of her husband, whom they have murdered, and, that she may not disclose the names of her ravishers, has her tongue cut out and her hands cut off. Later, she traces the names on the earth with a stick held between her stumps, and her father proceeds to revenge, which involves the killing of the rapists, the baking of their flesh in a pie (bones ground for flour, a laborious but ingenious notion), and the serving of this treat to their mother, whose bad idea, among others, that dual ravishing was. And there is Aaron, the Moor, who has given her a black bastard and has his own line in villainy. He ends like Barabas, unrepentant and cursing:

Ah, why should wrath be mute and fury dumb?
I am no baby, I, that with base prayers
I should repent the evils I have done;
Ten thousand worse than ever yet I did
Would I perform, if I might have my will.
If one good deed in all my life I did,
I do repent it from my very soul.

Not really unrepentant, then.

I see in this incredible work nothing but a tongue-in-cheek (or tongue-spat-out-of-cheek) exercise in a horror-and-revenge medium that Shakespeare, inexperienced as he was, could not take seriously except from the angle of box-office returns. It is the other side of that coin on which *The Comedy of Errors* is engraved—cold-blooded ingenuity, impossible complexity, a purging of an exaggerative faculty which could not, as in Marlowe, express itself as a strange magnificence.

In the three and a half months from early February to the closing of the playhouses in June, Lord Strange's Men acted on one hundred and five days. *Harry the Sixth* drew the most cash, and it is estimated that about ten thousand people altogether came to see it. Greene's plays did badly, and Greene was resentful, but he had no real right to be, since he professed a scorn for the stage. He had, he had said, no desire to see his verses "jet upon the stage in tragical buskins, every word filling the mouth like the faburdon of Bow Bell, daring God out of Heaven with that atheist Tamburlaine." He had always wished to produce great literary art for select readers, but he had to go

where the money was—in plays and pamphlets. But he made
the mistake of assuming that the popular audiences were made
up of fools, and that insincerity, bad workmanship, and improb-
ability of plot and character could get past them. On the other
hand, they should be grateful for the orts of scholarship thrown
at them by a master of arts:

> Lordly sir, whose conquest is as great
> In conquering love, as Caesar's victories,
> Margaret, as mild and humble in her thoughts
> As was Aspasia unto Cyrus' self,
> Yields thanks.

The girl who speaks these lines is the simple country wench of
Fressingfield, with whom the Prince of Wales falls in love in
Friar Bacon and Friar Bungay. It is not a bad comedy—it has
fine lyrical splashes and, in the scenes with the two magical
friars, it has the science-fiction gimmick of a closed-circuit
television set—but it is not quite good enough.

The case of Robert Greene is a sad one. He was about six
years older than Shakespeare, handsome, well made, with an
unshorn red beard. In 1592, this last year of his life, he had
come as low as any hack in Grub Street history, churning out
pamphlets on the rogues, cardsharpers, and bawds of the London he knew well, too well. He had a cutpurse follower called
Cutting Ball, who was quick with a dagger when his master was
threatened by any of his creditors. Once, when a writ was
served, Greene had forced the server to eat it up, wax seal and
all, from a fine dish in a tavern. He had a wife, but he lived
with Ball's sister, a decayed whore who had given him a brat he
named Fortunatus. He drank too much, and pamphlets like *A
Notable Discovery of Cozenage* and the two parts of *Conycatch-
ing* were dashed off to buy a quart of ale or a bottle of Rhenish.
His liver and kidneys were rotting, and he had accessions of
maudlin repentance for his wasted and dissolute life. The
disclosures of London crime that made up his later pamphlets
were written in, we are made to believe, no spirit of sensational-
ism but out of a sincere desire to protect the unwary through
foreknowledge. Greene was growing pious, but there is nothing

devotionally anemic about his last summer's work. He was a vigorous writer, and he is still good to read.

On June 11 there was a riot in Southwark. In the morning the Knight Marshal's Men, somewhat brutal peacekeepers, arrested the servant of a feltmaker on no real charge and cast him into the prison called the Marshalsea. In the afternoon the Rose put on a new play, A *Knack to Know a Knave*, followed by a jig, or brief bawdy farce, that Will Kemp had devised. The theatre was full of apprentices resentful of the Marshal's Men's high-handed brutality, and they marched off after the performance to demand that the prisoner be released from jail. The Marshal's Men laid into the mob with daggers, cudgels, eventually swords, but they got the worst of the battle. The Lord Mayor and his men rode in and restored order. The Council took a serious view of the matter, saw the danger of playhouses as places of free assembly, especially for unruly apprentices, and ordered that no more plays be shown until the following Michaelmas—September 29. The players went off on tour. The enforced closure of the Rose proved a blessing, for the summer was hot and dry, the city filthy and airless, and the plague broke out.

Greene was left alone in squalid lodgings, with a scolding mistress, a howling brat, and an awareness that he was far from well. He got drunk with Nashe, another pamphleteer, perhaps a greater one than Greene, and ate greedily of pickled herrings. His body began to swell, but he still had to push on with his hand-to-mouth writing. The players had all gone, and he brooded bitterly if unreasonably on their ingratitude. They had come to him asking for plays, and he had written plays, and they had made money on his plays and gone off on their horses to make more money on his plays in the provinces. He, meanwhile, was left alone among lice and fleas and the smell of the city's ordure. Buboes were swelling in people's armpits, and the death-carts were coming round. Intimations of mortality:

> Beauty is but a flower
> Which wrinkles will devour;
> Brightness falls from the air;

Queens have died young and fair;
Dust hath closed Helen's eye;
I am sick, I must die.
Lord, have mercy on us!

Nashe's lines, but Nashe himself had left stinking London. Greene looked at his body and saw the dropsy fast at work. His bitterness fastened on one image, that of a quiet unlettered smiler from somewhere in the barbarous provinces. The bitterness broke in an open letter he wrote to his fellow scholars, financial failures, magnanimous men battened on by the play-hungry players. He warned them to beware of the players, and he attacked from a full heart of resentment one particular player:

> Yes, trust them not: for there is an upstart crow, beautified with our feathers, that with his "Tiger's heart wrapt in a player's hide" supposes he is as well able to bombast out a blank verse as the best of you; and being an absolute *Johannes factotum*, is in his own conceit the only Shake-scene in a country. O that I might intreat your rare wits to be employed in more profitable courses: and let those apes imitate your past excellence, and never more acquaint them with your admired inventions.

This, like that earlier play-list, needs slow digestion. One fact unrevealed by the play-lists is that the second part of the *Henry VI* trilogy had been performed before June 11. For here is Greene parodying a line from it. The captive Duke of York addresses the vindictive Queen Margaret as "She-wolf of France, but worse than wolves of France," and, a few lines later, says: "O tiger's heart wrapt in a woman's hide." The *Johannes factotum*, Johnny Do-all or Jack-of-all-trades, refers to the play-mending, speech-vamping, walking-on Will who has now bloomed into a dramatic poet whose lines are memorable— even to a rival who resents finding them so. "Shake-scene" is one of those jealous deformations of the great name to which the great name seems to lend itself—Shakebag or Shagbeard and even perhaps the Shagnasty which is used today for hated people whose names are not Shakespeare. The whole thing is a nice piece of invective but it is totally unjust. It is implied that this country crow without a graduate's gown picks at the fur in the master's hoods of his betters and clothes himself in it, whereas Will is doing no more than draw on the common stock of the poetic drama—available to all without reader's ticket or diploma of graduation. The true bitterness, though, lies in a realization that the literary men have failed to capture the popular theatrical market, and that its future seems to lie with grammar-school upstarts.

To be fair to Greene, he did not himself publish this very personal attack. He died on September 2, sometime in the night, leaving many papers which the printing buzzards were quick to swoop on. His end was pathetic, and Shakespeare may have had it in mind when, in *Henry V*, he described the death of Falstaff. Greene's landlady, Mrs. Isam, told how he cried for a penny pot of malmsey wine, how he crawled with lice, how his doublet and hose and sword were sold for three shillings and his winding-sheet and burial came together to ten shillings and fourpence. He left a letter to the wife he had deserted, asking her of her charity and former love to pay his debts to his landlord and landlady, for if they "had not succored me, I had died in the streets." Mrs. Isam, with some vague memory of what was due to a poet, crowned the poor head with a garland of bays.

Wright, Burby, and Chettle grabbed such publishable material as they could find and ran off with it. Chettle, a real *Johannes factotum* of the book trade, ready to write, print, playmake, or do anything with words that would make money, had a book in Greene's name ready by September 20—piping-hot stuff, straight from the grave in Bedlam churchyard. It was called *A Groatsworth of Wit Bought with a Million of Repentance*, and in it the attack on Shake-scene the upstart crow was set down for the delectation of the enemies of promise. Burby was late with *The Repentance of Robert Greene, Master of Arts*. It was not ready till October 6, when Greene had been in his grave a whole month.

In that October of 1592, Lord Strange's Men were probably all back in London. On the 22nd there was a wedding: Ned

Alleyn married Joan Woodward, Henslowe's stepdaughter, to his financial advantage—probably a share in the freehold of the Rose. At the celebrations, Shakespeare must have brooded over Greene's attack with a mixture of feelings. He was worthy of a dying poet's venom; he was rising high, enough in the world to earn envy; he was being sniggered about ("There he goes, Shake-scene the Upstart Crow—caw caw caw. How dost thou, Johnny Fatscrotum?"); a noble name had made its first appearance in print in shameful deformation: his father would not wish it so. He had wished Robin Greene no harm—he had even bought him the odd pot of wine and lent him a groat or so without pressure of repayment. It was an unclean business, and Will sought to be washed free of it by, we must presume, going to Chettle and speaking his mind.

In December Chettle apologized. Wright brought out *Kindhart's Dream* and Chettle prefaced it with an epistle *To the Gentleman Readers*. He should, he admitted, have edited Greene's own words with more care. He had known nothing of Shakespeare at the time but he had met him since. He regrets the libel "because myself have seen his demeanor no less civil than he excellent in the quality he professes; besides, divers of worship have reported his uprightness of dealing which argues his honesty, and his facetious grace in writing that approves his art." The image is clear enough—Will quiet and polite, no Marlovian ranter or drinker, a man honorable in his financial dealings and a pretty and painstaking sort of writer. It is an image that will do to round off a busy year. At Christmas, the Rose due to open on December 30 with *Muly Mulocco*, it was in order for Will—not too deeply and with various reservations—to toast the future.

8

Patron

※※※※※※※※※※※※※※※※※※※※

The year 1592 had been remarkable, with new plays, plague,
and the death of a dissolute poet. Even more remarkable was
1593. In addition to new plays there were new poems, important ones. The plague was so virulent that, at its worst, it took
off a thousand a week. And there was a poet not merely dissolute but atheistical, doomed not just to die but to be murdered.

The cold beginning of 1593 damped down the plague, and
January was a hard-working month for Lord Strange's Men at
the Rose. They performed *The Spanish Tragedy*, *The Jew of
Malta*, *Titus Andronicus*, poor Greene's *Friar Bacon and Friar
Bungay*, an anonymous work called *The Jealous Comedy*, and
Marlowe's fiery, bloody *Massacre at Paris*. There was also *Henry
VI*, probably the whole trilogy. On Candlemas Day, February
2, the anniversary of the christening of the Shakespeare twins,
the playhouses were closed down: there were over thirty plague
deaths a week, and the situation failed to improve when spring
came. This plague was a great nuisance but, like cancer of the
lung, it was probably only there to kill other people. Shakespeare and his fellows had no real desire to rush out of London
to avoid it; they would have been happier to go on playing at the
Rose while the death-tumbrils rumbled through the streets.

We know all about this scourge now, but the Elizabethans did
not. When Henslowe's brothels had to close down, and the odd
stricken inmate had to be carried off on a shutter, there would
probably be more talk of God's judgment than of a causative
organism. The bubonic plague was a long accepted part of the
folklore of medieval and Renaissance Europe, and nobody

associated it with rats. Yet it was the rats of London, probably the stowaway ones, that brought it in. The rats' fleas sucked the diseased rats' blood, than attacked human beings and transferred the bacilli. The rat-flea-man process was the standard means of conveying the plague; unless it had become pneumonic, when it could be transferred by droplet infection, man did not give it to man. Nor did drinking water have anything to do with its spread, despite a common belief. The epidemic grew among human beings because it grew among rats, and the process was helped by rat-cannibalism, infected food, and even human feces. The outbreak of the disease among animals preceded human cases by about a fortnight.

The disease was characterized by enlargement of the lymphatic glands, usually the axillary ones, this forming the primary bubo—hence the term *bubonic*. There were secondary buboes in other parts of the body, but these were small and inconsiderable. After a maximum of ten days' incubation, the bubo appeared and heralded other symptoms—headache, chill, pains in the back, rapid pulse, restlessness, high fever. The symptoms galloped, drawing vomiting and delirium into the ride to an unavoidable conclusion. In seventy per cent of the cases, death usually followed in three to four days. It was nasty, painful, messy, and only a Nashe could make poetry out of it, though Nashe also described it realistically in his novel *The Unfortunate Traveller*. The "great visitation" of 1665 was the final assault on London, or any English city, and history has made it spectacular enough to render the plague Shakespeare knew seem a mere irritant. But it might have killed Shakespeare in that dangerous year 1593: he stayed in London while his fellows did not.

It was in May that Ned Alleyn got a small traveling troupe together: they would spend the rest of the year taking culture to the provinces. They secured a special license from the Privy Council to play anywhere seven miles out of London and beyond, and were even honored by an exhortation to provincial authorities to encourage and assist their playing. This was because Lord Strange's Men were looked on with royal favor, and they had to keep in trim in readiness for being called to Court. The troupe contained names we shall meet later: Thomas Pope, John Heminges, Gus Phillips, George Bryan, as well as William Kemp. They are among the names of the "principall actors in all these playes" prefixed to the collection of Shakespeare's plays which appeared (the First Folio) posthumously in 1623. They were already skilled players and were soon (except for Kemp) to become great ones.

Shakespeare's first phase as rising dramatist ended in 1593. If we discount *Titus Andronicus* and *The Comedy of Errors* as grotesque but vigorous exercises in, respectively, Italianate Senecan revenge tragedy and Plautine mistaken-identity farce, we can say that he had started with a very massive concept— nothing less than an epic chronicle of the Wars of the Roses. *Richard III* follows naturally on from the *Henry VI* trilogy, bringing the long story to an end with the reconciliation of the white and red roses in the marriage of Harry of Richmond and Elizabeth of York, and the inauguration of the Tudor dynasty which must die with the death of Elizabeth of England. The whole tetralogy was cunningly designed to exploit various popular emotions and certain artistic devices. There was anti-French feeling, articulate patriotism, fears about the succession; there was the new rhetoric—an instrument for Alleyn—and the new Machiavellianism, as well as the probing of character and motive which was Shakespeare's own contribution to drama. That weak king, Henry, is curiously appealing, the misshapen Richard of York is the ultimate villain, but neither can be written off as a mere instrument for eliciting audience responses. *Richard III* is, with all its crudities, an approach to the three-dimensional drama, in which men are not always what they seem. For the first time, in Clarence's dream speech, the unconscious mind is netted and landed. The response of Anne to Richard's wooing is a mixture of attraction and revulsion. Richard himself has power to excite a ghastly sympathy. The horror of the play is not spooned out of the Senecan stockpot, despite the conventional ghosts: there is a claustrophobic atmosphere in this agonized stage-England which is not merely new but inimitable. *Richard III* has, as all actors know, its own flavor, and it is to be found in no other play.

Shakespeare struck the camp of Bosworth and folded up the banners. In other words, he put away the copy of Holinshed's *Chronicles* which was his sourcebook for the English historical plays. He would need it again soon. *Richard II*, the two parts of *Henry IV*, and *Henry V* had to be written sometime, to make the story of usurpation and baronial conflict complete. Later the whole pageant might possibly come to an end with Henry VIII and the birth of the infant Elizabeth. He had plunged in in the middle, like an epic poet, but he needed a rest before dipping his pen in blood again. Now he began to dip it in honey. There was the story of Venus and Adonis to take up once more. The time was propitious for establishing himself as a narrative poet. That way, and not the way of stage thunder and being reviled as a *Johannes factotum*, was the true way to advancement. Classical amorousness was in the air. Lodge had written a rather dull *Scilla's Metamorphosis*, and a man called Clapham had done the story of Narcissus in Latin verse. More than anything, Marlowe was at work on his *Hero and Leander*, and Shakespeare had seen the manuscript. The description of Hero's garments confirmed him in his belief that his own amorous subject was a good one:

> Her wide sleeves green, and border'd with a grove
> Where Venus in her naked glory strove
> To please the careless and disdainful eyes
> Of proud Adonis that before her lies.

In May 1593 Marlowe was working on this poem in the manor of Scadbury, near Chislehurst, Kent, the country home of his friend Sir Thomas Walsingham, young cousin of Sir Francis. He had probably gone there not solely to work in quiet but to escape plague-racked London. But London called him back: the Privy Council wished to question him. There had been trouble, though none directly involving Marlowe. The recusants—Catholic and Puritan alike—had been active, and obscene libels on the Flemings, decent Protestant immigrant workers, had been circulating. Commissioners appointed by the Council began to search among London's literate irresponsibles, which meant chiefly poor men who tried to make a living out of pamphlets and plays, to see if they could find anything in writing which might provide a clue to the originators of the libels. These commissioners had considerable powers and could put a man on the rack or break his fingers if he were reluctant to give evidence. Broken fingers, it was recognized, could be a handicap to a writer.

The commissioners went to the lodgings of Thomas Kyd, well-known author of *The Spanish Tragedy*, arrested him, and carried him off to the Bridewell. While he sweated there, they examined his papers and found a number of heretical documents among them—denials of Christ's divinity, sneers at his miracles, gross arguments in favor of atheism. It sounded like Marlowe, and Kyd said it *was* Marlowe: Marlowe had left those papers in Kyd's lodgings two years before when they had been working together on plays. Now, whatever the Privy Council knew of the true Marlowe behind the long-tolerated mask of antireligious roarer, he had to be summoned formally to explain himself. On May 20 he was told to be ready to wait on the Council daily until instructed otherwise. He had ten days of life left: he does not seem to have been questioned on any one of them. He lodged at Deptford, near enough to both the city and his retreat in Kent. On May 30 he went to the tavern at Deptford kept by Eleanor Bull, a widow. The invitation to go thither probably came from Ingram Frizer, an unpleasant and devious character. Two friends of Frizer came along—Nick Skeres, a swindler, and Robert Poley, a perjurer and double-agent.

The party dined together at midday, walked in the garden of the tavern, talked a lot, then sat down to supper. After the meal—and, one assumes, a fair day's drinking—there was a quarrel. Some say it was about who should pay the reckoning, others, the honor of a wench. Marlowe, in a rage, grabbed Frizer's dagger and gave him two shallow wounds; Frizer tried to snatch the weapon back. In the struggle the dagger was driven into Marlowe's head over the right eye to a depth of two inches. His agony was extreme, and he died shrieking—some, of course, said swearing. At the inquest there were only three witnesses—Frizer, Skeres, and Poley. Frizer had acted in self-defense, said the jury.

Had he? Speculation can go on forever. Had the Spanish Secret Service paid good money to be rid of a dangerous spy? Had the friend or brother of a Catholic betrayed by Marlowe to the gallows paid out money in revengeful bitterness? Did Marlowe's own employers now find it convenient to have him silenced for good? We shall never know. To the simpler-minded, Marlowe's end had been engineered by a wrathful God. So perish all blasphemers. So, for that matter, perish all playwrights. Greene, in that letter that had attacked the upstart crow, had warned Marlowe: "Why should thy excellent wit, His Gift, be so blinded that thou should'st give no glory to the Giver? Is it pestilent Machiavellian policy that thou hast studied? O peevish folly!" And later: "Defer not, with me, till this last point of extremity: *for little knowest thou how in the end thou shalt be visited.*" The warning had gone unheeded; the prophecy of doom had been fulfilled.

We can only guess at Will Shakespeare's feelings about Kit Marlowe. That he admired him greatly as a poet we can be sure. But the tribute paid in *As You Like It* is more personal than literary:

Dead shepherd, now I find thy saw of might:
"Who ever lov'd that lov'd not at first sight?"

The saw comes in *Hero and Leander*, a most promising poem left, alas, unfinished. Marlowe is a shepherd because he wrote the exquisite "The Passionate Shepherd to His Love," a lyric well remembered in *The Merry Wives of Windsor*. Affection may have been mingled with strong disapproval of Marlowe's manner of live, for Shakespeare was a quiet man who wished to be taken for a gentleman. But Marlowe was also a scholar, and Shakespeare never despised learning. Learning, and the spirit of free enquiry which should be the best fruit of learning, were reserved for the private Faustus Marlowe, not the public Tamburlaine one. He had been a member of a sober discussion group called, by the suspicious, the School of Night and popularly believed to be a sort of warlocks' coven. It was led by Sir Walter

Raleigh, voyager, soldier, courtier, poet, historian, introducer to England of a great solace of life. The group contained other reputable names—the Earl of Northumberland, George Chapman the poet, Harriot the brilliant mathematician and astronomer (who, according to the public Marlowe, was worth ten of Moses), Gabriel Harvey, others. The tone of the sessions was serious, they went in much for the reconciling of science with revelation, and Sir Walter always called for prayers at the end. Whether Will ever attended we cannot know, but we can guess that he was not greatly interested in intellectual discussion. He arrived at his truths by intuition. As for ideas, they were the raw matter of poetry and drama, and the Ptolomaic cosmology would do as well for a sonnet or a speech as the Copernican. And he was taught by certain new friends that Sir Walt Stink the tobacco-man was despicable, given to slyness and treachery, a seducer of the Queen's Glories. Had not the Queen sent him to the Tower in '92 for defiling of a Maid of Honor's honor? He was friendly to the Puritans. And he was an atheist. How could such be reconciled, my lord? It is possible, Will, all things are possible.

Possible, for instance, that destiny was working towards the elevation of Shakespeare to England's best poet by getting two rivals out of the way—first Greene, now Marlowe. *Venus and Adonis* appeared nearly six weeks before Marlowe's death. He had probably seen a printed copy and said: "Mellifluous, too much so—candy with honey sauce. Too grossly man-and-woman. It lacks the delicacy of corruption. Ah, wait till *Hero and Leander* is finished—." It was a beautiful piece of printing, done by Dick Field, the lucky Stratfordian who had married the widow of his master the Frenchman Thomas Vautrollier and taken over the business. There were to be rumors later that Will had posted dexterously to her bed while Field was on one of his periodical trips to Stratford, perhaps with loving messages to Anne and the children as well as some gold. At the moment, though, Anne's husband had little time for adultery. He was seeking preferment. *Venus and Adonis* had an eloquent dedicatory epistle, real courtier's stuff: "I know not how I shall offend in dedicating my unpolished lines to your lordship, nor how the world will censure me for choosing so strong a prop to support so weak a burden..." The dedicatee was the Right Honorable Henry Wriothesley (pronounced Rizley), Earl of Southampton and Baron of Titchfield. "But if the first heir of my invention prove deformed, I shall be sorry it had so noble a godfather, and never after ear so barren a land, for fear it yield me still so bad a harvest." *First* heir? Either this was the first literary work Shakespeare had ever attempted, back home in Stratford, or else the plays were not to be regarded as literary work. He was concerned enough with publishing his poems, but not his plays. Poets like Greene had taught him that plays were nothing to be proud of.

Southhampton was nineteen years old—beautiful, self-admiring, with no inclination to become entangled with women. George Chapman wrote him a poem on the theme of Narcissus, which (the subject more than the knotty involved verses) went down well. *Venus and Adonis* also had an apt subject, and it was a far better poem. It achieved immense popularity among the young men of the Inns of Court, and it was said that some slept with it under the pillow. The honor was more Southampton's than the poet's. Anyone can be a handsome young nobleman; few can be the godfather of a work like *Venus and Adonis*. There goes his lordship. It is to him that *Venus*—Yes, yes, the facetious conceits, the mellifluities. Oh, sweet Mr. Shakespeare.

The earldom was a fairly new one. Henry Wriothesley's father, the second Southampton, had died in 1581—a Catholic who had upheld the rights of faith of the Duke of Norfolk and been sent to the Tower. His son, at the age of eight, became a royal ward, and he was placed in the care of Sir William Cecil, Lord Burghley, Lord High Treasurer of the realm. Lord Burghley sent him up to Cambridge—St. John's College. A freshman at twelve, he was a Master of Arts at sixteen. Then he was entered at Gray's Inn to complete his education. The Inns of Court had a sort of finishing-school function for the sons of gentlemen: they taught law but they also taught manners. Now, young as he was, it was proposed that Southampton marry. Lord Burghley had a very suitable match lined up—the Lady Elizabeth Vere, his own granddaughter. Southampton's mother, the widowed Countess, urged on him the need to secure the succession. One knew not the day nor the hour: the plague raged, earls have died young and fair. And this business of securing the succession obsessed the nobility for another reason: the Queen was setting such a bad example. Understandably, Southampton pleaded his unreadiness for the married state: he asked for at least a year of bachelor freedom. His grandfather, Lord Montacute (or Montague) of Beaulieu, brought in a faux-bourdon to his mother's descant. In the middle, Lord Burghley sang loudly of his ward's duty. Later he grew harsh, later still angry and vindictive.

Southampton did not want to look after his estates and raise a family. He wanted to be a soldier and follow the Earl of Essex to the wars in France. Robert Devereux, born in 1566, was, to Henry Wriothesley, a glamorous elder model of gallantry. Master of the Horse in his twenty-first year, distinguished participant in Drake's expedition to Portugal in his twenty-third, he commanded the entire Normandy expedition in his twenty-fifth. He was married, but his marriage was not unglamorous: his wife was the widow of Sir Philip Sidney, heroically dead after Zutphen in 1586, poetically very much alive with his *Astrophel and Stella* sonnet-sequence. Southampton tried hard to accompany his hero on the French expedition of 1591, but he was told to stay at home and think about the succession. The Queen eased his sulks by making much of him. He was handsome, witty, knew his classics. He was an ornament of the Court and, to a man as ambitious as Shakespeare, an ideal prospective patron. He was also wealthy.

We do not know whether the Earl and the poet had met each other before the dedication, or whether permission to dedicate was obtained vicariously. A useful go-between would be John Florio, Southampton's secretary, the son of an Italian Protestant refugee who had settled in London. Florio had been a professor of languages at Oxford but was now working on his Italian-English dictionary—an important contribution to philology, published in 1598. A secretarial post with Southampton gave him leisure and opportunity to observe the spoken English of the capital. That he came to the Rose to see the plays we can hardly doubt: Florio was word-mad (his dictionary was to be called A *World of Words*), and Shakespeare was a rising word-man. From Florio Shakespeare might have learned something about Montaigne, father of the essay, and stored up something of his spirit for *Hamlet*. Montaigne, dead in 1592, his *Essais* translated by Florio and published by him in 1603, was a Frenchman good for the English. He was intellectually curious but totally undogmatic: his big question was *"Que sais-je?"*— what do I know? He was dedicated to easy benevolence, toler- ance, empiricism. He was unlike, say, Archbishop Whitgift. *Hamlet* is really about the impact on a Montaigne-like man of the harsh world of power and intrigue. The tragedy of the prince derives from his having to act, and to base that action on a premise which a Montaigne-like man is bound to find uncomfortable. If one's father's ghost talks of murder and calls for revenge, it is hard to shrug and say *"Que sais-je?"*

It is possible that Shakespeare met Southampton as easily as he met (if he did) Florio. Young Inns of Court men flocked to the playhouse. Actors and playwrights have always been able to mix with comparative freedom in aristocratic circles. Think of Noël Coward and Earl Mountbatten. But we have to push a mere acquaintanceship further—not just to the formal postures of patron and patronized, but to something like friendship. Just over a year after the publication of *Venus and Adonis*, Shake- speare dedicated another long narrative poem to Southampton. This was *The Rape of Lucrece*, the story of Tarquin's forcing of the chastity of a noble matron. The whole prefatory epistle is worth quoting here:

> The love I dedicate to your lordship is without end; whereof this pamphlet, without beginning, is but a superfluous moiety. The warrant I have of your honorable disposition, not the worth of my untutored lines, makes it assured of acceptance. What I have done is yours; what I have to do is yours; being part in all I have, devoted yours. Were my worth greater, my duty would show

greater; meantime, as it is, it is bound to your lordship, to whom
I wish long life, still lengthened with happiness.

Your lordship's in all duty,

WILLIAM SHAKESPEARE.

Shakespeare had evidently been very close to his lordship in this
memorable year—a year in which the plague strengthened and,
in September, killed a thousand a week. The playhouses remained shut till December 26, 1593, but it was Sussex's Men
who played at the Rose—till Candlemas, 1594, when plague-
panic closed the theatres till April. Will may have been composing plays, but he was not acting them. Lord Strange's Men were
away. Will, one thinks, was living at Southampton House in
Holborn, or at Titchfield, one of the Earl's retinue, a tame
poet, a sort of friend. It is doubtful if he liked the life as much
as he had expected, but this was a mere inn on the long road to
fulfilment—an opulent inn, but no home. The route from
Henley Street, Stratford, to New Place, Stratford, was remark-
ably circuitous.

9

Friend

❧❧❧❧❧❧❧❧❧❧❧❧❧❧❧❧

"With this key," wrote William Wordsworth, "Shakespeare unlocked his heart." He was referring to the sonnet form, that
imported lyrical apparatus of fourteen lines, which the publication of Sidney's *Astrophel and Stella* made suddenly popular in
the early 1590s. Shakespeare, never slow to follow fashions,
produced one hundred and fifty-four sonnets between 1593 and
1600. In the first flush he turned them out in abundance; later
he was a more desultory sonneteer. They were published in
1609 by Thomas Thorpe, probably against the poet's wishes.
There was in those days no law of copyright; there was nothing
to prevent an enterprising printer from putting out whatever he
could get hold of, with neither apology nor recompense to the
author. Piracy sounds more romantic, more Elizabethan, than
theft. It was difficult to find a moral basis for condemning
literary piracy, since the bigger and more profitable marine
piracy of Francis Drake had gained him a knighthood.

Shakespeare and his fellow actors suffered a great deal from
pirates in the playhouse. Any play written was automatically the
property of the company it was written for. When Alleyn came
to Lord Strange's Men from the Lord Admiral's Men, he could
not bring *Tamburlaine* with him, for Marlowe had sold the play
to the company, not its chief actor. Theatrical companies played
fair with each other; not to play fair would have meant chaos,
the cheapening of a proud art. But printers had no such
scruples. If they could not steal a jealously guarded playscript,
they could at least send men to its performance in the theatre
and have them take it down in shorthand. The shorthand used

was not the phonetic notation of a Gregg or Pitman; it was based on ideograms, characters which made semantic sense on the principle of Chinese, and it was called *charactery*. If the piratical shorthand writer could not take down the sound of what he heard on the stage, only the sense, then the result would often be pitiful. *To be*—down goes the character meaning *to exist* or *to live*; *or*—straightforward enough; *not to be*—the opposite of *to be*—*to die* will do; *that is the*—a sort of copula symbol or equals sign; *question*—a character meaning not only *question* but *point, consideration, argument*. Taking his charactery home, the shorthand writer would remember some of what he heard, but not all. He could transcribe Hamlet's line, with fair semantic accuracy, as "To live or to die—aye, there's a point." But the poetry and magic would be gone.

In 1603 a "bad" quarto of *Hamlet* was published, full of the bathetic horrors of insensitively reconstituted charactery. The only way to drive out the bad was to publish the good—a sort of Gresham's Law in reverse. And so *Hamlet* as Shakespeare wrote it appeared in 1604. It was not poet's pride or vainglory that lay behind the other quartos published in his lifetime: it was his company protecting itself from the pirates. The argument, a sound one, was that people would usually buy the genuine if they could get it, and that would liquidate the false.

The publication of Shakespeare's Sonnets in 1609 had nothing to do with charactery or the illiterate travestying of great art. Thorpe got hold of fair copies of poems which, once having been written, would pass from hand to hand privately, being further copied on the way. Somebody had procured a whole chestful of Shakespeare's sonnets for Thomas Thorpe, and Thorpe was duly grateful. His (not Shakespeare's) dedication reads: "To the onlie begetter of these insuing sonnets Mr. W. H. all happinesse and that eternitie promised by our ever-living poet, wisheth the well-wishing adventurer in setting forth." It has usually been assumed that the "Mr. W. H." is the poet's own dedicatee, the man who begot the sonnets as a father begets a son, the fertilizer of the poet's imagination, but *beget* and *get* in Elizabethan English could mean the same thing, and Mr. W. H. was quite possibly the man who got the sonnets for Thorpe.

But if we play the scholars' game and puzzle over the identity of a Mr. W. H. in Shakespeare's life, or come out confidently with an assertion as to who he was, then we enter a dangerous world of time-wasting dissension, where monomania thumps and lunacy beckons. Those who say that Mr. W. H. was William Herbert, Earl of Pembroke, clash with those who are sure that he was Wriothesley, Henry, Earl of Southampton (a man told to put his family first), and there are side skirmishes involving scholars like Dr. Hotson, who has written a book to prove that Mr. W. H. was William Hatliffe, glamour boy of Gray's Inn, and—though his theory has long been exploded—Oscar Wilde, who said that he was Will Hughes, a young actor. Let us leave all this speculation for the moment and look at the Sonnets themselves.

The sonnet tradition which the Elizabethans inherited from the Italians was exquisite and courtly, essentially aristocratic and somewhat impersonal, concerned with the expression of love for a mistress who might or might not really exist. Petrarch was the great exemplar of the form, and the Italian sonnet structure is often named after him. Milton, Wordsworth, and Gerard Manley Hopkins used it with great success, but the Elizabethans found it unsympathetic—too much rhyme ingenuity was required. An octave, or eight lines, presented a theme, and a sestet, or six lines, qualified that theme or even contradicted it. The octave rhymed on the pattern *abba abba*, so that there were only two rhymes—easy enough in Italian, where many words have identical endings, as with *amore, cuore, fiore, dolore*, but not so easy in English, which is short of rhymes. The fact of this shortage, you will remember, sends a poet to Room 101 in Orwell's *Nineteen Eighty-Four*: he can find only one suitable rhyme for *rod*, and that once holy name is inadmissible in the superstate. The sestet was more manageable, since you could have *cde cde* if you wished, as well as *cdc dcd* or (difficult) *ccd ccd*. But the Elizabethans preferred to organize the fourteen lines into three four-line stanzas and a final couplet. At this point I may as well introduce the name of Michael Drayton, another Warwickshire man and well known to Shakespeare. In the sequence called *Ideas Mirror*, published in 1594, there is a very fine sonnet indeed:

Since there's no help, come let us kiss and part,—
Nay, I have done, you get no more of me;
And I am glad, yea glad with all my heart,
That thus so cleanly I myself can free.

Shake hands for ever, cancel all our vows,
And when we meet at any time again,
Be it not seen in either of our brows
That we one jot of former love retain.

Now at the last gasp of love's latest breath,
When, his pulse failing, passion speechless lies,
When faith is kneeling by his bed of death,
And innocence is closing up his eyes,

Now if thou would'st, when all have given him over,
From death to life thou might'st him yet recover!

The main virtue of Drayton's sonnet, apart from its drama, its reconciliation of speech rhythms with the demands of a strict lyrical form, and its immense simplicity of language, is what we must term, using a debased word, its sincerity. It is not a conventional adieu; it sounds as if wrung out of experience. Sir Philip Sidney was teaching English sonneteers that poetry had to be more than a trinket for a lady or a patball game in a summer arbor. In the first of the *Astrophel and Stella* sonnets he imagines himself, like any adolescent poetling, searching for a subject and a style:

Thus, great with child to speak, and helpless in my throes,
Biting my truant pen, beating myself for spite;
"Fool," said my Muse to me, "look in thy heart, and write."

The story of this sonnet sequence was true, bitterly so. Sidney was Astrophel, and Stella was Lady Penelope Devereux, the Earl of Essex's sister. His love was thwarted; she married Lord Rich and became poor Penny Rich, for the marriage was unhappy. Essex's marrying of Sidney's widow (Walsingham's daughter, incidentally) was a sort of obscure amends. As for the sonnets, they were written out of genuine passion and heart-break.

When Shakespeare came to the sonnet form, he had an autobiographical precedent to follow, and we assume that he followed it. There is a measure of convention in the Sonnets— admiration pushed to extravagant adoration in the courtly tradition, pain exaggerated to cosmic disaster—but the characters are real people and the emotions unfeigned. The earliest of the Sonnets, when copied out and passed from hand to hand, must have struck their readers with a delicious surprise, for one tradition of the form had been ruthlessly broken. There were amorous phrases like "thy sweet self" and "unthrifty loveliness" and "Shall I compare thee to a summer's day?" but these were addressed not to a woman but to a young man. Did this mean a pederastic fixation? Not necessarily; perhaps just the desire to impart an aesthetic shock through the language of heterosexual love in the service of friendship and admiration. A man of twenty-nine may admire a youth's beauty; if he is a poet he will find the right words, and only to the naive will the right words suggest a wrong relationship. And the passion expressed in the early Sonnets has in it no desire of physical possession. Rather the opposite: the elder man urges the younger to marry, so that his great beauty may be transmitted to posterity.

The younger man was, I think, Southampton. Those who urge the claim of William Herbert, since he fits in so well with Mr. W. H., have powerful grounds. Herbert's mother, the Countess of Pembroke and Sir Philip Sidney's sister, wanted the young Earl to marry, and he was unwilling—the situation there is identical with that of Southampton. Shakespeare may well have been commissioned by her, great patroness of learning and the arts as she was, not slow to see Shakespeare's persuasive worth if she had already read Venus's speeches, to write poems to her son which should more subtly prevail than mere prose counsel. Of the literary sensibility of the Countess of Southampton we have no knowledge. But Pembroke did not come to London till 1598, and it is hard to think of the Sonnets as being torn off in white-hot hurry from that year till the end of the century: moreover, there are references in the Sonnets to long absences on the player-poet's part (on tour?) from his beloved friend, and a very long period of friendship—all of three years;

there is also a celebration ("The mortal moon hath her eclipse endured") of the Queen's passing out of her grand climacteric, or sixty-third year, in 1596. Pembroke, so the dedication to the First Folio seems to show, was kind to Shakespeare in later years, but in the nineties there was only one noble friend and patron.

Southampton's unwillingness to beget heirs would hardly keep Shakespeare awake at night; hence one's conviction that the so-called "breed" sonnets were commissioned, probably by the Countess, to whom in his third sonnet Shakespeare makes a graceful reference ("Thou art thy mother's glass, and she in thee/Calls back the lovely April of her prime"). He was probably paid with pieces of gold that he could send home to Stratford. The money was needed: the theatres were closed, and it is hard to imagine that a salary was doled out to Will by the careless lovely youth who called himself friend, not employer. Gifts there would be, but these were no substitute for hard cash paid in respect of work done. I sometimes think the poet was making a literal if oblique plea for money under the fiscal metaphors of the fourth sonnet:

> Then, beauteous niggard, why dost thou abuse
> The bounteous largess given thee to give?
> Profitless usurer, why dost thou use
> So great a sum of sums, yet canst not live?

After the sonnet had been read, Will might say: "While we are on the subject of money, my lord——."

If Southampton would not marry, it might have been not only because he wished to enjoy bachelor freedom, but because he had a distaste for women—temporary only, perhaps a pose assumed by others of his circle. To have catamites or kiss and clip the male friends of one's own age would be accounted a kind of chic Platonism. At that time of plague, moreover, it was suicidal to go around the brothels or to import women of the town for a night's pleasure. One slept with the ladies of the Court at one's peril: the Queen would savagely punish the defilers of her Glories (this had happened to Raleigh; it was to happen also to both Pembroke and Southampton). There was, of course, no shortage of clean sleeping partners—from citizens' wives to aristocratic adulteresses—but, for some reason or for various reasons, the Southampton set inclined to a mixture of the Bedouin encampment, the well-appointed monastery, and the Hellenic agape, during the period of Will's initiation into the joys of aristocratic life. Will would not be shocked by evidence of homosexuality: he may have been inclined to it himself: he was, after all, a member of the theatrical profession. The sexual orientation of Elizabethan actors may have been influenced by the fact of boys taking women's parts and taking them well. Will certainly took well to the laudation of male beauty. If it was the pose of the self-seeker, it was a pose not hard to assume and sustain.

As the young Earl's professional counselor of marriage, Will was in an awkward position. I myself have a wife and a son, my lord: I feel myself fulfilled.—Aye, so I notice: filled full of them—that is why you go not home to pay visits. And that must have been true: we cannot somehow see Shakespeare eagerly galloping back to Stratford as soon as a theatrical run ended or was brought to an end by plague or riot. All women are shrews, Will—you yourself show it on the stage. Unless, like Lavinia, they have their tongues cut out. Well, Will could read Southampton a comedy of the taming of a shrew, ending in marital bliss founded on male supremacy. The play was first acted, as far as we can tell, at Newington Butts in 1594. Shakespeare probably worked on it during his period in the Earl's service, learning about the Italian scene from his lordship or his traveled fellow lords. He was to become very Italianate in his comedies, and all the sun and elegance came to him secondhand. His Italy was London-bottled Chianti.

The Taming of the Shrew was not aristocratic comedy—it has a good playhouse reek about it—but it may well have been an amateur performance at Southampton House. There is an induction or prologue which has no relevance to the play that follows, but it makes sense if we consider Will's position at the time. A drunken Warwickshire tinker, Christopher Sly, has a hoax played on him: he is wakened from crapulous sleep and told that he is a great lord who has lost his memory. Installed in a fine chamber, he makes the expected comic rustic *gaffes,* and then has *The Taming of the Shrew* performed by interlude players. Will was a Warwickshire rustic installed in a noble chamber. "Ask Marian Hacket, the fat ale-wife of Wincot, if she know me not," says Sly. Wincot, or Wilmcote, was Shakespeare's mother's own village. And there is a cunning reminder to Southampton that his poet has already served him well:

Dost thou love pictures? We will fetch thee straight
Adonis painted by a running brook,
And Cytherea all in sedges hid,
Which seem to move and wanton with her breath
Even as the waving sedges play wi' the wind.

Will avoids mentioning his own name: "The Slys are no rogues. Look in the chronicles: we came in with Richard Conqueror." If we subscribe to the Joyce theory of Will's brother usurping his bed, then this will do for a prophetic text. Will presents himself totally in disguise, though it is a thin one: a man who tinkers with plays, who tried to be a Christopher like Marlowe, who is essentially sly. This fancy is, of course, unsound.

Another comedy, and a far inferior one, must certainly have been composed solely for a well-bred audience. This was *Love's Labor's Lost,* which probably dates from late 1593. Shakespeare had been taking note of John Lyly's plays, written for the Children of the Chapel Royal and St. Paul's—highly refined and rather charming comedies, full of euphuistic wordplay (Lyly, with his novel *Euphues,* had already shown himself well qualified to purvey that). These little dramas were not for the public playhouses: their delicate petals would wilt under the garlic blasts of the groundlings. They were performed before the Queen and in private houses. Southampton's circle probably liked them or affected to like them. In the nineties some of them were published—*Galatea, Midas, Campaspe, Endymion*: all good classical themes—and the honeyed language and ingenious conceits could be examined at leisure. Shakespeare examined them, and then proceeded to a refined and courtly comedy of his own, full of witty quibbles, big words, and allusions to foreign travel. *Love's Labor's Lost* is almost painfully aristocratic.

Its theme was highly relevant to the Southampton circle's view of the good life. The main characters—the King of Navarre, Berowne, Longaville, and Dumain—have sworn to keep away from women for three years and get down to some hard study. The names themselves, in that context, were good for a laugh. For Henry of Navarre was well known as a man who could not keep away from women for three days, let alone years. His commanders—Marshal Biron and the Duc de Longueville—were also ladies' men. As for Dumain or de Mayenne—he was Henry of Navarre's main enemy in the Catholic League, and as likely to be willing to share the Navarre cloister for three years as to pray to Saint Martin Luther.

Inevitably the vow of celibacy, after intrigue, comedy, a great deal of sonneteering (the play shows Shakespeare to be obsessed with the sonnet form), is broken; heterosexual love must win. Berowne falls heavily if reluctantly for Rosaline, one of the ladies attendant on the Queen of France:

A whitely wanton with a velvet brow,
With two pitch balls stuck in her face for eyes;
Ay, and, by heaven, one that will do the deed,
Though Argus were her eunuch and her guard.
And I to sigh for her! To watch for her!
To pray for her!

A dark lady and a lusting disgust which prefigures Troilus's for Cressida. Is Shakespeare speaking for himself? There is also a Rosaline in *Romeo and Juliet*—merely described, not presented, but her thigh quivers. Later, in *As You Like It*, Rosalind is to be purified into a girl to be loved, not just hotly desired.

There are many references to the School of Night, and the pedant Holofernes—perhaps played by Judith Shakespeare's father—has been taken as a caricature of Raleigh's wizard Harriot. Armado, the fantastical Spaniard, vain, ridiculous, self-dramatizing, melancholy, involved with a serving wench, may be Raleigh himself as Southampton wished him to be seen: the Earl of Essex had taught him to hate that able and ambitious man. Shakespeare fires shots at George Chapman, the poet of Night, the obscure and knotty metaphysical who called Night his mistress and communicated with spirits. He is, without doubt, the Rival Poet, the man who praised Southampton as Narcissus, while Shakespeare dramatized him as Adonis. And here is Chapman in one of the Sonnets:

Was it the proud full sail of his great verse,
Bound for the prize of (all too precious) you,
That did my ripe thoughts in my brain inhearse,
Making their tomb the womb wherein they grew?
Was it is his spirit, by spirits taught to write
Above a mortal pitch, that struck me dead?
No, neither he, nor his compeers by night
Giving him aid, my verse astonishèd.
He, nor that affable familiar ghost
Which nightly gulls him with intelligence,
As victors of my silence cannot boast;
I was not sick of any fear from thence:
But when your countenance fill'd up his line,
Then lack'd I matter; that enfeebled mine.

This may have been written in 1594, when Chapman published *The Shadow of Night*. He was then thirty-four and still had forty years of writing in front of him. To most he is the man who spoke out loud and bold in the translations of Homer which drove John Keats to a laudatory sonnet. But he was also a skilful playwright and a narrative poet capable of completing Marlowe's *Hero and Leander* as well as producing his own involved works. He has power, and sometimes it sounds like a Shakespearean power:

Presume not then ye flesh confounded soules,
That cannot beare the full Castalian bowles,
Which sever mounting spirits from the sences,
To looke in this deepe fount for thy pretences:
The juice more cleare than day, yet shadows night,
Where humor challengeth no drop of right:
But judgement shall displaie, to purest eyes
With ease, the bowells of these misteries.

That comes in *The Shadow of Night*. Chapman seems to be having a dig at Shakespeare in the reference to "Castalian bowles." The epigraph to *Venus and Adonis* tells of bright Apollo bringing to the poet *pocula Castalia* full of the crystal water of inspiration. But, thinks Chapman, the fleshiness of Shakespeare's poem in his mind, here is a poet too carnal for the rarefied element. Cattiness, but Shakespeare could be catty too: his sonnet about Chapman has its own digs.

The Sonnets record an unequal friendship, marred by the jealousy not only of a rival poet. Southampton did not keep up the posture of misogynist for long: Will fell heavily, as we shall see, for a dark woman, and the younger, prettier, more exalted man took her from him. But first he had to learn to like women, and *Love's Labor's Lost* was only a theoretical lesson from an older man who knew about love. A strange anonymous poem appeared in October 1594, and we are entitled to suppose that it recorded an amorous escapade in which both Shakespeare and his patron took part. The title is *Willobie His Avisa or The true picture of a modest maid and of a chaste and constant wife*. A character called H. W. greatly desires to sleep with a lovely girl who is an innkeeper's wife, and he goes to "his familiar friend W. S." for advice on how to encompass his aim. There are references to a "new actor" and an "old player" and (in the forty-third Canto, which is in prose) we learn that "this Comedy was like to have grown to a Tragedy by the weak and feeble estate that H. W. was brought unto." W. S. urges his friend on, but Avisa will have none of him.

This kind of publicity—whether the story was true or false—would be embarrassing to Southampton, who had to think of his position and the impropriety of having a mere player as friend. Perhaps in this autumn of 1594 Will wished to break the bondage, however sweet, of a tame poet's life in a great house. Friendship would continue, as well as a more distant patronage, but the time had come for the player-playwright to resume his career. Nearly two years had elapsed since the enforced closure of the theatres and the resumption of playing at the Rose in May 1594. New companies began to be formed. Ned Alleyn, who had served the Lord Admiral before serving Lord Strange, now went back to his old troupe and reorganized it. Ferdinando Stanley, Lord Strange, had succeeded to the earldom of Derby in September 1593, but in the following April he died—mysteriously and in great pain, some said of witchcraft. His acting protégés had to seek a new protector, and they found him in Henry Carey, Lord Hunsdon, Lord Chamberlain. The Lord Chamberlain's Men, the greatest body of actors of all time, with the greatest playwright of all time, were at last in existence. In October 1594 they found a theatre—literally the Theatre, one of the two playhouses in Shoreditch—and when they opened, Will Shakespeare was with them.

10

Mistress

A good deal spilled into Shakespeare's new plays from his life among the aristocrats, and it was not all wit and quibbling, horses, hounds, fine silks, and gold trenchers. There was, for instance, the rather sordid quarrel between Southampton's friends and Southampton's neighbors. The friends were the Danvers brothers—Sir Charles and Sir Henry—who were the sons of Sir John Danvers, country magnate and justice of the peace. The neighbors were Sir Walter Long and his brother Henry, whose estate was close to Southampton's own near Titchfield. There had been enmity between the two families for a considerable time, its roots lost perhaps in the Wars of the Roses, but a particular phase of nastiness arose in 1594, when Sir John Danvers, from the magistrate's bench, committed one of Sir Walter Long's servants for robbery. Sir Walter rescued the servant from the justice, and, after due complaint to the judge at the next assizes, Sir John saw Sir Walter locked up in the Fleet prison. Then, to drive home the lesson, he committed another of Sir Walter's servants on a charge of murder. When Sir Walter left prison, he and his brother provoked various brawls between their own followers and Sir John's, so that one servant was killed and another grievously wounded.

But it was the Danvers family itself that the Longs were after, and Henry wrote insulting letters to Sir Charles, calling him a liar, a fool, a puppy dog, a mere boy, and promising that he would whip his bare arse with a rod. Sir Charles was very angry. Accompanied by his brother and some of his men, he entered an inn at Cosham where Henry and Sir Walter were dining with some exalted friends, and he hit Henry twice with a truncheon. Henry drew his sword and wounded Sir Charles. Sir Henry Danvers drew his pistol and fired on his enemy namesake, who fell and shortly after died. The Danvers brothers got away and took refuge with the Earl of Southampton, who, despite the issue of warrants for their arrest, arranged for them to escape to France.

Shakespeare would recognize the dramatic utility of all this, but only if made sufficiently remote—antique and exotic. He was never happy about rendering the contemporary scene directly— that was for the new satirical school—and his topical references strike home all the harder for suddenly flashing out from an imagined past. The Danvers-Long conflict inspired him to present an "ancient grudge" between two families of Verona, and the irony of a boy in one family falling in love with a girl from the other. The story was an old one and well known. It had last been done in English verse two years before Shakespeare's birth, by a poetaster named Arthur Brooke. With the impact of the Danvers-Long affair to drive him, Shakespeare now attempted a new kind of tragedy—Italianate but not Senecan, the high color of the language outbraving the spilt blood.

It is interesting to note that three plays—*Two Gentlemen of Verona, Romeo and Juliet,* and *The Merchant of Venice*—were written closely on each other during, or just after, the period in Southampton's service, and that all three are set in the region of Venetia. In *Love's Labor's Lost,* Holofernes makes a sudden gratuitous reference to Venice and recites:

Venetia, Venetia,
Chi non ti vede, non ti pretia.

Venetia—meaning to Shakespeare Venice and, seventy miles away, Verona—had to be seen to be appreciated. Did Southampton take Shakespeare on a trip thither? Or did Florio tell him so much about it (even drawing the Grand Canal and the exact location of the Rialto) that he began to feel he knew it without paying it a visit?

Two Gentlemen of Verona was, so Shakespeare must have recognized, a stage failure. He tried to do for the popular theatre what he had done for the Southampton household—

namely, write a play loaded with wit, high-flown language, quibbling, romantic love, the contention of young aristocrats, and set it in a country noted for passion, sun, swords flashing in the sun. The popular theatre would take this if it could also have a convincing plot and compelling characters, and these *Two Gentlemen of Verona* did not supply. Today it is liked for two things—the lyric "Who is Sylvia?" (though it is Schubert more than Shakespeare who has made it popular) and the servant Launce, faithful in the English way to his deplorable mongrel Crab. Launce's master Proteus proclaims in his very name an inconstancy of character and affections which is in strong contrast to that simple fidelity. This is a very Shakespearean touch.

The two gentlemen do not do justice to Verona, and that city was too good to waste, so *Romeo and Juliet* came along to make Verona more important than it perhaps really was: if any foreigner visits Verona today, it is chiefly because Shakespeare wrote *Romeo and Juliet*. Of the virtues of this romantic tragedy, the first ever, there is no need to speak. The masterstroke of an opening scene in colloquial prose, the exploitation of the whole range of the stage as the interfamilial enmity is established, the swiftness with which the main characters are delineated—these show at once that we can expect brilliant entertainment. Shakespeare perhaps uses too many words, but they are charged with lyric fire—as in the "Queen Mab" speech of Mercutio (during the composition of which Shakespeare was perhaps already thinking of writing A *Midsummer Night's Dream*)—and there is the earthiness of Juliet's nurse to counteract that element. It is remarkable that so much action should be able to cohabit with so much static lyricism—those sonnets of the Chorus, for instance—and that the rhymed couplet homilies of Friar Lawrence should, far from boring, suggest a point of rest, a *canto fermo* to unify the counterpoint. Shakespeare was thirty, perhaps thirty-one, when he wrote the play, and he was no longer young, but this of all works of literature eternizes the ardor of young love and youth's aggressive spirit.

As a bitter quarrel of two families well known to Southampton may be taken as the starting point of this play, so a more public bitterness, in which Southampton was only indirectly concerned, may be thought of as bringing *The Merchant of Venice* to birth. In the spring of 1594, the Earl of Essex, who, in Southampton's eyes, could do little wrong, formally accused a certain Dr. Roderigo Lopez, a Portuguese Jew and physician at the Court, of having conspired with Spanish agents to poison the Queen. Behind this accusation was a record of enmity and bitterness of a purely personal nature. Lopez had good connections in Portugal, Portugal was next door to Spain, and Walsingham, as head of the Secret Service, had found Lopez a very reliable forwarding agent of information to and from English spies on the Iberian peninsula. After Walsingham's death in 1590, Essex took over Lopez's service. To be able to supply, as a personal gift to the Queen, odd gobbets of information from Spain through Portugal, seemed to Essex a useful device of ingratiation. But Lopez, more loyal to the Queen than to Essex, gave her his information first. When Essex, beaming, approached the throne with white-hot news from Iberia, the Queen was able to tell him that she knew it already. Essex hated Lopez for this double-dealing and determined on revenge.

He found an opportunity when a man named Tinoco confessed that he, and another man called Ferrara, had been sent over to England to persuade Lopez to work for the Spanish cause, and that Lopez, as an earnest of willingness, had accepted a valuable jewel from the Spanish king. Lopez was arrested and examined but, after the most thorough search through all his private papers, nothing of an incriminating nature could be found. The Queen now accused Essex of malice and sent him off in disgrace. Essex was enraged and spent the winter of 1593–94 in building up a case against Lopez of such plausibility that the attorney general had to take action. Lopez was formally arraigned at the Guildhall at the end of February 1594, and the jury, impelled by anti-Semitic prejudice as much as by actual evidence, found him guilty of plotting against the Queen's life. He, and Tinoco and Ferrara with him, were sentenced to be hanged and quartered at Tyburn. There was some delay in the carrying out of the sentence—the Queen continued to have doubts about the guilt of her little ape, as she called Lopez—and the great public entertainment of triple butchery was not presented till June.

One can imagine Southampton's boyish elation at the Earl of Essex's victory over his Queen and his enemy—an elation which Shakespeare would find very distasteful. The motivation behind the whole sickening business was less devotion to the monarch than personal vindictiveness. The cruelty of the execution was enhanced by the general laugh that went up when Lopez, with the rope round his neck and the butcher's knife winking in the sun, swore that he loved the Queen as much as he loved Jesus Christ—an ambiguous statement from a Jew. Essex and his party would be there to witness the shambles of that fine June day, among booing and laughing citizens with sucket-eating children on their shoulders—a good day out, and all free. Shakespeare, one feels, was not there. But he was not above exploiting the general bitterness towards Jews by writing a play in which a Jew is the villain—not a treacherous one, however, but a usurious one. Barabas in *The Jew of Malta* is a Machiavellian monster; Shylock merely, and literally, wants his pound of flesh.

That Shylock is, against the convention in which Shakespeare was working, not altogether an unsympathetic character is evident to our own age, but the Elizabethan audiences would see only a thick-nosed usurer in a greasy gaberdine. At the end of the trial Shylock goes off quietly, a subdued human being who says he is not well, fading out in humiliation. He does not enjoy the cursing full-orchestra final defiance of Barabas. He is real, and he is more like Shakespeare than Shakespeare is like the prissy Christians of that intolerable and intolerant Venice. Shakespeare believed in making money and saw nothing wrong in high interest so long as he himself was not paying it. The pound of flesh is, of course, going too far, but it is somehow cleansed of horror when we consider that Shakespeare is working on two levels—one that, since nobody dies, cannot be tragic and hence must be comic, though there are no laughs—only the strange taste of lyrical anti-Semitism; and an allegorical one, in which the symbols are more important than the characters. The play is about flesh and gold. Flesh is living and, through the music of love, capable of being transfigured above the muddy vesture of decay; gold is dead, but it breeds hate like maggots. Flesh cannot be weighted as gold can, and love, as Portia's suitors find, cannot be evaluated as if it were a precious metal. Gold is redeemed when it is fashioned into a ring, symbol of marriage, and heaven itself does not then disdain to be thick inlaid with gold patines. On the level of narrative, the fifth act is redundant; on the level of symbolism, it completes a poetic statement.

In *Romeo and Juliet*, mercurial Mercutio indulges in a flight of fairy music. Shakespeare is discovering in himself a vein of folk fancy that needs fuller working out than in a brilliant but irrelevant cadenza. The fourth play of this group, A *Midsummer Night's Dream*, is a comedy obviously intended to celebrate a wedding. Comedies are now to depend on the falling-out of lovers. But to have such falling-out motivated by failure of affection in the lovers themselves, or indeed produced by any human agency, would be indiscreet in a wedding piece, so Shakespeare introduces the fairies. Since Sir James Barrie and Enid Blyton, fairies have become debased and whimsical, but in Will's Warwickshire they were tough and dangerous, with no Tinker Bell among them. They were demons more than figurines in ballet shoes, not essentially malevolent but, to use the theological term, uncovenanted powers. They were the pre-Christian gods reduced to wood spirits. There is no whimsy in the language Shakespeare gives them.

That A *Midsummer Night's Dream* is a play for important nuptials we take for granted. Whose nuptials were they? On January 26, 1595, the Lord Chamberlain's Men were commanded to perform at a wedding at Greenwich, with the Queen and the entire Court present. The bridegroom was the Earl of Derby, son of the Chamberlain's Men's old patron; the bride was—we will come to her in a moment. One presumes that A *Midsummer Night's Dream* was the play performed on this occasion—a play easy to rehearse quickly (a royal summons requesting a new play rarely gave much time), since it is full of separable sections, the lovers' scenes, the fairies' scenes, the artisans' scenes all capable of isolated rehearsal. The play had everything except Mendelssohn, but time has made good that omission. As a vehicle for the varied powers of the Lord Chamberlain's Men, it was superb. If there was no place for tragic rhetoric, there was tragic parody, which was just as good.

The bride was the Lady Elizabeth Vere, the lady whom Southampton had refused to marry. In despair, Lord Burghley had let the matter drop and blessed a match in which there was no reluctant partner. But, at the height of his anger at his ward's recalcitrance, he had imposed a fine of five thousand pounds on him—evaluating Lady Elizabeth's frustrated affections as if they were precious metal. If he had seen *The Merchant of Venice*, he had not taken in its deeper message. One presumes that, on his granddaughter's happy marriage to Lord Derby, he rescinded the fine.

If so, this was an auspicious time for Shakespeare to obtain money from his patron and friend. There is a persistent tradition that Southampton gave him—not lent him—a thousand pounds, a lot of money in those days. With the formation of the Lord Chamberlain's Men on a shareholding basis, Shakespeare needed capital, and Southampton was the man to provide it. The sum given, if it was given, might have been only a hundred pounds, enough for a share, but the tradition of the thousand pounds holds chiefly because of the last scene of *Henry IV* Part Two where Falstaff says to his friend, Master Shallow, a very small country magistrate, "Master Shallow, I owe you a thousand pound." If Shallow could lay his hands on the sum, so, much more easily, could Southampton. And if Shakespeare did not have to pay the sum back, it was because Southampton preferred the equivalent of a pound of flesh.

It was with the opening up of the Theatre in Shoreditch that Shakespeare, his long apprenticeship over, began his dramatic career in earnest. The playhouse was a good one, built by James Burbage who, having started life like Snug, as a joiner, became a considerable actor and even led the Earl of Leicester's Men while Shakespeare was still a baby. Burbage had acquired his land in Shoreditch—no more than a patch of waste ground full of weeds, bones, and dog merds—in 1576. The landlord, Giles Alleyn, no relation of Ned's, granted a twenty-one years' lease.

It was assumed there would be no difficulty about obtaining a renewal. On this land, cleared and leveled, Burbage built a very fine playhouse, calling on his brother-in-law, the rich grocer John Brayne, to provide most of the capital. This became a well-appointed home for the Lord Chamberlain's Men, at the head of whom was James Burbage's own son, Richard.

Dick Burbage, three years younger than Shakespeare, had learnt his acting technique from Ned Alleyn. Alleyn had been, and still was, a great actor, but his range was restricted to the heavily rhetorical, and there was no humor in him, nor was he capable of the romantic delicacy needed for the new Italianate lovers' roles. If Burbage, as he probably did, played the part of Bottom in A *Midsummer Night's Dream,* then he was given an opportunity to parody the Alleyn style in the Pyramus and Thisbe interlude, thus, in a single stroke, displaying all its limitations:

> O grim-look'd night! O night with hue so black!
> O night, which ever art when day is not!
> O night, O night, alack, alack, alack,
> I fear my Thisby's promise is forgot!

The tone would be that of Alleyn playing Hieronimo in *The Spanish Tragedy.* Burbage, besides possessing a considerable emotional range and great physical litheness, knew a good deal about the visual possibilities of the new drama, including the value of realistic makeup. He was a portrait painter as well as an actor. What he and his fellow actors now needed was a repertory, and they needed it quickly. Shakespeare, newly installed in lodgings near the Theatre—St. Helen's, Bishopsgate—got down to providing it.

He was not able to give all his attention to the needs of the Lord Chamberlain's Men, however, for it was about this time that he was heavily in love. Anne in Stratford was forgotten or, if remembered, remembered guiltily; his affections were centered on a lady cultivated enough to play the virginals:

> How oft, when thou, my music, music play'st,
> Upon that blessèd wood whose motion sounds

With thy sweet fingers, when thou gently sway'st
The wiry concord that mine ear confounds,
Do I envy those jacks that nimble leap
To kiss the tender inward of thy hand,
Whilst my poor lips, which should that harvest reap,
At the wood's boldness by thee blushing stand:
To be so tickled, they would change their state
And situation with those dancing chips,
O'er whom thy fingers walk with gentle gait,
Making dead wood more blest than living lips:
Since saucy jacks so happy are in this,
Give them thy fingers, me thy lips to kiss.

(The jacks are the pieces of wood attached to the plectra which pluck the strings.) The accomplishment, very well observed by Shakespeare, suggests that the beloved was either a lady of some social position—perhaps a beauty of the Court—or else a high-class courtesan equipped with geisha skills. She was very dark, in a period when to be dark, either in skin or hair or eyes, was to be unfashionable, but the poet glories in her darkness: ". . . I will swear beauty herself is black, / And all they foul that thy complexion lack." In one of the Sonnets the glory is much qualified, and Will looks at his mistress with eyes clearer than is proper for a lover:

My mistress' eyes are nothing like the sun;
Coral is far more red than her lips' red;
If snow be white, why then her breasts are dun,
If hairs be wires, black wires grow on her head:
I have seen roses damask'd, red and white,
But no such roses see I in her cheeks,
And in some perfumes is there more delight
Than in the breath that from my mistress reeks.
I love to hear her speak, yet well I know
That music hath a far more pleasing sound:
I grant I never saw a goddess go;
My mistress when she walks treads on the ground:
And yet, by heaven, I think my love as rare
As any she belied with false compare.

Shakespeare here reacts violently against the romantic exaggeration current in so many love lyrics—an exaggeration he himself reserves, in his perverse way, for praising the beauty of a man. It is an honest poem, but it is impossible to imagine any woman being pleased with it. If Shakespeare's mistress appreciated this candor (black wires and reeking breath, indeed), she must have had an exceptional sense of humor. Or she must have been bred in a tradition that did not admit the devices of poetic flattery. It is easier to think of Shakespeare's addressing this sonnet to a young man guilty of amorous overpraise rather than to the sonnet's subject: the man who has seen the world educating a boy who has not.

Who was the Dark Lady? There have been many candidates or, to be pedantic, nigrates. We have first to decide whether she is black only in her eyes and hair, being otherwise the "whitely wanton" of Berowne's outburst, or black, meaning dusky or dun or coffee-colored, all over. That there were dark women in the brothels of Clerkenwell, near enough to Shakespeare's lodgings, seems evident from odd contemporary references—the Moor discussed by the Gobbos, *père et fils*, in *The Merchant of Venice*; Denis Edwards's letter to Thomas Lankford, asking him to "secure my negress: she is certainly at the Swan, a Dane's beershop, Turnbull Street, Clerkenwell"; the "Lucy Negro, Abbess de Clerkenwell," brought in with a "Choir of Nuns" at the Christmas revels of Gray's Inn in 1594. Shakespeare's plays are not lacking in dark skins—from Aaron to Cleopatra; the status of Othello shows, incidentally, that there was no color prejudice in those days, however much anti-Semitism was rife. Possibly Shakespeare's falling for a dark skin was no poetic eccentricity, though the initial contact may have come from poetic curiosity.

We may, if we wish, judge from the *triste post coitum* sonnet beginning "The expense of spirit in a waste of shame / Is lust in action," that the transports Shakespeare knew with his Dark Lady were very violent and wholly carnal. The strength of the ensuing revulsion would argue that. I know of no deeper disgust than that expressed in the phrase "had, having, and in quest to have," where the poet seems to hear himself panting like a dog after a bitch in heat. It was an affair of lust not love, and the woman is best thought of as anonymous, an instrument of elemental pleasure, then remorse. When the poet's friend took her from the poet, he was taking a commodity—a pound, or many pounds, of flesh. After the postures of celibacy, or homosexual dalliance, he wanted a woman—not Mistress This or Lady That. The business sounds sordid, and I hear the chink of money in the background.

Those who see the Dark Lady as white put forward the claim of Mary Fitton above all others. Mary, or Mall, Fitton was a Maid of Honor to the Queen. Knowing what could happen even to a man of high rank who meddled among those jealously guarded Glories, Shakespeare might be very cautious. But if Mr. W.H. is the Friend and Patron of the Sonnets, and Mr. W.H. can be none other that William Herbert, Earl of Pembroke, then Mall's claim is very plausible, for Herbert seduced her. Mall even bore Herbert a son, very short-lived, in 1601. So there are the mistress and the friend, both of whom prove false. But, to my ear, both the attributions ring false.

If Shakespeare had fallen so heavily for Mall Fitton, a flirtatious minx by all accounts and unlikely to bestow on a poor poet the treasures of her body, there being no hope of advancement there, he would be unlikely to remember her with anything but sad and still lustful bitterness. He would not be sneering and facetious about her. But *Twelfth Night*, produced at Court in the period of Mall's pregnancy and disgrace, has a sneering and facetious reference which we can stomach only if we think of Shakespeare the professional dramatist drawing on the current gossip of the Court for an in-laugh and being himself indifferent to the personages involved in the gossip. Sir Andrew Aguecheek boasts of his skill in dancing, and Sir Toby Belch says: "Wherefore are these things hid? Wherefore have they a curtain before them? Are they like to take dust like Mistress Mall's picture?" Dr. Hotson, in his *The First Night of Twelfth Night*, asks us to think that Mistress Mall is present in more than a casual quip. He suggests that Malvolio, melancholy majordomo of the Lady Olivia, is a caricature of Sir William Knollys, Controller of the Queen's Household, who, though married and old, paid ridiculous court to Mall. In the very name there is a plain statement of his lechery: *Mall voglio*—I want Mall. If Shakespeare had suffered from Mall, he would hardly wish to make comic capital out of another man's suffering.

It is best to keep the Dark Lady anonymous, even composite. Shakespeare was a long time in London, and we cannot think that he limited himself to one affair. The Sonnets make statements of permanent validity about some of the commonest experiences known to men—obsession with a woman's body, revulsion, pain in desertion, resignation at another's treachery. Shakespeare was no John Keats, mooning over Fanny Brawne, but a realist aware of self-division, the tugging of the black and the white spirits, and the irresistible lure of the primal darkness that resides in all women, whether white or black.

I I

Gentleman

❧❧❧❧❧❧❧❧❧❧❧❧❧❧❧❧❧❧❧

Rioting in the city. Heads smashed in Billingsgate. Martial law proclaimed. Apprentices hanged, drawn, and quartered on Tower Hill.

It was the summer of 1595, and the main cause of the riots was high prices. In default of public-spirited students, today's specialists in protest, the bloodier demonstrations were left to the apprentices, who beat up the egg vendors and butter-women for doubling, and more than doubling, their prices. Eggs at a penny each, butter at sevenpence a pound—this was not to be tolerated, so the butter had to smear the pavement and the eggs be used as preliminary ammunition. The young have always been delighted to be angry, but the old have not always been tolerant. To execute mere boys on the scene of their crime seems to us to be going too far, but this was Merry England. Naturally, the playhouses—places where apprentices could assemble easily—were shut down, and the Lord Chamberlain's Men were out of work for at least two months.

In the playhouse Shakespeare had recorded, very lengthily and rather beautifully, the disastrous summer and autumn of the previous year. Titania had blamed it all on the dissension between herself and her husband Oberon: it was an act not of God but of the uncovenanted powers. Now England was suffering from the failure of the crops and the murrain on the cattle. That Shakespeare, like other small capitalists, had foreseen the scarcity of grain in London and already bought a bushel or so is not hard to believe. To buy cheap and sell dear is a venerable way of making money.

To augment the national misery, it was known that the Spaniards had a new and bigger Armada ready, and that Drake and Hawkins had, most inopportunely, set off on what was to be their last voyage. The times were terrible, and astrologers found little comfort in their knowledge that the Queen was about to enter on her grand climacteric. On September 7, 1595, she began the sixty-third year of her life. Sixty-three was nine times seven, a combination of numbers highly charged and portentous. In 1588, the year of that other Armada, nine and six had been the mystic numbers—the six not so tricky as the seven, but dangerous enough. That 1588 had ended gloriously, mocking the sad presage and augurs, was no comfort now: England might not be so lucky a second time, especially with so much sin, complacency, and treachery about.

For potential treachery, it was already time to look in the direction of Will's patron's hero, the Earl of Essex, Robert Devereux, once the Queen's bonny sweet Robin, now not Robin Bedfellow but Robin Badfellow, so they said. "And Robin shall restore amends," smiled Puck at the end of A *Midsummer Night's Dream*, but Robin still brooded over his humiliation at the Queen's hands over the Lopez affair. He was talking about the senility and incompetence of the sovereign lady who, in the flowery Court of Love tradition which made all courtiers wooers but some more than others, once had all his heart. In the November of 1595, thirty-seventh anniversary of the Queen's accession, a book entitled A *Conference about the next Succession to the Crown of England* came into her hands. The author, Doleman, had very indiscreetly dedicated his work to the Earl of Essex, and the Queen wished to know what connection there was between subject and dedicatee. Whatever answer Essex gave, he was put temporarily out of the Queen's favor.

The new Catholic threat from abroad made many loyal subjects anxious about the situation at home. The Queen was old, and the preachers rubbed it in. The Bishop of St. David's, preaching in the Queen's presence, stupidly reminded her that she was at an age when the senses fail and the strength diminishes and the powers of the body decay. If she suddenly died, as she might, she would leave the question of the

succession unsettled: it was not at all certain that James VI of
Scotland's candidature was acceptable to every party in the state.
The truth is that she was, in a sort of correspondence course,
grooming James for the succession, but was fearful of making
her choice of him public knowledge. The Catholic enemy
might arrange his assassination before he got to the throne and
throw the country into most promising confusion. And so the
popular speculation went on, along with a popular fear that the
Queen herself was trying to render groundless.

The question of Elizabeth's being deposed by an ambitious
Protestant subject could not have been much talked of, or else
Shakespeare would not have written and presented *Richard II*
around this time. Here, though, if anyone wanted it, was a
reminder that there was a precedent for deposition, and that the
second centenary of Henry Bolingbroke's usurpation was approaching—1599. Shakespeare, with more interest in his private
affairs than in public ones, was merely getting on with his job.
After comedies set in Venetia or in Athenian Warwickshire
Fairyland, the time had come to resume the epic drama of the
Wars of the Roses. He had written the end; now he had to write
the beginning, showing that the York-Lancaster conflict was a
curse stemming from one man's sin, a sin that no number of
pilgrimages to the Holy Land could expiate. Henry IV, no less
than Oedipus, had brought misery and death on his people
through a primal wrong. There was no crime worse then regicide.

Shakespeare learned from Marlowe's one historical drama,
Edward II (now available as a printed book), that a mere
procession of events, in the village-pageant manner of the
Henry VI trilogy, was less compelling than an examination of
the motives behind the events. Edward is a feeble ruler, given to
the unnatural love of his minion Gaveston, neglectful of his
queen and his kingdom alike. He is deposed and brutally
murdered, but at least his son takes over. Richard is also
deposed and brutally murdered, but his blood dies with him.
The Tudor blood was so to die.

Temperamentally, Richard is emotional, an aesthetic dreamer,
rather like Edward, but Shakespeare could not, in fairness to the
true historical Richard of Holinshed's *Chronicles*, make him a

pederast. For sexual self-indulgence Shakespeare substitutes a lust for language, quibbles, conceits—the poet's own failing. The soliloquies, public and private, are as long as Richard wants them to be, and his creator is very indulgent. There are also tantrums, showings off, manic changes of mood. He is more queenly than kingly. The part of Richard calls for all the resources of a virtuoso, and Shakespeare had a virtuoso in Burbage.

Was the composition of *Richard II*—at this time, not some time later—altogether Shakespeare's idea? The Essex party was growing: it needed a program, perhaps also a poet. Southampton, a faithful friend to Essex to the last, had given Will money. He had two great poems dedicated to him, and his beauty had been eternized in many sonnets; he had also taken, or was going to take, Will's mistress. But he may have thought himself entitled to more—if only vicariously. He may have suggested a poem or play which showed an England ailing under incompetent rule, and a strong patriot, wronged by his ruler, saving his country through usurpation. Will may have said that he proposed writing *Richard II* anyway and, sick of comedy and ready for a return to tragedy or history, he might as well start on it now. As for propagandist possibilities—that was no concern of his, since these resided in the theme; he certainly would not falsify history for other than artistic ends, and he would not underline contemporary relevance. Very well, then: get on with it.

In getting on with it, Shakespeare kept, as he always did, an eye on the public mood. His audiences were ready, as they had been in the old *Henry VI* days, for patriotic slogans, since the Spanish threat was powerful and embattled Englishmen like nothing better than to be told, memorably, that they are both big and little at the same time. In John of Gaunt's dying speech—one long implausible sentence—there are plenty of pokerwork phrases—"This precious stone set in a silver sea . . . This blessed plot, this earth, this realm, this England . . . This land of such dear souls, this dear dear land . . . ," but the embarrassment of the appositive riches is mitigated by a predicate which, coming twenty lines after the start of the sentence, affirms bluntly that England is in a bad way. Most patriotic memories, strong on the precious stone part, are weak on the "made a shameful conquest of itself." Noting the cynicism which is to come in *Henry IV*, we may wonder whether Shakespeare piled on the royal-throne-of-kings rhetoric to make the puncturing of the chauvinistic emotions thus aroused the more painful. It is as dangerous to assume patriotism in Shakespeare as it is to assume atheism, vegetarianism, or freemasonry.

The year ended with the Lord Chamberlain's Men performing four times at Court. It is doubtful if they put on *Richard II*: it was a season for comedy. Seriousness was reserved for real life and the bad year that followed—1596. It was a very bad year for Shakespeare, as we shall see, but at least he lived through it. Too many people died in the streets for want; food prices reached a famine level; money that should have bought relief for the poor continued to drain into the foreign war. Henry IV of France complained that England was providing insufficient help in his struggle against the common Catholic enemy; Elizabeth was enraged by the Gaullist tone of his ambassador's demands. The French had always been a treacherous nation, said the English. The new year began with the alliance as good as broken.

When spring came, the news from France was dangerous. The perfidious French were saying that they would prefer to have the Spaniards in Calais rather than the English, for, with the Spaniards there, there was always a good chance of regaining the town through the mediacy of the Pope, whereas the English, once they repossessed it, would never let it go. This was good Gallic logic, and very infuriating to the English. In April the Spanish were established in Calais and preparing to cross the Channel in force—not in the gnat-bite sort of raid that had already annoyed Cornwall. On Good Friday, six thousand men were in readiness to march to Dover but, with news coming that Calais could not hold out any longer, the levies were dismissed. On Easter Sunday, while the Bishop of St. David's was preaching to the Queen about her decrepitude and composing a humble prayer for her, one suited to a decrepit state, levies were once more demanded. They were easily enough found: it was merely a matter of closing the churches while the worshipers were inside, then pressing enough men into service. This time they were marched to Dover, but they did not sail for Calais. Calais had fallen. It was rumored that a seasoned force from the Netherlands had broken through the Spaniards and reached the garrison, but the wretched French had caused them to be slain. The Spaniards, they said, were more *smypathiques* than thick-speaking Northern Protestants.

An alternative English plan, one long pondered, was now brought into operation. This was to send a fleet to Cadiz, under the command of Lord Charles Howard, the Lord Admiral, and the Earl of Essex, now restored to favor. A few weeks before it sailed from Plymouth, the ships of Drake and Hawkins returned from their piratical venture, but Drake and Hawkins were not with them. They were dead, and the enterprise had failed. The auguries, in this climacterical year of the Queen, were not good. But, followed by the Queen's prayers, the fleet and troops sailed for Spain on June 3.

Meanwhile, Shakespeare's bad summer had started. A certain William Gardner, a corrupt and bad-tempered justice of the peace in Southwark, was maintaining that Shakespeare, together with Francis Langley, owner of the Swan Theatre, had threatened his life. It was probably all nonsense: Shakespeare was no Kit Marlowe, drunk and ever ready to draw; it was malice, no more, but it meant a lawsuit. With this on his mind, Shakespeare tried to push on with his new history, which was based on an old play once performed by the Queen's Men—*The Troublesome Reign of King John*. In the Shakespeare manner, it was a means of commenting on the present while presenting the past, and it was full of fickle France and defiant England, with an anachronistic Protestantism in John's scorn of the Pope's temporal power. It also had the patriotic fanfares Will was always ready to sound:

Come the three corners of the world in arms,
And we shall shock them. Nought shall make us rue,
If England to itself do rest but true.

But it is, without doubt, the worst play of Shakespeare's maturity. It has fine lines, but the characters are pasteboard. And yet, knowing the special grief of the poet that summer, we can find odd stabs of poignancy. The words of Prince Henry, for instance, where the "who" is ambiguous:

> 'Tis strange that death should sing.
> I am the cygnet to this pale faint swan
> Who chants a doleful hymn to his own death,
> And from the organ-pipe of frailty sings
> His soul and body to their lasting rest.

Or the dying King John:

> There is so hot a summer in my bosom
> That all my bowels crumble up to dust.
> I am a scribbled form drawn with a pen
> Upon a parchment, and against this fire
> Do I shrink up.

The Swan of Avon, wearing the Lord Chamberlain's swan on his livery, scribbling away through the hot summer—these are the materials out of which the metaphors are made. And his cygnet has died. Pembroke says:

> I'll go with thee
> And find the inheritance of this poor child,
> His little kingdom of a forcèd grave.

Most poignant of all, here is Constance, mother of Arthur, who is to die:

> Grief fills the room up of my absent child,
> Lies in his bed, walks up and down with me,
> Puts on his pretty looks, repeats his words,
> Remembers me of all his gracious parts,
> Stuffs out his vacant garments with his form.

It was at the beginning of August that Hamnet Shakespeare died. He was eleven and a half. Anne Shakespeare was forty and perhaps considered her childbearing days over. Will must resign himself to dying with no son to inherit the social glory he was struggling to win. Anne, that tough countrywoman who kept away from the hazards of towns like London, would probably outlive him. Those sonnets to Southampton on the joys of fatherhood would strike Will ironically now. And then, on October 29, with the poor child scarcely cold in his little kingdom, Garter King of Arms granted at last to John Shakespeare the title and blazon he had sought for so long:

> Gold, on a Bend sables, a spear of the first steeled argent. And for his crest or cognizance a falcon his wings displayed Argent standing on a wreath of his colors; supporting a spear gold steeled as aforesaid set upon a helmet with mantels and tassels as hath been accustomed and doth more plainly appear depicted on this margent: Signifying hereby and by the authority of my office aforesaid ratifying that it shall be lawful for the said John Shakespeare, gentleman, and for his children, issue and posterity (at all times and places convenient) to bear and make demonstration of the same blazon or achievement on their shields, targets, escutcheons, coats of arms, pennons, guidons, seals, rings, edifices, buildings, utensils, liveries, tombs or monuments or otherwise for all warlike facts or civil use or exercises, according to the Law of Arms, and customs that to gentlemen belongeth without let or interruption of any other person or persons for use or bearing the same.

The motto was *Non Sans Droict*—not without right.

This was the ultimate irony. Hamnet could have been the first born gentleman of the family—apart from those shadowy ancestors invoked by his grandfather—but now it might not be. Nobody could know in 1596—Gilbert thirty, Richard twenty-two, Edmund sixteen—that the whole Shakespeare male line would be finished in exactly twenty years. The time for bearing or making demonstration of the coat of arms was not long.

Still, Shakespeare the gentleman could ride back from the Stratford funeral with a grim sense of achievement. There was this matter of the relationship he had, but three years before, inaugurated with a noble lord, pressing him to the fatherhood that would pump a great blood to posterity. The social gap between lord and player had been too wide for comfort, but now it had narrowed. There had been an estrangement, but now it might be healed. Southampton, indeed, had had little time for the company of poets and players. He had been much at Court, and it was rumored that he was dangerously intimate with one oft the Queen's Glories—Mistress Vernon. He had tried to follow Essex, first to Calais, later to Cadiz, but the Queen had kept him at home. The Cadiz expedition had ended gloriously, and Southampton was bitter at not being allowed to share in the glory. He would be in no mood for humble sonnets seeking a renewal of friendship.

But the mood of England, and of its thwarted nobles, changed during that hot August. The Cadiz adventure went without a hitch, and it was in the tradition of romance, long thought to be dead. Essex threw his hat into the sea with joy when the English ships sailed into the harbor. Raleigh, Essex's enemy but now, for a space, his comrade in arms, blasted fanfares of trumpets back at the warning cannon of the Spaniards. The town walls were scaled with a fine disregard for danger. The town, once possessed, met courtesy and humanity from Essex. If only all the commanders could have shown the scorn of plunder which Essex, with all his faults, regarded as the mark of a good victor, then the whole expedition could have been one of the true glories of the reign. But the soldiers grabbed what they could as quickly as they could, often ignoring the richer prizes with the myopia of greed. The Spaniards burned forty great ships and many smaller, rather than let them pass into English hands. Loot which should have gone to the Queen and paid for the whole enterprise was brought home by individual captains in specially chartered ships. It was a great victory, but there was trouble in store for the authors of the victory. The Queen would see to that.

Essex, now bearded, rode through London in triumph, his men flaunting beards of the same cut. Already ambitious, he was to increase his ambition to the limit. But now was the time for bells and bonfires. August ended, and the Queen sailed out of the dangerous waters of her climacteric. Shakespeare wrote his patron a sonnet celebrating the fact:

The mortal moon hath her eclipse endured,
And the sad augurs mock their own presage;

Incertainties now crown themselves assured,
And peace proclaims olives of endless age.
Now with the drops of this most balmy time
My love looks fresh, and Death to me subscribes,
Since, spite of him, I'll live in this poor rhyme,
While he insults o'er dull and speechless tribes:
And thou in this shalt find thy monument,
When tryants' crests and tombs of brass are spent.

They were friends again. Doubtless this sonnet, written fair on good parchment, was sent to Southampton House with a proud seal on the cover—spear, falcon, helmet, and the motto *Non Sans Droict*. Not without right and not before time. As for that son, dead of fever or blood-poisoning or a fall from a tree or the bite of a mad dog, Shakespeare had to find substitutes in the creations not of his body but of his imagination.

12

Globe

❧❧❧❧❧❧❧❧❧❧❧❧❧❧❧❧❧❧❧❧❧

There had been a time, the time of Spenser's *Faerie Queene*, when the English Court had been a scented roseate bower of adoration, full of handsome fine-legged gallants prostrating themselves before a paragon of wit and beauty. Elizabeth had sustained the myth of the goddess into old age, but now the paragon was becoming, God bless us, a thing of naught—at least in the eyes of the younger nobles. She employed her feminine arts still—caprice, mind-changing, vacillation, tantrums, honey after aloes—but these no longer fascinated while they irritated. For she was an old woman with a long thin face, her teeth yellow and broken, her sparse grey hair covered with a red wig. True, her mind was as vigorous as ever. The storm of improvised Latin she loosed on an insolent ambassador became a legend. She handled French and Italian as skillfully as a trained interpreter. She was still the great intellectual, the only one ever to occupy the English throne, and no European prince could outdo her in the attitudes of pride and dignity becoming a monarch. But she could no longer command the loyalty of her own young men, meaning chiefly Essex. And, to give Essex his due, he had cause, if not for disloyalty, certainly for resentment.

After the English success at Cadiz, the King of Spain, though bankrupt, managed to prepare another Armada. The Queen thought he could best be frustrated by a double venture—an attack on the Spanish port of Ferrol and then the waylaying of the fleet that called at the Azores with its load of West Indian treasure. Essex, hero of Cadiz, insisted on sole command, and he got it. When, after delay, the expedition sailed, there was the inevitable discord between Essex and the Rear Admiral, Raleigh. Blinded by personal animosity, Essex conducted the venture with gross incompetence, allowing the Ferrol fleet to sail for England—only storms prevented it from attacking Falmouth— and failing to intercept the treasure argosies. Back home he was in bad odor, and the Queen rubbed it in by making the Lord Admiral, Howard, Earl of Nottingham—a senior earldom—and representing him in the citation as the joint victor of Cadiz. This was defensible, but it was indiscreet; there were too many of the fiery young who saw Essex as sole hero of that expedition. Essex sulked, kept away from Court, made himself ill with brooding on his wrongs.

As the menace of Spain diminished, the problem of controlling rebellious Ireland increased. Elizabeth called a meeting to decide on the appointment of a Lord Deputy there: Essex, Nottingham, the younger Cecil, and a clerk of the signet alone were present. When Elizabeth stated that she wished to give the post to Sir William Knollys, Essex urged the appointment of Sir George Carew—a personal enemy he wanted removed from the Court. The Queen rejected this candidate, Essex grew enraged and turned his back on her. She struck him on the ear and told him to go off and be hanged. He instinctively started to draw, but Nottingham restrained his sword arm. Essex swore that he would not tolerate this insult and indignity. He strode out of the presence.

The Court split into factions. It turned into a kennel full of barking dogs. That spirit of unity which had animated the nation when Armadas threatened changed to a mood of cynicism. The death of Southampton's guardian, Lord Burghley, signaled the end of an era of dignified statesmanship: it was men like Essex who saw themselves as the statesmen of the new age. The death of Philip II—a mass of suppuration which made even his doctors vomit—marked the end of a period of struggle which had been glorious for the English. Henry IV of France had given in to Catholicism, saying that Paris was worth a mass. England had neither great allies nor great enemies any more. She turned from grappling with galleons to the putting down of tribes of ill-smelling kerns in an island that was all bogs.

The tone of the drama changed. Man was no longer the flawed colossus of Marlowe; he was a wretched creature whose follies had, for his own good, to be castigated. Satire was to be the new mode in the playhouses. Life here and now, not in dead Rome or distant Verona, was the concern of the new dramatists. Shakespeare, although his genius was acknowledged, already seemed to some to belong to an earlier epoch. In a sense this was true. If he, Burbage, Kemp, and other members of the Lord Chamberlain's company ever stole into the Rose on the Bankside, to see what the Admiral's Men were doing, they would find that George Chapman, in comedies like A *Humorous Day's Mirth*, was exhibiting to applause the manners of contemporary London—jealous old magnates with young wives, witty men around the Court, self-conscious melancholics. The term *humor* was becoming modish, and it did not directly refer to comedy. It was used in connection with a sort of mechanistic psychology that the satirists delighted in. As is often the way with up-to-the-minute trends, it was really very old-fashioned. Shakespeare, whose psychology was not mechanistic, was so modern that the modernists could not see his modernity.

The theory of humors derived from the science of the ancients. If matter was compounded of different proportions of the elements—air, earth, fire, water—so mind, or rather temperament, was made up of varying proportions of basic fluids that, entering the body, determined the nature of the owner of the body. There were four fluids or humors, corresponding to the four elements—blood, phlegm, choler or yellow bile, and melancholy or black bile. If blood predominated, a man's temperament was sanguine; if phlegm, it was phlegmatic; the choleric or angry and the melancholic or depressed were the result of the predominance of one or the other of the two biles. By subtle mixing, other temperaments could be produced. In a normal man there would be a perfect balance of humors. But it was the abnormal which the new comedians wanted—the choleric soldier and the black-hatted melancholic. The "humorous man" Hamlet refers to when talking to the players is not a funny man; he is a sort of dramatic artifact made on pseudo-scientific principle and not out of observation—Will's way—of real human beings.

The king of humors was Ben Jonson, eight years younger than Shakespeare, and coming into his force in 1597, the year of Essex's so-called Islands Voyage. He claimed to be of gentle stock, mocker of Shakespeare's pretensions to gentility, and he gave a character in one of his plays a coat of arms with a boar's head on it and the motto "Not Without Mustard." His father, he said, had lost his lands under Queen Mary and then entered the church, dying a month before his son was born. His mother had then married a bricklayer and, though Ben had been to Westminster School through another man's kindness, he had been forced into his stepfather's trade as an apprentice. He hated laying bricks, so went off to fight in the Low Countries, where, so he said, he had killed an enemy before both camps—in the classical manner—and claimed the dead man's goods as lawful spoils. He had then taken to acting with third-rate touring companies—Hieronimo in *The Spanish Tragedy* was his big part—but, now in London, was writing plays for Pembroke's Men at the Swan.

The play of his that was produced in 1597 was *The Isle of Dogs*—a topical satire to which Nashe, the poet and pamphleteer and friend of dead Greene, had contributed a couple of acts. It was clever comedy in its brash way, but, in those inflamed times, it was unwise to put on anything that hit so hard at local and contemporary folly. It was seditious and slanderous, said the Council. The Lord Mayor of London went further and condemned all plays as corruptive, unchaste, lascivious, lewd, prone to inculcate in the auditors the very vices that, in the modern mode, they pretended to chastise. He asked the Council to close down all theatres. The Council more than met that modest request. They ordered the demolition of the playhouses on both sides of the river. It was an awe-inspiring enactment—the liquidation of the Elizabethan drama. The embittered players, who could hardly yet take in that their occupation was gone, blamed it all on that damned bricklayer.

That damned bricklayer (he hath dropped his load of bricks on everybody's toes) was put in the Marshalsea, along with Gabriel Spencer and Robert Shaa—both members of Lord Pembroke's troupe. Nashe was sought after, but Nashe had gone off to live in Yarmouth, there to eat herrings and write about them in *Nashe's Lenten Stuffe*, a Joycean work ("Saint Denis for France, Saint Iames for Spaine, Saint Patrike for Ireland, Saint George for England, and the red Herring for Yarmouth"). Jonson, no fool, joined the Admiral's Men before his arrest and got four pounds advance from Henslowe: this would keep him handsomely in jail—till it ran out, that is. An empty summer stretched for the theatrical companies: they did not dare think of the autumn and winter. We can be sure that Shakespeare went back to Stratford at this time. He had at last compounded his elevation to gentleman by buying Clopton's old house—New Place. The tragedy of the situation would strike him again. A coat of arms and the finest house in Stratford, and no son to inherit the glory.

Things are rarely as bad as they seem. The Council's anger at the disruptive and seditious influence of the playhouses died down. If the orders to demolish them had ever been taken seriously, they had certainly not been acted on by the time autumn came, for at the beginning of October 1597 they all reopened. A good season beckoned, for Parliament had been summoned and the city was full. On October 8 Jonson and his fellow actors were released from the Marshalsea. On October 11 they were with the Admiral's Men at the Rose.

If Burbage had ever begged Shakespeare to try his hand at the newfangled comedies, complete with sharp satire and a large variety of humors, then he probably said no more after the affair of *The Isle of Dogs*. But, ironically, what might seem to Shakespeare and Burbage a sufficient argument against the representation of contemporary manners—namely the danger of a charge of sedition—was hovering over one of Will's harmless historical tragedies. He had written *Richard II* because it was the logical beginning of a War of the Roses epic, and now his play had been published by Andrew Wise—though with the depositon scene cut out. People were reading it not for its literary excellence but because they saw in Bolingbroke the lineaments of Essex. The hotheaded followers of the aggrieved Earl were looking for parallels in the two periods, and Shakespeare's play was their text. The man of business, innocent in his intention, unmoved by the forcing of his work into an area of propaganda, merely considered that it was time to continue the great historical sequence and see what Holinshed's *Chronicles* could teach him about Henry IV.

But the Lord Chamberlain's Men were having theatre trouble. The lease of the land on which the Theatre stood was running out, and the landlord, Giles Alleyn, was not anxious to renew it. The players would, it seemed, have to look elsewhere for an outdoor theatre, but they were considering the possibilities of an indoor one. James Burbage, who died in February 1597, had himself seen that the future of the drama might lie less with the popular audiences—groundlings who chewed sausages and garlic and booed and spat—than with those cultivated gentlemen who could appreciate a well-turned epigram, a melodious line, and an apt classical reference. Lyly had run a successful private theatre in the Blackfriars, in which his little boys had performed those refined little plays which the better sort had loved. The building consisted of a large hall, in which the plays had been presented, and a number of rooms let out as apartments. Lyly had had trouble with the landlord and seen the hall turned over to an Italian fencing master. Now there was no fencing, and Burbage had, at considerable expense, acquired the hall and turned it into a theatre suitable for the Lord Chamberlain's Men. But the monied residents of the adjacent apartments begged the Privy Council to forbid the acting of plays there, and the Council had been only too happy to listen. At the moment—October 1597—the Lord Chamberlain's Men felt understandably insecure. Admittedly, since James Burbage's death, Giles Alleyn had changed his tune somewhat concerning the renewal of the lease of the ground on which the Theatre stood. Probably owing to Dick Burbage's professionally persuasive powers, he had begun to hold out vague hope to the players, but he could not be induced to put anything on paper—not even a signature to the new lease that Dick and his brother Cuthbert had helpfully drawn up. Meanwhile, having no legal right to be on the premises, the Men moved out of the Theatre. Fortunately, James Burbage and John Brayne had acquired the neighboring Curtain about ten years before, but nobody wanted to think of it as an alternative home. It was a building in poor repair and lacking in amenities.

Shakespeare pushed on with the reign of Henry IV, assured that uneasily crowned Bolingbroke would pack them in. Wise's edition of *Richard II* was ready for a second printing; its readers would want to see how the story continued. It was a long story, Shakespeare was finding, and the length had little to do with what King Henry did. Indeed, King Henry was interesting him far less than his son, Prince Hal. Trying, somewhat grudgingly, to be in the fashion, Shakespeare was surrounding the prince with a gang of humors—Bardolph, Pistol, Poins, and a fat man called Sir John Oldcastle. Shakespeare had found the character in an old play of the Queen's Men—*The Famous Victories of Henry V*—but he had a historical namesake, a Lollard martyr burnt in Henry V's reign. This Oldcastle had the title of Lord Cobham, and the title still survived. The present Lord Cobham objected to finding one of his ancestors libeled with fatness, drunkenness, cowardice, and dishonor in a stage play. The character had to be renamed; he became Sir John Falstaff.

The background of the chronicle—both Parts One and Two—was war, civil war, with an unrulable Harry Percy very like Lord Essex, much, like him, given to talking about his honor. But the abiding voice is Falstaff's, and Falstaff will have nothing to do with honor: "What is in that word, honor? Air. A trim reckoning. Who hath it? He that died o' Wednesday. Doth he feel it? No. Doth he hear it? No. 'Tis insensible then? Yea, to the dead. But will it not live with the living? No. Why? Detraction will not suffer it. Therefore I'll none of it: honor is a mere scutcheon; and so ends my catechism." Falstaff at least is no hypocrite. If there is to be war, he will get out of it what he can. There had been, during the recent Essex expeditions, abuses of the press system in Gloucestershire, and it is in Gloucestershire that Falstaff and Justice Shallow dig out recruits from the parish. Falstaff lets Mouldy and Bullcalf go, taking three pounds for the pair. Real-life Gloucestershire captains had been greedier than that—five pounds a leg had been the price for buying one's way out of army service.

That Falstaff should be one of the great lovable characters of all literature is—to those who equate lovability with moral excellence—an eternal mystery. But to those who see no virtue in war, government propaganda, sour puritanism, hard work, pedantry, Rechabitism, and who cherish fallen humanity when it reveals itself in roguery and wit, then there is no mystery. The Falstaffian spirit is a great sustainer of civilization. It disappears when the state is too powerful and when people worry too much about their souls. When we talk of the Shakespearean spirit, we sometimes mean chiefly the Falstaffian. When, in Orwell's *Nineteen Eighty-Four*, Winston Smith wakes up with the name Shakespeare on his lips, his unconscious has not been invoking the patriotic orator or the pleader for order and obedience in the state; it has been dipping down to Shakespeare-Falstaff the folk-spirit, the witty, irreverent scoffer at political slogans, the old raspberrying Silenus. There is little of Falstaff's substance in the world now, and, as the power of the state expands, what is left will be liquidated. We cherish Falstaff with a powerful nostalgia.

There is, I think, something of Shakespeare the man, as well as Shakespeare the imaginative projector, in this gross god of wine and cowardice. He is not just the fat rebel trying to get out of the thin conformist. He is the witty jester of a small court—Shakespeare in Southampton House. He is tolerated but fundamentally despised. At the end he is rejected by the friend who has become a king and told to fall to his prayers. He owes a thousand pounds.

And, about this time of writing the *Henry IV* plays, the end of Will's friendship with Southampton must at last have come. The Queen's Glory the Earl had seduced—Mistress Vernon— was seven months gone with child. He had played the man, taken her secretly over to Paris and married her, but on their return the Queen had struck viciously, clapping both Southampton and his countess in jail. From now on, Southampton's cause would be totally Essex's. There would be no more time for listening to good advice from a plebeian poet, or for conducting raffish friendships among players. But he had, though belatedly, taken one piece of advice; and he had followed his mentor slavishly by impregnating first and marrying after.

So, for Shakespeare, the consolations of his craft and the piling up of money. Falstaff was, as he was bound to be, a popular success, and the Court smiled on him. The tradition is that *The Merry Wives of Windsor*, which shows Sir John in love, was composed because the Queen wanted more Falstaff. It is perhaps unlikely that Shakespeare would, of his own free will, wish to show more of him that he had already shown. *Henry V*, whose theme was a just and noble war, had no room for a vinous cynic, and Shakespeare wisely, and in one scene of marvelous pathos, killed him off. The Falstaff of *The Merry Wives* is not sympathetic; lechery does not suit him, and he has played out his wit in a more congenial setting.

Ben Jonson must have approved of Falstaff, despite his disapprobation of Shakespeare's lack of art and classical learning. Falstaff would look to him like a moderately well-engineered humor set in a not very well-engineered play. To Ben, Shakespeare's plays lacked form—they sprawled. They did not fulfill the rules of the ancients, who taught the art of concentrating the audience's attention through limitation of time and space. Have your action bounded by a single set, enacted in a single day—if you can, that is. But never follow Shakespeare in making action work itself out over whole years, moving from town to town, even from country to country. The audience becomes confused; there is too much for it to take in. Such would be Ben Jonson's advice to the new playwrights. Ben and Will, over a fish dinner in the Mermaid, or over ale in the Triple Tun, argued much about their art. Ben, we are told, was as ponderous as a Spanish galleon, but Will had the speed of an English man-of-war.

They went their own ways. Shakespeare left history and went back to comedy—*Much Ado About Nothing*. Ben came over to the Lord Chamberlain's Men and gave them *Every Man in his Humor*. Alleyn was annoyed at his desertion of a company that had given him welcome even after the scandal of *The Isle of Dogs*. Henslowe, remembering that four pounds advance, spoke of ingrates. Gabriel Spencer, who had been in jail with Jonson but had remained loyal to the Admiral's Men, picked a quarrel with him. In Hoxton Fields, not far from the Curtain, they had a sword fight. Ben was stout but little, and his sword was ten inches shorter than Spencer's. Nevertheless he ran Spencer through the right side and left him dead.

Naturally, Ben was arrested. At his trial he pleaded benefit of clergy. This was an old casuistical device which depended on the ambiguity of the word *clerk*. A clerk was a clergyman. A clerk was one who could read and write. Ben Jonson could read and write, therefore he was a clerk. Therefore he was a clergyman. You did not hang a clergyman. Argal, you did not hang Ben Jonson. But you branded his thumb with a T for Tyburn, a reminder that he would not escape hanging next time. And you confiscated his goods. But, as with most playwrights and poets, Ben Jonson's goods were in his head.

It was during the period of waiting for trial (or, alternatively, during the serving of his penance for the *Isle of Dogs* affair) that a strange thing happened to Jonson. He was visited by a priest and converted to Catholicism. According to his own account, he remained in the faith till 1610, when—in token of his reconciliation with the Anglican church—he drank off the whole of the Communion chalice. The business is strange because his career was in no way hindered by the conversion: the Privy Council seemed to bother as little about Jonson's Catholicism as it had done about Marlowe's atheism. The strangeness dissolves if we consider that Jonson had been secretly enrolled into the Secret Service, and was now, in more than one sense, the heir of Marlowe. To anticipate, he became ostensibly friendly with Robert Catesby, the instigator of the Gunpowder Plot, and it may have been as much through Jonson's agency as anything that the attempt to blow up the English Parliament was frustrated. It would be a decent gesture to sing "Drink to me only" at Britain's annual fireworks celebration of the foiled plot. Everybody knows the song, though not everybody knows "Hark hark the lark" or "Who is Sylvia?" It is a small victory for Ben, but Shakespeare is big enough to concede it.

Shakespeare, who continued doggedly to have nothing to do with espionage or politics, was now about to start on the most remarkable phase of his playwright's career. We associate the great plays with a great theatre, and this was now to come into being. If Giles Alleyn had renewed the lease of the ground in Shoreditch, there would not have been that stimulus to new work which a new physical medium will give—so, at least, it is possible to argue. Anyway, at the end of September 1598, it was evident that the Lord Chamberlain's Men would have to give up all hope of a renewal. Out of despondency came a new elation. The story is romantic and, one might say, typically Elizabethan.

One clause in the original lease of 1576 stated that the building erected on the Shoreditch site should belong to the Burbages if it was removed before the date of expiry. Cuthbert and Richard Burbage, believing that Alleyn would renew, let the Theatre stand, assured that they would soon return to it. But when Alleyn came along with a new lease in 1598, the conditions to it were so outrageous that the Burbages refused to sign. Alleyn had expected this; indeed, he had so contrived the lease that it was inevitable. His aim was to use the Theatre building for his own ends. He did not want a renewal; he wanted his own land and a free playhouse.

The Lord Chamberlain's Men fumed. Then they began to look around for a new site. They found one near to the Rose and their rivals, the Lord Admiral's Men. It was a garden plot near Maid Lane, and they signed a lease that entitled them to move in on Christmas Day. Capital was needed, of course. The Burbage brothers would provide half; the other half was to be divided among Shakespeare, Heminges, Phillips, Pope, and Kemp. This would give Shakespeare a tenth part of the new playhouse as well as his share in the company itself. The contract for erecting the new theatre was given to Peter Street, master builder. Where were they to get the timber?

There was only one answer to that. During the Christmas holidays, when Alleyn was out of London, a dozen or so demolition workers, with the Burbages at their head, went to the old Theatre in Shoreditch and began tearing the structure down. Then they transported it across the river on carts, piling up the timber on that garden site on the Bankside. The last days of December were bitterly cold, and the Thames froze over. But the work went on, and there was no need to use London Bridge.

It was like the Israelites crossing the Red Sea. God was on the side of the Lord Chamberlain's Men.

All through the following spring the workmen toiled overtime at erecting the finest theatre that London had ever seen. The players knew what they wanted—something circular, a wooden O, with all the old appurtenances which had made the Elizabethan drama the swift, intimate, rhetorical medium it was: jutting apron, curtained-off recess or study, tarrass or gallery above, musicians' gallery above that. A fair cellarage and a trapdoor. They yearned towards the moment when the playhouse flag would be unfurled for the first time—Hercules with the world on his shoulders. The motto would be *"Totus mundus agit histrionem,"* roughly translatable as "All the world's a stage." The name of the theatre would be the Globe.

13

Poets' War

❧❧❧❧❧❧❧❧❧❧❧❧❧❧❧❧❧❧❧

In the early spring of 1599, while what was to be the Globe was in the halfway stage of its erection, and Giles Alleyn stormed impotently about the loss of his timber, Shakespeare must have considered that it was time to have done with the Wars of the Roses. Soon, the whisper went, it would be forbidden to represent any phase of English history on the stage: wherever one looked in English history, one seemed to find some inflammatory parallel to the present times. A foolish Cambridge lawyer, Dr. John Hayward, had published in February a book on the deposition of Richard II by Bolingbroke, and he had dedicated it fulsomely to the Earl of Essex. The Archbishop of Canterbury himself demanded the excision of the dedication: the church, to whom deposition of the Lord's anointed was blasphemy as well as treason, might yet be a more formidable enemy to playwrights and pamphleteers than the Council could ever be. Shakespeare worked fast on *Henry* V: it would be a pity to have to leave the long saga unfinished.

It would be a good rousing trumpeting play for the new theatre, perhaps indeed for its very opening, and, probably for the last time, the old Elizabethan spirit of aggressive patriotism could be invoked without absurdity. Though the coolness between Essex and his Queen continued, yet Essex was the only man to resolve the Irish problem. He was temporarily a legitimate hero again, and aspects of him could, without danger, flash off the warrior king of the new play. Shakespeare could even make the chorus mention him directly:

Were now the general of our gracious empress—
As in good time he may—from Ireland coming,
Bringing rebellion broachèd on his sword,
How many would the peaceful City quit
To welcome him!

He had in mind the noise of acclamation which sped Essex
and his army on their way on March 27. "God bless your
lordship—heaven prosper your venture." And Essex, plainly
dressed, as humble as Bolingbroke doffing his bonnet to an
oyster wench, said something like "Thanks, my countrymen,
my loving friends." Southampton, out of jail now, was with
him. Essex proposed making him General of the Horse, but,
knowing the Queen would disapprove, left this elevation till
they were safely, or unsafely, in Ireland.

The Venetian ambassador had termed Ireland the English-
man's grave, and it was true that ironclad soldiers had so far
failed to subdue the courageous and crafty Irish leader of the
rebels against English rule—Hugh O'Neil, Earl of Tyrone, ruler
of central and eastern Ulster. His men might be mere tribal
savages, but they were well disciplined. Behind them, it was
feared, the Spanish power, though much diminished now, was
waiting to mop up the remnants of the English army that the
Irish would rudely hack, against all the rules of civilized war.
But Essex had sixteen thousand men and thirteen hundred
horses, the biggest army that had left England during the whole
of the reign. He was confident. It was a pity that a bad omen
struck as they were marching north through Islington. A black
cloud swooped from the northeast, bringing hail and lightning.
The Elizabethans were a healthily superstitious race: those who
now feared the worst were wise to do so.

Elizabeth had proposed sending Charles Blount, Lord Mountjoy, in place of Essex. Essex had fought a duel with him some
years before, but he was now the lover of poor Penny Rich,
Essex's sister. In *Henry* V, Shakespeare names the French herald
Mountjoy, and it might be thought that there is a significant
allusion here, though the significance is obscure. But Shakespeare was merely using a convenient French name, and it

happened to be the name of the Huguenot family with whom he had lodgings in Silver Street, Cripplegate. Christopher Mountjoy, his name now thoroughly Anglicized, was a maker of tires or ornamental headpieces for ladies. He was a useful landlord to have while Shakespeare was working on that ribald scene of *Henry V* which is wholly in French and contains a number of words which, though dirty, are foreign and hence unlikely to corrupt English audiences. It is probable that the boy actors who played the French ladies were brought along to Silver Street for coaching.

The Mountjoys had a marriageable daughter, Marie, and Shakespeare's name appears in the documents of a lawsuit relating to her marriage. Stephen Belott, the apprentice who married her, complained that Christopher Mountjoy had not produced the dowry of sixty pounds he had promised and, moreover, had not ratified in his will a verbal promise of a legacy of two hundred pounds. In court, the Mountjoys' maid said that "one Mr. Shakespeare that lay in the house" had been deputed by his landlord "to perswade the plaintiff to the same marriage." Will, in his deposition, made while he was in Stratford, proved himself to be a not very reliable witness. He said that, in his view, Belott was a good boy, but he could remember nothing of the verbal transactions. From this we may conclude that he was distracted, writing a play or something, while the marriage negotiations were proceeding. Kindly, a little absent-minded, hard-working, still in London lodgings and not the fine London house he could afford now—again a shadowy portrait emerges.

Ben Jonson was much in Shakespeare's mind when he was writing *Henry V*. There even seems to be a caricature of him in Nym, a new member of the Falstaff gang, though Falstaff, of course, is dead. Nym tells Pistol that he will prick his guts a little, "in good terms, as I may; and that's the humor of it." Pistol, who is a kind of comic Alleyn, clings to the old Ercles vein for his reply: "O braggart vile and damned furious wight!" and so on. But Ben's jibes about the devices of the chronicle play, in which there was no room for the new realism (how, for instance, could you get a whole army on the stage?), were striking home—hence the chorus, who is always apologizing for what the "wooden O" cannot adequately do.

That wooden O, an octagon really, crowned with a fine thatch that, fourteen years later, was to cause trouble, opened in July. *Henry V* went down well; there was great popular hope that Essex would trounce Tyrone, and the jingoistic tone of the play was apposite. But pessimism and fear must have been at work in high places, else why did the Archbishop supervise, in good Nazi style, the burning of books deemed to be too free-speaking? There had been a fine bonfire in June, with satire and amatory poems, even *Willobie his Avisa*, going up in flames. As for Dr. Hayward's book on the deposition of Richard II, the whole of the new edition of fifteen hundred copies had been burnt, and there was a general ban on all works dealing with English history. The effect of this was to make writers go further back in time and publish books on Roman history. It is doubtful if Shakespeare would, at that particular period of his career, have gone to North's Plutarch unless stimulated both by the ban and the new interest in antique Rome. If you wanted a historical parallel to the dangerous times, you could get it as easily from the assassination of Julius Caesar as from the deposition of Richard II.

But before writing *Julius Caesar*, Shakespeare had a certain vein of comedy to get out of his system. He was convinced that the Jonsonian approach to the form was wrong: both satire on the times (dangerous, anyway) and pasteboard humors represented a shameful limitation on a mode that was potentially rich in wit, romance, and even philosophy, and could take fair comment on topical events in its stride. Besides, he had seen possibilities in a new kind of clown—not the old leering buffoon, full of improvised cracks and trippings over, but one with a capacity for learned wit, subtle observations, melody, and pathos. In other words, the day of Will Kemp was over. There was a young man called Robin Armin who could, with the right lines, revolutionize the comic aspects of the drama—whether in self-styled comedy or in tragedy. Armin was to be Touchstone in *As You Like It* and Feste in *Twelfth Night*. He was also to be the Fool in *King Lear*.

But first, in that summer of 1599, Kemp had to go. There was probably acrimony, and a good deal of instinctive histrionics, in the greenroom that still smelled of new paint. Kemp said, doubtless, that he had been in the profession before most of them were wiped, and as for Shakespaw here, butcher's boy hence Not Without Mustard, had he not taught him all he knew while he was still unhandily botching plays for the Queen's Men? A sort of ingrates, the lot, but Shakebag especially. Well, he would be glad to be out of it, the theatre was not what it had been, all words words words now, honorificabillibus, and no wooing of the muse of improvisation. He sold his shares in the Globe and went away. He planned something that would bring him more fame and wealth than ever he could gain from continued service with a fellowship of word-struck pedants, full of references to poets like Metamorphosis and Virgil. He planned to dance from London to Norwich, with his trill-lillies on his legs, and make himself rich by opening a book (three to one he couldn't do it) and later writing one.

The book was written, and we have it. (If only Shakespeare had written a book as silly, cocky, and self-revelatory.) It is called *Kemps Nine Daies Wonder* and it was produced in 1600, the year when, accompanied by "Thomas Slye my Taberer, William Bee my seruant, and George Sprat, appointed for my ouerseer, that I should take no other ease but my prescribed order," this "onely tricker of your Trill-lillies, and best belshangles between Sion and mount Surrey" frolicly footed it as he had said he would, nine days between the two towns, welcomed everywhere, Cavaliero Kemp, one in the eye for those who had cast him out, and particularly a person called "my notable Shakerags." Later he tried to dance across Europe, over the Alps to Rome, but the high Head-borough of heighs (or antic hays) was not so well known on the Continent and the venture was not successful.

There was no Kemp, then, in *As You Like It*, but there was so much else that he was not greatly missed. If the groundlings wanted lavatory mirth, then they should have it in a very refined form. Sir John Harington had, a few years earlier, written a book about his own cleanly invention, the water-closet, and entitled it *The Metamorphosis of Ajax*. Ajax was a Jonsonian humor, a man with too much black bile, a melancholic malcontent. It seemed appropriate to metamorphose him into that best throne for all costive brooding, so Ajax became A Jax or A Jakes. Shakespeare—to whose heart anything with *Metamorphosis* in the title would travel straight—took the name, frenchifying it to Jaques, for his own melancholy character. This courtly brooder on man's folly, exiled with his duke to the Forest of Arden, is a genuine character, not a mere humor, and he has one of the best of Shakespeare's set pieces to deliver. This expands the motto of the Globe into a philosophical meditation on the parts man plays from babyhood to senility, for if the globe is the world and the Globe is a theatre, then the world must be a theatre.

The Globe did well, but it could not do well on Shakespeare's plays alone. Runs were short, the repertory had to be large, and jumpy, capricious, critical audiences had to be fed with a variety of plays, as well as with variety within any given play. The audiences, meaning the citizens of London, were very jumpy through the summer of 1599, what with new rumors of Spanish landings on the Isle of Wight, the city gates locked and chains across the streets, talk of defending London with a bridge of boats at Gravesend. And the news of Essex's expedition to Ireland—such of it as leaked out from the Council—was generally bad. Essex seemed to be doing little but knighting his followers, knighting being one of his obsessions, and, as the Queen put it, going on progress to the tune of a thousand pounds a day. Shakespeare got the jumpiness, the portents of danger to the state, the fickleness of the mob, the hell that follows the disruption of order, in his first Roman tragedy, *Julius Caesar*. And, reading Antony's life in Plutarch, he could see another tragedy stirring.

But the Globe also put on Jonson's *Every Man out of His Humor*, the play in which Ben sneers quietly at Shakespeare's genteel pretensions (Not Without Mustard). Ben also sneered at Shakespeare's presuming to write a Roman play when he knew so little Latin: one of these days he, Jonson, would show them how a Roman play should be made. And he scoffed particularly at the line "Caesar did never wrong but with just cause." Shakespeare obligingly changed it to:

Know, Caesar doth not wrong; nor without cause
Will he be satisfied.

According to the cast list, Shakespeare played in Jonson's earlier comedy, *Every Man in his Humor*, but he does not seem to have wished a part in the sequel. The Lord Chamberlain's Men did not like it greatly—too long, too sermonical with its chastisement of manners. They cut it, and no playwright likes his work to be cut. Ben went back to the Lord Admiral's Men, very huffy.

The whole of the year, and the year following, was characterized by uneasiness and snarling, in the theatre as much as in the world of affairs. The Admiral's Men at the Rose were only a stone's throw from the Chamberlain's Men at the Globe, and perhaps that proverbial distance was literally tested. The Rose tried to beat the Globe on its own dramaturgical ground: if, for instance, the Globe was doing well with Falstaff, then the Rose would put on a Falstaff play of its own, but they would get back to the truth—the real Sir John Oldcastle, not the fat travesty concocted by Shakespeare. And so, in the manner of Henslowe's more urgent commissions, the task of making *The True and Honorable History of the life of Sir John Oldcastle, the good Lord Cobham* was parceled out among poets—Munday, Drayton, Wilson, and Hathway. The Drayton was Michael, a man of Shakespeare's county and a friend; the Hathway was no relative of Anne. The play was a success, but posterity has rejected it, preferring the false Sir John to the true one.

Still, one play in those days did not make a season. Gloomily, Henslowe and his son-in-law recognized that the Bankside now belonged to the Globe, and the Rose was past the days of its summer bloom. So they went north and bought land in St. Giles's parish, between Aldersgate and Moorgate. They proposed building a square-shaped playhouse called the Fortune, and they drew up a detailed blueprint which still survives and shows us what the *fin de siècle* Elizabethans thought suitable in a theatre. Thus the Fortune stage was to be forty-three feet wide and to jut over twenty-five feet into the auditorium. The total cost, exclusive of painting, was to be £440—more than seven times the price Shakespeare had given for New Place in Stratford. The theatre, of course, is long gone, but the site remains— Fortune Street, between Whitecross Street and Golden Lane, E.C.I.

Giants fought giants, and dwarfs fought both. If the Admiral's Men and the Chamberlain's Men suffered from each other, they both suffered, and so did the lesser companies, from the child actors, the little eyases of *Hamlet*, who were popular again with the better sort. One could visit the singing school of St. Paul's and see sweetly pretty dears going through the motions of an old-fashioned classical-type comedy, and not be affronted by rude apprentices jeering and discharged soldiers falling over drunk. The Earl of Derby had revived this acting troupe of choirboys, and he sought playwrights for them. One of the new men was John Marston, an enigmatic character who died in 1634, though at what age we do not know. He revised an old piece called *Histriomastix*, retaining the desperately antiquated personifications of the moralities—Peace, War, Envy, Plenty, and so on. But with *Antonio and Mellida* and *Antonio's Revenge* a more original vein appears—lines like "While snarling gusts nibble the juiceless leaves / From the nak'd shuddering branch" and "The black jades of swart night trot foggy rings / 'Bout heaven's brow . . ." Jonson hated this clotted style, and he was annoyed that Marston should profess himself a disciple of his. There would, in these times of enmity, be trouble between Marston and himself. The criticism of the poet "Mellidus" —evidently the author of *Antonio and Mellida*—in *Every Man out of His Humor* would start things off perhaps: "A slight bubbling spirit, a cork, a husk." Jonson liked war. Whether the story he eventually told was true, we do not know—that he beat up Marston and took away his pistol—but he would certainly want to do it.

The Paul's Boys were so popular that Henry Evans, who had worked with John Lyly in the old Blackfriars days, and Nathaniel Giles, who had been Master of the Children of the Chapel Royal since 1597, got together and formed a new children's company. Evans knew that the Blackfriars Theatre was empty, that Burbage and his friends were forbidden to perform there because the gentlemen in lodgings had pleaded that it would mean loss of amenity, but children's performances might be a very different thing. So it proved. Evans arranged with Burbage to take out a twenty-one-year lease, and thus a home was found for a new band of little eyases. It was a good band, and it contained the young actor Salathiel Pavy, who was to impersonate old men so well and, on his death at the age of thirteen, elicit a fine elegiac poem from Ben Jonson. Jonson, who would write for any company that did not question his authority as an expert on drama, willingly wrote for the Blackfriars children. He wrote *Cynthia's Revels*, for instance, which failed to get put on at Court during the Christmas holidays of 1600–1, *Twelfth Night* being preferred. Ben, naturally, did not like this. He liked his own play, though—"This precious crystal work of rarest wit," as Cynthia herself puts it. Cynthia was meant to be Queen Elizabeth, and the words were set in proleptic elevation of Ben to Royal Poet. Nobody, in Ben's view, could write like Ben.

Marston, stealing the subtitle of *Twelfth Night*, wrote a play for the rival boys' company of St. Paul's. *What You Will*, in the gentlest way imaginable, suggests that Ben Jonson (disguised as Philomuse) is hypercritical and has no real right to abuse audiences (as he does in *Cynthia's Revels*) for not liking what they are told to like. "Rules of art," he is told, "were shaped to pleasure, not pleasure to your rules." Who is he to "spit defiance on dislike?" and so on. Jonson became very mad at this subdued remonstrance. He planned a play in which his contemporaries and inferiors should be trounced, though—to exhibit his own restraint and basic decency—not under their real names. He talked in the taverns about this project, and the Lord Chamberlain's Men inevitably heard him. They considered that Jonson, the satirist, needed satirizing himself. No player was happy about the manner in which he sneered at players—the mere fiddles that played the tunes of him, the master composer, and played them badly. Moreover, the men of the Globe had no love for playwrights who worked for the boy actors and drew custom away from their betters. Burbage could not expect satire from Shakespeare, so he commissioned Thomas Dekker to have a slam at Ben on the stage.

Dekker, who was about thirty at the time, was best known in the theatre for his *Old Fortunatus* and *The Shoemaker's Holiday*, the latter the first real "citizen's play" of the period. It deals with a recognizable London of tradesmen and apprentices, and it has an admirable comic character in Simon Eyre, the healthily Rabelaisian cobbler ("She hath a privy fault—she farts in her sleep") who becomes Lord Mayor. Dekker was also a delightful writer of pamphlets about this real London: his *The Gull's Hornbook* is a classic guide to the manners of the city. As a poet he was inferior to Ben and even Marston, but he produced one lyric which, like "Drink to me only," everyone knows. This is the lullaby beginning "Golden slumbers kiss your eyes." Before Dekker could answer Jonson's attack on the players, the attack had first to appear. Jonson was always a slow worker, and it took him four months to write *The Poetaster*. While writing it he learned that Dekker was going to reply to it, so Dekker too became an enemy, one to be mocked on the stage.

When *The Poetaster or His Arraignment* was first performed by the boys at the Blackfriars, it impressed more with its smell of the lamp than by the sting of its satire. Ben shows off his learning in speeches of great length (one can hear those children crying as the lines were beaten into them: Evans and Giles were used to the old modes of school discipline), but, when it is a matter of his own strong feelings, he can be brisk and salty enough. Thus, this on the players: "An honest decayed commander cannot skelder, cheat, nor be seen in a bawdy house, but he shall be straight in one of their wormwood comedies. They are grown licentious, the rogues; libertines, flat libertines. They forget they are in the statute, the rascals; they are blazoned there; there they are tricked, they and their pedigrees; they need no other heralds, I wiss." Ben seems unable to forgive Shakespeare for that coat of arms.

The setting of the play is Rome under the Emperor Augustus, and the main characters are the Roman poets—Ovid, Virgil, Horace. Horace, little and fat but a genius, is meant to be Ben himself. The envious Crispinus and Demetrius ("a dresser of plays about the town") are, respectively, Marston and Dekker. They conspire against Horace, but they do not win. In the presence of the Emperor himself, Horace makes Crispinus vomit up all his ridiculous doggerel, spewing out (it is not a very good joke, really) tough words like *spurious, snotteries, turgidous, ventosity.* Shakespeare might also be expected to come in for this Rabelaisian sort of critical attack, but we wonder whether he is actually in the play. Ovid opens it with these lines:

> Then, when this body falls in funeral fire,
> My name shall live, and my best part aspire.

They sound like the final couplet of one of the Sonnets, but turn out to be the end of an interminable poem in heroic couplets. Shakespeare loved Ovid, and young Francis Meres had recently compared him to Ovid, but it is doubtful if Ben would give him the satisfaction of being Ovid on stage. He recognized also that, little as he approved his undisciplined art, he could not shove Will in with the rest of the poetasters. He was too big for easy lampooning. Moreover, Ben—as he acknowledged later in print—could not deny Will's free and open nature, his lack of niggling jealousy. In spite of everything, they were friends.

Dekker's reply to *The Poetaster* was called *Satiromastix, or The Untrussing of the Humorous Poet.* The main characters are the same as in Jonson's play, but this time Crispinus and Demetrius are decent talented poets, and Horace—who has an admirably named follower, Asinius Bubo—is a braggart and scold who is ultimately forbidden to identify himself with the Quintus Horatius Flaccus of Augustus's Rome. "Horace loved poets well and gave coxcombs to none but fools, but thou lov'st none, neither wise men nor fools, but thyself." So says Tucca, on whom Ben-Horace has written scurrilous epigrams. Dekker is able to present his Horace as a mere simulacrum of the true one by setting his play not in Rome but in the reign and country of King William Rufus. Our heads swim at the ease with which the Elizabethans fuse, or confuse, disparate times and cultures.

Ben was hurt rather than angry. He had only, he said, done what he had done for the good of art. And as for answering this libel of Dekker's, well—

> ... for to revenge their injuries,
> Were to confess you felt them. Let them go,
> And use the treasure of the fool, their tongues,
> Who makes his gain, by speaking worst of best.

And, later:

> ... I leave the monsters
> To their own fate. And since the Comic Muse
> Hath prov'd so ominous to me, I will try
> If TRAGEDY have a more kind aspect.

This, and much more, is in an epilogue he added to *The Poetaster* after long digestion of his hurt. The tragedy was to be *Sejanus*, a real evocation of Rome, not the botched business that was *Julius Caesar*.

Shakespeare, as we see, kept out of this little war, but he was believed to have some connection with it in an aftermath of which we know nothing. A Christmas play put on by the students of St. John's College, Cambridge—*The Return from Parnassus*—is full of references to theatre business in London, and it takes retrospective sides in the late controversy. Ben Jonson, says one character, is "so slow an inventor that he were better betake himself to his old trade of bricklaying; a bold whoreson, as confident now in making a book as he was in times past in laying of a brick." Shakespeare, it is conceded, would do well if he wrote on graver subjects: too much love in his "heart-throbbing line." It is the poet rather than the dramatist who is meant. And then, as though the anonymous author had not heard of the split between the Lord Chamberlain's Men and their old chief clown, Kemp and Burbage are brought on the stage to give a lesson on acting. Kemp ("Kemp," rather) pours scorn on the learned school of dramaturgy:

> ... they smell too much of... that writer Metamorphosis, and talk too much of Proserpina and Jupiter. Why, here's our fellow

Shakespeare puts them all down; aye, and Ben Jonson too. O that Ben Jonson's a pestilent fellow; he brought up Horace giving the poets a pill, but our fellow Shakespeare hath given him a purge that made him bewray his credit.

This shows no inner knowledge. Kemp had as little time for Will as, presumably, he had for the other learned playmaker, and was probably inclined to rate their erudition about equally. But there is a reference here which seems to relate to something that Will did to Ben, and we do not know whether to take it personally, professionally, metaphorically, or what. "Bewray his credit"—a gross step further than vomiting. Was it, as Dr. Hotson thinks, this business of *Twelfth Night* being accepted for the Court Christmas junketings and *Cynthia's Revels* rejected? Was there a play, now lost, in which Shakespeare, in classical guise on *Poetaster* lines, administered some bowel-cracking draught to a pseudonymous Jonson? Did he put senna and rhubarb secretly in his wine in the Mermaid? We shall never know. Infuriatingly, whenever Shakespeare does something other than buy a lease or write a play, history shuts her jaws with a snap.

14

Rebellion

These bitings and scratchings of poets were very small stuff
compared with the big public tragedy, or farce, that now began
to go into rehearsal. The leading actor was the Earl of Essex, a
disgraced man. He had done little in Ireland except create new
knights, and the Queen raged. He had met Tyrone by a
river—Essex on the bank, Tyrone in midstream on horseback—
and, it was believed, had told the rebel that soon there was to be
a change of regime in England, and if Tyrone were friendly it
might be much to his advantage. Shortly after—autumn 1599—
he took ship for England, rode at once to the Palace of
Nonsuch, and confronted the Queen, travel-stained as he was,
in her bedchamber. He was not at once rebuked, merely told to
go and change his clothes: a breach of protocol was no more
than a match struck in an inferno. Later that day there came
the closeted interviews and, after those, Essex's committal to the
charge of the Lord Keeper. By this time, all London knew that
Essex had concluded a truce with Tyrone.

His followers were no whit abashed. The Earl of Southampton
was seen a good deal in the playhouses, enjoying himself. What
he and his old protégé had to say to each other we do not know:
perhaps Shakespeare was too disillusioned to wish to effect a
reconciliation. His dramatist's brain was becoming preoccupied
with a puzzle that hardly existed for Ben and the other humor
men—the puzzle of the good intention that could produce evil.
Essex and Southampton honestly believed that the Queen's
deposition was good for the realm; Essex spoke only of honor
and patriotism, not of personal advantage. Yet high motives

could throw the country into bloodshed and chaos, the slaughter of innocents. It was an anomaly he had worked out in *Julius Caesar.* Brutus was a murderer but still the noblest Roman of them all. The conscience of the killer was to become an obsessive theme in the tragedies Shakespeare was preparing to write.

Essex grew ill. The Queen relented temporarily of her anger and sent eight of the best physicians of the day to examine him. There was no physical ailment, they reported: it was all in the mind. The Queen relented of her relenting, and Essex remained confined, disgraced, untried till the summer of the following year.

It was on June 5, 1600, that a formal trial was inaugurated, a Star Chamber matter. Essex was accused of having disobeyed orders: he had been sent to Ireland, at very great expense, to subdue the wild Irish, and he had concluded a truce instead. The prosecution spent eleven hours on its opening speeches, and the Attorney General, the Solicitor General, and Sir Francis Bacon—to whom Essex had once proved a good and influential friend—were in their best rhetorical form. Essex was physically weak, but only at the end of the long day was he allowed to sit: kneeling had seemed to the court to be the most appropriate posture for him. As for the verdict, that was a foregone conclusion. The punishment? The Tower, dismissal from his profitable offices, a huge fine—all these were proposed, singly or together. Finally it was agreed that the Queen should decide. More waiting then, and Essex back to the charge of the Lord Keeper. He was beginning to elicit great sympathy from the general public—his humiliation, his humility, his patience.

On August 26 he was freed. The royal anger over the Irish affair was becoming much mollified by the reports of Lord Mountjoy's success over there, and the very contrast between his quiet ability and the empty flamboyance of Essex was enough of a punishment for the latter: perhaps he would now learn to grow up. But he was forbidden to come to Court. Essex could bear that, but he could not bear the prospect of a more piercing punishment—the Queen's failure to renew the farm of the tax on sweet wines, a monopoly that had been one of the many marks of her favor to him, and exceedingly profitable. The date for renewal was Michaelmas; Essex was heavily in debt to the vintners; he wrote the Queen letters full of love and self-abasement; he sweated with apprehension. The Queen saw through the gestures of repentance and questioned the sincerity of the love: she told Francis Bacon as much, and Bacon told others. And then, after keeping Essex dangling till All Hallows, she announced that his monopoly would not be renewed: she would hold the farm of the sweet wine tax in her own hands.

Four days before Christmas, London was briefly shaken by an earthquake—no huge Asiatic tremor, but a sufficient portent for the superstitious. Essex House was now a sort of party headquarters, where all assembled who believed that their causes could best be furthered by the Earl and not, to use the Earl's own words, an old woman whose mind was as crooked as her body. Courtiers out of favor mingled with captains who had lost their commissions. Puritans gave sermons which stated how the rule of the sovereign was subject to higher authority, and that this authority could be seen in them that knew they were saved—a doctrine to be fulfilled in the regicide of fifty years later. A follower of Essex, a man called Cuffe, a sort of blunt Casca, spoke about the disgrace of submitting to humiliation, and how my lord, already robbed of certain of his rights and his riches, would systematically be reduced to poverty if he did not act now. Essex, thus encouraged, spoke out of his own anger, and his words were promptly borne back to the Queen. With so many welcome at Essex House, it was hard to keep spies out.

It must have been at this time that Shakespeare wrote his *Troilus and Cressida*. It was still forbidden to write books on English history, and it was dangerous to put English history on the stage, but the whole of the classical past was available and—since political man is always the same—there were plenty of piquant parallels to Elizabeth's troubled reign in Rome and Greece. Greece had recently become more popular than Rome, as witness the *Troy's Revenge, Agamemnon,* and *Orestes His Furies* put on at the Rose, as well as a *Troilus and Cressida* written by Chettle and Dekker. And, in 1598, Chapman's translation of seven books of the *Iliad* had appeared, with a dedication to the Earl of Essex, "living instance of the Achillean virtues eternized by divine Homer." Virtues? At present Essex was exhibiting the Achillean vice of sulking in his tent.

The story of Troilus and Cressida had been told by Chaucer, but told as a romantic tale of love. Shakespeare left out the love, or rather purified it into lust. It is likely that he was again undergoing transports and agonies of the kind that he had known with the Dark Lady, or else—with Southampton very bitterly in his mind these days—was remembering how he became passion's slave in vain. Shakespeare was a highly sexed man, and in his own time his chambering had bred at least one legend. In the diary of John Manningham of the Middle Temple is the following entry for March 13, 1601:

> Upon a time when Burbage played Richard III, there was a citizen grew so far in liking with him, that before she went from the play she appointed him to come that night unto her by the name of Richard the Third. Shakespeare, overhearing their conclusion, went before, was entertained and at his game ere Burbage came. Then, message being brought that Richard III was at the door, Shakespeare caused return to be made that William the Conqueror was before Richard the Third.

The anecdote does not have to be true, but anecdotes of this kind are not circulated about men who dislike women. Shakespeare's tragedy may have been that he liked them not wisely but too well, that he could not take them lightly—as Ben seemed able to do—but tended to conceive love where only lust was in order. He valued the sexual act too highly as an expression of genuine affection, and then found the affection was not returned. Left stranded with an emotion too great for its object, he knew accessions of profound disgust—chiefly with himself. He saw himself, Will the lover, as a dog with a bitch, panting. In *Troilus and Cressida*, the pander Pandarus sings a dirty little song in which the sighs of the lover "ho ho ho" are converted into both the pantings of the dog and the orgasmatic cries of the bitch—"ha ha ha." The play is about the disillusion-ment of lust, with Troilus first mad for Cressida then nauseated by the transformation of a goddess into a prostitute.

This theme of the disillusionment of love or lust is closely

associated with the political theme. Ulysses, giving his opinion
on the Greek failure to take Troy, blames it on the Greek failure
to maintain order. There is a hieratic pattern in the universe,
which men, for the sake of communal health, must be willing
to imitate. "Take but degree away, untune that string, / And
hark! what discord follows. . . ." The Greek army is untuned:

> The general's disdained
> By him one step below, he by the next,
> That next by him beneath; so every step,
> Exampled by the first pace that is sick
> Of his superior, grows to an envious fever
> Of pale and bloodless emulation:
> And 'tis this fever that keeps Troy on foot,
> Not her own sinews. To end a tale of length,
> Troy in our weakness stands, not in her strength.

"A tale of length" is too true. *Troilus and Cressida* has more talk
than action, and this is why it failed on the stage. But the excess
of talk is a sure sign that Shakespeare is more concerned with
expressing his own personal convictions than with making a
play. Never did he contrive better verse or more telling images,
but the verbal brilliance gets the better of the dramatic design: it
rules where it should serve, degree has been taken away. As for
the cause of the Greek untuning, it is to be found in Achilles,
the bass-peg of the fighting army, who

> Having his ear full of his airy fame,
> Grows dainty of his worth, and in his tent
> Lies mocking our designs.

And, in the same way, Essex's scoffing at the hierarchical
pattern of the English kingdom portends impotence and ruin,
anarchy and chaos.

But wherein lies the association of the disillusionment of lust
and the decay of the state? It is a double parallel. There is, first,
the simple failure of trust. If lovers' vows can so easily be
broken, how much more easily the subject's vows to the sovereign. Then there is the metaphor which (as, at length, in
Coriolanus) turns the state into a body, complete with head,

limbs, and belly. Indiscriminate love can lead to the decay of the body: the term *venereal* connotes both love and disease. It is so easy to talk of honor, which is higher than love, and yet make honor the means of ruining the fair body of the state. Pandarus, in his epilogue, mentions the "Winchester geese" of the Bankside— those prostitutes whose brothels come under the jurisdiction of the Bishop of Winchester—and ends by bequeathing his diseases to the audience. It is a means of conveying a double disgust. Had Shakespeare, disturbed at the disease of the greater body, also at this time seen the beginning of disease in his own?

Mere artists must observe great events, not participate in them. Yet sometimes the work of art itself will be forced, by the makers of events, into the arena of action. This was now to happen with one of Shakespeare's works, and it was evil, as is any perversion of art into propaganda. On Friday, February 6, 1601, some of the Earl of Essex's followers came to the Globe and requested that *Richard II* be given a special performance the following afternoon. The Lord Chamberlain's Men replied that the play was now old stuff and unlikely to attract much of an audience. The Essex men then said they would indemnify the players against a loss at the box office; they would pay forty shillings for the performance. They were men of high rank— Lord Monteagle was among them—and it was hard to refuse. Burbage and his fellows were only players.

And so on the Saturday, prompt at three in the afternoon, the preludial trumpets sounded and the play began. Essex was not present, nor apparently was Southampton, but there were a number of distinguished names in the audience—a lord and many knights, not all the latter of Essex's making. The significance of the choice of play would not be lost on the groundlings. The deposition scene came and went: let it now be noted that once, out of honor and, as it proved, for the good of the realm, a nobleman deposed a monarch, capricious and hysterical tyrant who overtaxed the people and sent one of England's best men into exile. Finally came the regrettable necessity of regicide. The play ended. God save the Queen.

The uneasy Council summoned the Earl of Essex that

evening, but he refused to go: it was not safe to stir abroad, he said, with so many enemies after him. That night and the following morning he and his followers made their preparations to seize the city. Another historical precedent than that shown in *Richard II* was now being invoked. The Duke of Guise, seen on the stage in Marlowe's *The Massacre at Paris*, had taken Paris in 1588, helped by a few followers but welcomed by the whole city; he had driven the king out of the capital. Could not Essex, London's favorite, achieve a success as easy? At ten o'clock on Sunday morning, the Lord Keeper, the Chief Justice, the Earl of Worcester, and Sir William Knollys came in the Queen's name to Essex House, bidding him refrain from any rash act he might have in mind. There was a huge crowd there, and some cried "Kill them!" Essex made the four notables prisoners, and left them guarded in Essex House as hostages. Then he and his two hundred followers, all young men, rode to the city.

Up Ludgate Hill and all through Cheapside, Essex shouted that a plot had been laid against his life: "For the Queen! For the Queen!" Then a herald proclaimed him a traitor, but Essex believed that the Queen knew nothing of his intent: a herald would do anything for two shillings. At the sound of the word traitor, some of his followers left him and mingled with the crowd. The sheriff had promised Essex arms, but the promise was broken. Essex sweated now; he saw that he must make his way back to the fortress of Essex House. But Ludgate Hill had chains across it and an armed force waiting. His men charged, and Sir Christopher Blount killed a man, but he was at once taken prisoner. Essex managed to get back to Essex House by way of the river, but here he found that his hostages had been released and the land side of the fortress was under siege. In the evening the Lord Admiral threatened to blow up the house, so Essex, having destroyed all the incriminating documents he could find, gave himself up. The news was imparted to the Queen while she was eating her usual solitary dinner. She went on eating, unmoved.

"A senseless ingrate," she said next day, "has at last revealed what has long been in his mind." The city was put under a strong guard and the Court now became a fortress. Some adventure-loving apprentices aimed to raise a company of five thousand to release Essex, but this was romantic nonsense: they had—probably at the Rose—been watching the equivalent of too much television. A more serious plot was conceived by Captain Lea, who resolved to seize the Queen and force her to release Essex and his followers. He reached the door of the room where she usually dined and there was seized himself.

A week later, Essex and Southampton were brought to trial. Essex wore black and was disdainful of his judges. "I am indifferent how I speed. I owe God a death." The woman's tailor in *Henry IV*, pressed into service by Falstaff, had spoken similarly: "I care not; a man can die but once; we owe God a death." Essex was on a sort of stage, desirous of leaving in men's minds the memory of a good performance. He eloquently washed his own brain of all its treasonable stuff, confessed all, and called himself, when he was back in the Tower waiting for execution, "the greatest, the most vilest, and most unthankful traitor that ever has been in the land." He asked for a private death, for he did not want the danger of being corrupted at the last by the acclamation of the mob.

On February 24, 1601, Shrove Tuesday, the Lord Chamberlain's Men were summoned to Court to perform. We do not know what play they gave: it would have been typical of the Queen's sardonic humor to ask for *Richard II*. They must have felt uneasy; they had, after all, and for forty pieces of silver, sounded the fanfare for that Sunday revolt. The following morning, Ash Wednesday, Essex was beheaded in the courtyard of the Tower. "He acknowledged, with thankfulness to God, that he was thus spewed out of the realm." He was only thirty-four—young to us, to his contemporaries too old for ungovernable madness. As for the Earl of Southampton, he languished in the Tower and was still languishing two years later, when the Queen died. King James released him, and he prospered in the new reign.

The Lord Chamberlain's Men were suspected by the Council of having had their part to play in the rebellion: why perform that inflammatory tragedy at that inflammatory time? Augustine Phillips, one of the actors, perhaps the one that had played

Richard, gave the company's version of the event on oath. They had been requested to put on a revival of *Richard II* by their betters, lord and knights of the realm; it would have been unseemly to refuse. Their innocence was accepted; no further action would be taken. Still, the art of the drama could not any longer be regarded as a mere harmless frippery for the passing of an idle afternoon. Drama, with men like Shakespeare, had learned to touch life on the raw.

Shakespeare wrote nothing for the greater part of that year. Then, in the autumn, he wrote the play which, of all plays ever written, the world could least do without.

15

Royal Deaths

It is coming up to three in the afternoon, and the Lord Chamberlain's Men are making ready for the world premiere of *Hamlet*. Dick Burbage, playing the lead as ever (and the biggest and most eloquent lead there has ever been), is in black, like Essex at his trial, and he is busy with paintbrush and delicately mixed colors on the faces of the two boys who are taking the women's parts. The backstage area is crammed: there are parts for everybody—Jack Heminges, Gus Phillips, Tom Pope, George Bryan, Harry Condell, Will Sly, Dick Cowly, Jack Lowin, Sam Cross, Alex Cook, Sam Gilburne, Robin Armin, Will Ostler, Nat Field, Jack Underwood, Nick Tooley, Willie Ecclestone, Joseph Taylor, two more Robins (Benfield and Gough), Dicky Robinson who is Ben Jonson's favorite, and two more Jacks or Johnnies—Shank and Rice. Rice is really Rhys or Ap Rhys, a Welshman notable for Sir Hugh Evans and Fluellen as well as, earlier, Glendower.

There is also Will Shakespeare, who is making up for the Ghost. At thirty-seven he is grey enough; he needs but little art on his receding hair and his beard. He has walked hither from his lodgings in Silver Street, turning his eyes away from the baiting of the bear Sackerson (or is it Harry Hunks?) in Paris Garden: he is growing squeamish about blood, there has been enough blood spilt these last ten years in London. This part of the Ghost reminds him how much death he has seen—this year his father, not so many years ago his son. He, a living father, is about to play a dead one. The living son of the play has very nearly the same name as that son who died. How strangely things work out.

He has put much of himself into this tragedy, but he did not choose to write it. Burbage came across that old *Hamlet* of Tom Kyd in the play trunk and suggested that, since revenge tragedy had become popular again, it might be a good plan to do something sophisticated and modern with the old tale of the Danish prince who feigned madness to encompass revenge of a murdered king and father. Well, the groundlings, by the sound of them, expect a treat on the lines of *The Spanish Tragedy*, which Ben has refurbished for the Admiral's men. The better sort, in the galleries and on the sides of the stage (tablets at the ready to take down notable lines and maxims), have seen Marston's *Antonio's Revenge*. All have lived through the real-life tragedy of Essex's rise and fall. Hamlet, though, is not an Essex; nor is he, despite the inky cloak, the conventional melancholic. He looks back to a folk legend, the green man Amloth that acted mad. Had not the Earl of Derby used to say: "I'll play Amloth with thee, lad," meaning he would be furious?

Denmark is in the news. It seems certain now that the succession will go to James Sixth of Scotland and that none, since the shock of the Essex rebellion, will oppose it. It will not be long before a Danish queen, with her Danish friends, will be in London. At present the Danes are not much liked—something to do with their poaching on English fishing preserves in the North Sea, something to do with their shocking drinking habits. The man who owns the Dansker beershop—Yaughan, or some such name—drinks till he vomits. Soon it will be vaguely treasonable to dislike the Danes: at present it is in order.

Most of the actors are mouthing their lines; some are taking Dutch, or Danish, courage out of a firkin sent over from Yaughan's, or whatever the name is. There is an unknown man there brought in for walking-on parts. He has the look of a shorthand writer: he will work his piracy from the very stage or wings. He looks foolish. He will have Claudius saying: "Lights lights I will to bed," as though merely tired, not shocked by the revelation of the play within a play. A good device of Tom Kyd's, that. Worth retaining.

Music. Trumpets. The flag flies from the high tower. The play begins. On the tarrass or gallery a nervous officer of the watch: there have been nervous officers enough during the Essex troubles. All these Danes have Roman names, Italianate anyway: the groundlings cannot conceive of a tragedy without hot Southern blood in it. Francisco, Horatio, Marcellus, Bernardo. It is broad daylight and the autumn sun is warm, but words quickly paint the time of night and the intense northern cold. Eerie talk of a ghost, Horatio skeptical in the modern manner. Then the Ghost appears, Will Shakespeare, the creator of all these words but himself, as yet, speaking no words. Reminiscences from Horatio about the recently performed *Julius Caesar*, the portents before the assassination.

> And even the like precurse of fierce events,
> As harbingers preceding still the fates
> And prologue to the omen coming on,
> Have heaven and earth together demonstrated
> Unto our climatures and countrymen.

Denmark is, for the moment, England; the audience still remembers that Christmas earthquake. Backstage, Armin does a skillful cockcrow. The Ghost glides off. While Horatio and the soldiers finish their scene on the tarrass, the main stage below fills up with the court of Denmark.

Trumpets and drums for Claudius, the boy Gertrude beside him. Every inch a king, he delivers his address from the twin-throned dais. Too long? Well, the auditors have Hamlet's sour sad face to look at, counterpoint to that kingly strength and discretion. Hamlet leans against a downstage pillar, as far away as possible from the upstage king. Now for his first soliloquy: they will see now that he is not one of Ben's melancholics, a black weed of depression lacking roots. The roots are powerful enough: his black is the black of mourning, he is wretched for the death of his father and for a rottenness in the state figured in his own mother's faithlessness and, worse, her incestuous marriage. And now the rage of his invective against the unweeded garden of the world and the frailty of women, its flowers, is balanced by the entrance of the sane scholar Horatio, not easily movable, and, in the scene following, the sweet innocence of Ophelia (surely there is nothing of Gertrude in her, but Hamlet

will, in his bitterness, see much), and the sententious maxims
of Polonius.

Now the tarrass again, and the air biting shrewdly, a nipping
and an eager air. Hamlet, censuring the Danes for their drunkenness, is in danger of becoming dull. Good, the attention of
the groundlings is wandering, there are some coughs. Now into
that dullness the Ghost thrusts himself again, and the growing
inattention is jolted awake. The Ghost beckons Hamlet away,
which means that both leave the tarrass and take the stairway
quickly, reentering on the main stage below. The five lines
shared by Horatio and Marcellus are just enough to cover their
passage. So this great speech of the Ghost can be made in the
main acting area. The bookholder is ready to prompt, for Will
is not always reliable, not even with the lines he has himself
written. And now the Ghost's morning dissolution: no cockcrow
this time, since an effect is diminished by repetition. The
gallants from the Inns of Court, on their stools left and right of
the stage, are already writing down odd lines on their tablets:
they will quote them that evening at supper. Hamlet also has
tablets. He takes the gallants aback by himself writing that one
may smile, and smile, and be a villain. Horatio and Marcellus
have been able to make their way down to the main stage more
slowly—perhaps there was time for a quick swig backstage—and
the Ghost has had time to get below the stage, into the
cellarage. From deep below comes the injunction "Swear."
Horatio, the skeptic, is filled with wonder. Hamlet tells him
there are more things in heaven and earth than are dreamt of in
his philosophy. Some of the gallants, despite Hamlet's previous
gentle mockery, are busy with their tablets. The Ghost, perturbed
spirit, is bidden rest. Will can take that literally. His next and
last entrance is many scenes off.

Soon we forget the unfolding tragedy, for Rosencrantz and
Guildenstern have arrived to tell the prince that the players are
coming, and we settle down to a long discussion of the stage of
the London theatre. Guildenstern and Rosencrantz—these are
pawnbrokers' names. Hamlet's two schoolfriends smile and
smile and are villains. Curiously, though, Rosencrantz's name
seems to prophesy a pathetic death which is none of his

concern: Ophelia goes to her watery end with rose garlands; at her funeral she has her "virgin crants." But the only hard fate discussed at the moment is that of "the tragedians of the city"—the Lord Chamberlain's Men, who have come on tour as far as Elsinore in Denmark. Why are they not at home in London? Because the little eyases or young hawks of the children's theatres are taking all the custom. "Do the boys carry it away?" asks Hamlet. "Ay, that they do, my lord," replies Rosencrantz. "Hercules and his load too." They all look up a moment at the flag fluttering from the tower of the Globe, which shows this same loaded Hercules.

The players enter, and Hamlet mentions a play that was acted "not above once." It "pleased not the million; 'twas caviare to the general." The first player delivers a long speech from this play—about the siege of Troy, Priam, Pyrrhus, and Hecuba. At once we realize what the play is called—*Troilus and Cressida*. The speech is not in the printed version: it was probably cut during rehearsal. Nobody liked the play: it was never "clapper-clawed" by the mob. But Shakespeare still thinks it a fine piece of work, and he is determined to impose that excised speech on players and public alike. Good work must not be wasted.

When, very soon, we come to Hamlet's "To be or not to be" soliloquy, there will be some puzzled frowns among the more naive members of the audience. For here is a man wondering whether there is anything after death—"the undiscover'd country, from whose bourn / No traveler returns"—when he has already been given proof, and by his own dead father at that, that heaven and purgatory exist. But the brighter of the auditors will know that this new *Hamlet* is really two plays—the old revenge tragedy of Thomas Kyd, with a real hell to which the avenger can send his slain villain, and a close study of a very contemporary agnostic mind. Can the two really blend?

And how very piquant is this juxtaposition of suicidal meditations, mad invective against all women in the shape of poor Ophelia, and obsession with the conduct of the drama. "Speak the speech, I pray you," says Hamlet to three of the players, "as I pronounc'd it to you, trippingly on the tongue," and he goes on to give a most comprehensive lesson on acting technique, ending with an eloquent justification of the expulsion of Kemp from the Lord Chamberlain's Men. Just before the play within the play commences, Polonius tells Hamlet that he "enacted Julius Caesar; I was kill'd i' the Capitol; Brutus kill'd me." Gratuitous and irrelevant? Not altogether, for it is likely that the actor who takes Polonius also took Julius Caesar at this very theatre, only a few days before. And Brutus, of course, was taken by the man who is now playing Hamlet—Dick Burbage. There is humor here: the two men get outside their present parts for a moment and perhaps bow, smiling, as some members of the audience clap, remembering those other performances. Then, later, comes a very complex irony, for Brutus-Hamlet puts his sword through Polonius-Caesar when he is hiding behind the arrass. "It was a brute part of him to kill so capital a calf there." What is a joke now will be no joke later.

Later, after Polonius's slaying, the urgency of the action brings in reminiscences of more serious matters than the conduct of the drama. Hamlet becomes Essex. The King says:

How dangerous is it that this man goes loose!
Yet must not we put the strong law on him:
He's lov'd of the distracted multitude,
Who like not in their judgment but their eyes;
And where 'tis so, th' offender's scourge is weigh'd,
But never the offense.

Then, when Hamlet is sent away, it is Laertes, son of the slain Polonius, who becomes Essex. The rabble call him lord and cry: "Choose we; Laertes shall be king." And is there not an echo of dead Essex in mad Ophelia's fragment of song—"For bonny sweet Robin is all my joy"?

With Ophelia's death, Shakespeare homes straight to Warwickshire and his boyhood. Kyd's Hamlet play made Ophelia die by falling over a cliff-edge; Shakespeare drowns her amid a profusion of Warwickshire flowers:

... crowflowers, nettles, daisies, and long purples
That liberal shepherds give a grosser name,
But our cold maids do dead men's fingers call them.

The "grosser name" is bulls' pizzles. This periphrastic information about flower-naming is so irrelevant here (after all, a queen is telling a distracted young man about his sister's death) that one has to conclude that Will has allowed Warwickshire reminiscences totally to swamp the business in hand. For he is thinking of a girl who lived not a mile from Stratford when he was a boy, and who drowned herself—some said for love—in the Avon. Her name was Kate Hamnet. She merges with Ophelia and his own dead son.

And in the gravedigging scene, before the first clown sends his assistant off for a stoup of liquor from the Dansker beershop kept by "Yaughan," the Stratford coroner's arguments about Christian burial rights for a suicide are recalled. When Hamlet appears with Horatio, the throwing up of skulls affords opportunity for meditation on three aspects of Shakespeare's career, personified in a dead lord ("Here's fine revolution, an we had the trick to see't. Did these bones cost no more the breeding but to play at loggats with them?"), a dead lawyer (with a firework display of legal knowledge, as though the poet is demonstrating what he learned in the musty office at Stratford), and a great dead clown, Yorick, surely Dick Tarleton, who—if Shakepeare's career really began with the Queen's Men—metaphorically carried the apprentice playwright on his back.

The play moves to its conclusion. Evening is coming on, so that the final scenes can be played with lights, and Hamlet's corpse can be carried off with a cortège of torchbearers. The corpses that litter the stage come back to life to take their bow. Polonius and his daughter return from the grave to accept their plaudits, and the Ghost makes his own shy acknowledgment. The audience knows that this is the author, but they do not know his greatness. Some of them would have preferred to see *Hamlet* in its old form. Burbage, very justly, takes the lion's share of the applause. There is a prayer for the Queen, and the audience leaves. The days of the bawdy jig—a brief kickshaws after the heavy meat—are over: they went out with Will Kemp. The actors have finished, but they must look over another play for tomorrow—a revival of something, probably a comedy. All this tragedy has taken it out of them.

We can fancifully reconstruct the outward deatils of an Elizabethan stage performance, using conjecture and guesswork as to what the audience saw. But we have a fair idea of what the audience heard, and it was not what we hear today. Shakespeare's plays *look* the same now, in quarto or folio, as they looked nearly four centuries ago, but English pronunciation has undergone many changes since then, and we would most of us be shocked, transported by time-machine back to *Hamlet* at the Globe, to note how *provincial* Shakespeare's English sounds. To give a general impression of is phonetic impact, we have to try to imagine Burbage speaking with an accent that is part Lancashire, part New England, part Dublin. When the play within the play is performed, Hamlet tells Ophelia that it is called *The Mouse-trap* and that this title figures "tropically." "Tropically" was pronounced in the modern American way, almost like "trapically." There is a pun there which is lost in the modern Queen's English way of saying it. So also in "O that this too too solid flesh would melt," the "solid" would sound like a mixture of "solid," "sallied," and "sullied." The digraph *ea* always carried the value it today carries in *steak* and *great*, so that, as in Dublin English, *raisins* and *reasons* would sound much the same (Falstaff puns on that, talking about reasons being as plentiful as blackberries). *See* and *sea* were not homophones; *love* and *above* rhymed with *prove* and *move*; the r-sound was always pronounced; a word like *noble* carried a noble round low vowel, not the pinched high diphthong of today. A provincial-sounding language, then, but one, as *Hamlet* shows, capable of bearing a limitless burden of cosmopolitan complexity.

In less than ten years the English stage had progressed from creaking melodrama to an intellectual sophistication few post-Elizabethan playwrights have been able to touch, let alone surpass. This is in itself an achievement stupendous enough to glorify any monarch's reign, but it was, as we know, only one achievement among many. All the great work of that age seems somehow stamped with the very quality of the genius that Elizabeth, uniquely in the history of the English crown, possessed. *Hamlet* is hers, but so also are Byrd's anthems, the Royal Exchange, the circumnavigation of the Golden Hind, the

Virginian settlement, the *Laws of Ecclesiastical Polity*, the joint stock companies, the defeat of Spain—a few of many monuments to the reign now about to end.

The shadow of the Essex tragedy was slow in lifting, but none could deny that justice had been done, and that the Queen had suffered more than any in exacting that condign punishment. Her reign ended in a kind of sad serenity. Mountjoy achieved in Ireland what Essex had failed to do: Tyrone surrendered at Kinsale, and the Spanish army behind him, thus discouraged, was quick to capitulate. There was an echo of Drake and Hawkins in Sir Richard Leveson's exploit in Cezimbra Road, when he took a Portuguese carrack, crammed with gold, in the face of seemingly impossible opposition. But to recall the past was not to renew it. A sort of optimism had died, a belief that men, given the opportunity, would act well rather than ill. The story of Richard II still played on Elizabeth's mind. "He that will forget God," she said, "will also forget his benefactors. This tragedy was played forty times in open streets and houses." Mountjoy, now her Lord Deputy in Ireland, had once been as ready as Essex to lead an army against her. Men could not be trusted to follow one pattern. (This was what Shakespeare was trying to say in his new plays.) And there was Henry IV of France, whom Elizabeth had helped unstintingly and who now, when England needed money, would give only fair words. "Antichrist of ingratitude" Elizabeth called him. And yet the existence of trust and love in men could sometimes seem more than a fiction. Elizabeth's last Parliament, prepared to complain bitterly about what they regarded as the scandal of royal monopolies (like that wine-tax farm that Essex had held), ended by acclaiming her, so that she was able to reply: "Though God hath raised me high, yet I account the glory of my crown, that I have reigned with your loves."

Like everything in the world, it was both true and not true. "Good neighbors I have had, and I have met with bad: and in trust I have found treason"—words she had spoken to Parliament two years before the Armada. And, "As for me, I see no such great cause why I should either be fond to live or fear to die." It was even more her philosophy in 1603, when she was in her seventieth year. Her health was still good, but she did not attempt to guard it. In the bitterly cold January of that year, she went boldly in light clothes while her Court huddled in furs. In February she appeared in all her regal glory before an envoy from Venice, but when the envoy felicitated her on her good health, she made no reply. Perhaps she did not wish to think her health an earnest of more years to come: she was not fond to live.

A week or so later, her cousin and friend the Countess of Nottingham died, and her system took this as a pretext to fall into a melancholy. She did not wish to recover: death was, it seemed, almost a matter of volition. She refused all physic. She had, a short while before, had the coronation ring cut from her finger. She retained till her death, however, a small ring that Essex had once given her. On March 19, 1603, word was sent to James of Scotland that he must hold himself in readiness: one actor was soon to quit the stage, another must listen for his cue to enter. Elizabeth did not keep him waiting long. She fell into a coma, her face turned to the wall. On March 24, between two and three in the morning, she quietly died.

The poets had nothing to say. There were no plays called *The Wonderful Reign* or *The Virgin Queen of England*. The actors had to have their eyes bent on him who entered next. Ten years were to go before Shakespeare, in *Henry VIII*, just before the Globe was to go up in flame, presented those past glories as future ones. All that professional pens could give was the obsequies of hack pamphlets, like Dekker's *The Wonderful Year*:

Shee came in with the fall of the leafe, and went away in the Spring: her life (which was dedicated to Virginitie), both beginning and closing up a miraculous Mayden circle: for she was borne upon a Lady Eve, and died upon a Lady Eve: her Nativitie and death being memorable by this wonder: the first and last yeares of her Raigne by this, that a *Lee* was Lorde Maior when she came to the Crowne, and a *Lee* Lorde Maior when she departed from it. Three places are made famous by her for three things, *Greenewich* for her birth, *Richmount* for her death, and *White-Hall* for her Funerall.

Perhaps nobody, not even Shakespeare, could find the really fitting words. Posterity itself goes on looking for them.

16

VI & I

❦❦❦❦❦❦❦❦❦❦❦❦❦❦❦❦❦❦

King James arrived in London, eager to assume a greater crown than that of Scotland. He had hunted all the way south—live hares brought along in baskets. He loved the chase. He had, at Newark, ordered the hanging of a cutpurse without trial. The monarch was above the law. He had knighted three hundred men between Edinburgh and London. He could be generous when it cost little. The common people he did not greatly like. They clamored to see him, but he lacked his predecessor's graciousness. "God's wounds!" he cried. "I will pull down my breeches and they shall also see my arse." He was given to homosexuality. He was not half the man his predecessor had been, but he saw himself as *Caesar Caesarum*—Emperor of emperors. No flattery was too gross for him. Adulatory ceremonies of a sickening fulsomeness were revived at Court. Great lords had to wait on him at table, presenting dishes on bended knee. He would hardly listen unless addressed by some such oriental honorific as *most sacred, learned, wise*. For his wisdom he was accounted a Solomon. The more cynical, recalling the association between his mother and the musician David Rizzio, said he was rightly called Solomon, since he was the son of David that played on the harp.

He was two years younger than Shakespeare. His appearance was tolerable. "Handsome, noble, jovial," said an Italian visitor, perhaps going too far. "A man happily formed, neither fat nor thin, of full vitality." His hair was brown and his complexion ruddy. In other words, he was an ordinary-looking man, with none of the slobbering or oddities of frame or gait that his enemies have attached to him and transmitted to posterity. His learning was genuine, and his prose writings—like the *Counterblast to Tobacco*, which seems to foresee lung cancer—are vigorous. He had no talent for verse. He loved food and often, especially under the influence of Prince Charles's friend George Villiers, Earl of Buckingham, got very drunk. He was deeply religious and devoted to the Church of England, one of the few English things he really liked. He had been brought up by rigid Scottish Calvinists, and his turning against them disappointed the English Puritans. Although his wife, Anne of Denmark, was Catholic, he had no love of Rome. But his bishops loved him, and he loved his bishops. One of the finest things he ever did was to order a new translation of the Bible. He never bathed or washed, but he would sometimes dip his finger-ends in rosewater.

There was a new kingdom now: England and Scotland had combined to become what Wales really was—the land of the British. Shakespeare later celebrated this in Edgar's poem in *King Lear*:

Childe Rowland to the dark tower came,
His word was still "Fie, foh, and fum,
I smell the blood of a British man."

The English, who had longed for the peace and security that the new reign seemed to promise, felt strangely let down when the Jacobean period started. London was full of Scotsmen on the make. There was grandeur at Court, but glamour seemed to have gone out of the national life. There were no great issues—such as the naval and military securing of the English Reformation—to inject adrenalin into Englishmen's veins. *Ichabod, ichabod*: the glory had departed. They had had the best of their time.

But the King, who had been brought up very austerely, reveled in such life-enhancing pastimes as the drama. His reign was glorious with dramatic achievement, though it was mostly achievement with a core, sometimes hardly discernible, of sickness and corruption. Instead of *Romeo and Juliet* there was *The White Devil*; instead of *As You Like It* there was *A Cure for a Cuckold*. To his period belong Shakespeare's greatest tragedies, the incredibly beautiful and moving products of disillusionment. Comedies like *All's Well That Ends Well* and *Measure for Measure* are not meant for laughs, and one is uneasy at the whiff of a looser morality than would have been seemly in the old Queen's reign—too much coupling with the wrong woman by intention and the right woman by accident, too many unrebuked sneers at virginity, too much coarse frankness between men and women. There is a burden of self-doubt in the very uncategorizability of these plays, and it comes out in the tortuousness of the verse in *All's Well*, qualifying the simple moral fable taken from Boccaccio. The pessimism of *Measure for Measure* is fitter for a tragedy than a play with a happy, or not unhappy, ending. One scene provides a title for the bitterest of all our post-atomic-war visions—Huxley's *Ape and Essence*. Another provides the most terrible speech about the fear of death in all literature, as well as the most potent cantrip to meet the coming of death. Excellent, but this is meant for a Court entertainment. The simple quality of gaiety has gone out of this grave man of ripening, or souring, years.

Whatever went on inside that fiddle-shaped head, the outer circumstances of Will, and the troupe of which he was a shareholder, could hardly have been better in the new reign. In its very first year, 1603, the Lord Chamberlain's Men turned into the King's Men. The senior members, of whom Shakespeare was one, became Grooms of the Bedchamber. In this capacity they formed part of the entourage of the Spanish ambassador, when he came to negotiate peace in 1604. The playwright who had composed great speeches of patriotic defiance now bowed to the friend who had been the enemy. The days of defiance were over: the soldier's pole had fallen. King James detested war and even shrank from the sight of a soldier's weapons (killing deer was a different matter). Queen Elizabeth would gladly have led her armies in the field; her successor was—all knew, though few said—a physical coward. No more fire-snorting plays like *Henry V*.

As a sort of royal officer, Will must now have regained entrée to high and desirable circles. The Earl of Southampton had been released from the Tower, but patronage and familiarity in that old shamed quarter were hardly to be renewed. It is probable that planetary Will now began to spin in a new solar system, whose bright center was less Southampton's mirror-image, William Herbert (HW—WH), than William Herbert's mother. Herbert had succeeded to the earldom of Pembroke in 1601, had been in the Queen's bad books over the Mary Fitton affair, but now, in the new reign, was free, ebullient, and in royal favor.

His mother, the Countess of Pembroke, was forty-two years old in 1603—beautiful, gracious, learned, a female paragon to match the male paragon who was her dead, but ever-living, brother, Sir Philip Sidney. The two of them had worked on the prose romance, *Arcadia*, at Wilton House, that country estate near Salisbury which, as John Aubrey put it, "was like a College, there were so many learned and ingeniose persons." After Sidney's death from wounds received at Zutphen, the Countess had edited his sonnet-sequence *Astrophel and Stella*. Thereafter she was to give patronage to other sonneteers, as well as scholars, perhaps even playwrights. Her qualities are best expressed in the obituary on her by William Browne:

Underneath this sable hearse
Lies the subject of all verse:
Sidney's sister, Pembroke's mother:
Death, ere thou hast slain another,
Fair, and learn'd, and good as she,
Time shall throw a dart at thee.

There is evidence that Shakespeare was at Wilton in 1603, though not in the capacity of a guest. James's accession in May was at once greeted by an outbreak of plague, and the Court, as well as the theatrical companies, left town. James was a guest of the Pembrokes in the autumn, while the plague still raged. The King's Men were at Mortlake, where Gus Phillips had his home. They were ordered to come to Wilton to put on a play, and it is recorded that John Heminges—business manager for the troupe—received the sum of thirty pounds for their trouble. The Lady Pembroke of two and a half centuries later swore there was a letter in the family archives from the great Countess to her son, telling him to bring the King to see *As You Like It*, and adding, "We have the man Shakespeare with us." The letter has disappeared, but the phrase—for some magical reason or other—sends a shiver of authenticity down one's spine. Not "Shakespeare"—author of plays and poems—but "the man Shakespeare," drinking, talking, easy, affable, witty, a person of distinction who has temporarily been detached from a cry of players. Something like that, anyway.

The Countess evidently liked plays, and she had even made a play herself—a translation of *Marc-Antoine* by the somewhat insipid French Senecan Robert Garnier. Perhaps she showed it to the man Shakespeare in 1603. Perhaps he said: this would do well, madam. There is grace and restraint and the lines flow easily. Perhaps he thought: This will not do at all. If there is to be a play about Antony's love life, then it must be instinct with passion and bold word-music, and the Egyptian Queen must be musky and seductive as any Moorish trull in the Clerkenwell brothels. I will set that down on my mental tablets.

Bernard Shaw suggested that Lady Pembroke was the model for the Countess of Rousillon in *All's Well That Ends Well*. He went too far, as he frequently did, by asserting that this lady "is the most charming of all Shakespeare's old women, indeed the most charming of all his women, young or old." But, in the relationship between the Countess of Rousillon and her son Bertram, who rejects a marriage arranged for the good of the family line, there is certainly a conjugation of the verb whose voice was so active both in the Southampton family and at Wilton. The Herbert recalcitrance is later than the Wriothesley one—closer to the date of composition of the play. Shaw's identification will serve.

What, though, were the favors and friendship of the Pembroke family compared with the supreme patronage of the Court? King James thought highly of the company that bore his name. If Elizabeth had paid ten pounds for a command performance, he—meaning the Privy Purse—paid twenty. True, prices were rising (one of the causes of the prevailing melancholy, so the Marxist critics tell us), but James did not have any possible cost-of-living index in mind. He loved dramatic entertainments, but he tended to equate dramatic excellence with high cost. What he loved best was a masque, and masques cost dear. Shakespeare could have given up five-act tragedies and made a lot of money out of one-act masques, but the artist got the better of the man of business. He never wrote any masques.

The masque was a mixture of the old-time morality or interlude and the newfangled opera (an anticipation of the latter, really: Monteverdi's pioneering *Orpheus* did not appear till 1607). It was brief but sumptuous, and its interest was more sensuous than intellectual. It was a composite art form, and poet, composer, choreographer, and stage designer had to work closely together, sometimes having to keep their refined gorges down when a menagerie-keeper was called in for special effects. When James I was still only James VI, there had been a masque at Stirling Castle with a pride of lions in it. The ladies had been frightened. Shakespeare knew about this while he was writing A *Midsummer Night's Dream*: "Masters," says Bottom, "you ought to consider with yourselves: to bring in—God shield us!—a lion among ladies is a most dreadful thing; for there is not a more fearful wild-fowl than your lion living."

The themes of the masques were abstract. Virtues and vices, personified in morality style but in very sophisticated costumes, contended, and the virtues inevitably won. There were fine stage effects, high words, dignity, nothing coarse. The anti-masque, which followed the masque as the jig followed the play, aimed at a grotesque contrast, with wild men, pygmies, blacka-moors, Turks, baboons, and buffoons prancing and gibbering about.

The court masques had an exhibitionist appeal. If the décor, text, and music were the work of professionals, the actors were usually amateurs of high rank—nobles who liked to show off a fine physique and a sonorous voice. The taboo of the popular stage, which made boys play women, did not apply in the masques, and the ladies were delighted to exhibit their pearly bosoms and even their lower limbs in dances and statuesque postures. Queen Anne, a very ungloomy Dane, wore, in a masque about the Twelve Goddesses, a very short skirt, so that, according to one observer, "we might see a woman had both feete and legs which I never knew before." These pretty displays did not always go as planned. The actors and actresses were sometimes drunk—presumably under the Danish influence— and not only slurred what lines they could remember but giggled, fell over, made unscripted exits to vomit. When the King of Denmark, a fair drinker himself, came to the British Court, he was entertained by a masque which was a monumental chaos of drunkenness, his own daughter leading all the rest in glassy eyes and hiccups. Such performances could be depressing to the scriptwriter, but, like a scriptwriter in Hollywood, depressed for different reasons, he could think on his high fee and be more cheerful.

If Shakespeare, to obviate such depression, never wrote a masque—except for the odd wisps of masquelike apparition in the later plays—Ben Jonson eagerly embraced the chance to show off his wit, learning, and lyrical skill in brief expositions for a high price. He jumped on the bandwagon early, being commissioned to create the pastoral masque, *Satyr*, which was performed at Althorp, in the open air, when the King was on his way from Scotland to London. Some of the masques he wrote are exquisite and have superb lyrics:

> The faery beam upon you,
> The stars to glister on you;
> A moon of light
> In the noon of night
> Till the fire-drake hath o'ergone you!
> The wheel of fortune guide you,
> The boy with the bow beside you;
> Run aye in the way,
> Till the bird of day,
> And the luckier lot betide you!

The form was good for Ben in more than a financial sense. It curbed two of his biggest faults—prolixity and preachiness. His audiences did not want to be lectured on their stupidity; his amateur performers could not learn long speeches. Strong and delicate conciseness was needed, and Ben, a very superior artist, could give that.

Belligerent and touchy in the popular theatre, Ben could achieve terrible jealous rages in this other medium, which, depending on collaboration, was marked by conflict of interests. The brilliant designer Inigo Jones developed the visual side of the masque to such a pitch of wonder that the mere words—so often ill-learned and ill-delivered—sank out of hearing. Jones, a year younger than Jonson, was a great man. He had studied the visual arts in Italy and brought the great Palladian vision to an England that, cosmopolitan in so many ways, was provincial in painting and architecture. He could do anything with his pencil, and his eye was as faultless when supervising the royal collection of pictures as when envisaging his architectural projects. Ben and he first worked together, if that is the right term, on a royal exercise in negritude called *The Masque of Blackness.* "It was her Majesty's wish," said Ben gloomily afterwards, "to have them blackamoors." The subject did not inspire him, and the work was saved only by Inigo Jones's ingenious costumes and contrivances. From then on he could do no wrong, except in the eyes of the poets. He designed elaborate machines for transformations, a *machina versatilis* or revolving stage, and set up the first English proscenium arch. These visual wonders, along with the fantastic costumes he designed, became, to the Court and nobility, the true essence of the masque: the words were a mere pretext. The visual heresy had entered the theatre, and Ben was disgusted. Think of the cost, too—thousands of pounds spent on one drunken performance, enough to back a whole season of sober humors comedies at the Globe or the Fortune.

Shakespeare was well out of all this. He was content to write his plays for the Globe, for royal command performances, and, from 1608, for the indoor theatre at Blackfriars. It is in 1608 that we meet his name on a document establishing him as one of the lessees of this theatre: it was to house the King's Men in the winter while the Globe continued as their summer home. The complaints about loss of amenity from the gentlemen in chambers at Blackfriars no longer carried much weight. The King's Men were important people.

Why did not these important people manage to get into the

Blackfriars playhouse earlier—say, in 1603? The answer is that the Children of the Revels were still there, and it was not possible, under the contract they had signed with the Burbages, to get them out. But they made the mistake of putting on a play which satirized the King of France. The French ambassador complained, and the Council forbade their playing further at the Blackfriars. The Council thus ended a phase of remarkable forbearance, for this was not the first time there had been complaints about the conduct of the children's company. Evans, in the manner of a recruiting officer, had virtually pressed promising boys into what he regarded as a kind of royal service. But one day he went too far. He kidnaped a boy, a Master Clifton, as he was on his way to school. The father, who was a gentleman, went to the playhouse and demanded his son's release. Evans sneered and said he had authority to press what boy he would into acting service, even a duke's son. Then, in Clifton's presence, he thrust a script into the boy's hands and told him to get it by heart, else he would be whipped. It took Clifton *père* two days to get his son freed from this bondage.

The Blackfriars children, or their masters, had a bad name then, and the Council was glad to see them replaced at that playhouse by those accomplished but respectable professionals who had at least one gentleman among them. So, then, at the Globe and the Blackfriars, Mr. W. Shakespeare, Groom of the Royal Bedchamber, property owner, small capitalist, playwright as good as the best of them, worked out the climax of his career. He had everything he had ever wished for, and he proceeded to present human life as a tragedy.

17

Sick World

In 1604, Shakespeare reached the age of forty. It is in order to enquire about the state of his health at this time and, in the absence of surviving medical reports and prescriptions, to guess that he was, or was going to be, or had recently been, not very well. If everybody owes God a death, the hardworking artist owes fate an occasional physical or mental breakdown: he cannot build so many new worlds without damaging his own fabric. Shakespeare had been driving himself hard for many years, as actor, playwright, and businessman. Some of the acting seems to us supererogatory: he had enough to do with his own work without taking a part in Ben Jonson's *Sejanus* in 1603. But his energy was evidently considerable, and one guesses that it mostly resided in his nerves. When not stuck in London, a badly drained, fly-haunted, plague-prone city, he was riding about England on tour or visiting his family and property in Stratford. In London he had only lodgings, and lodgings rarely did any man any good. He did not drink much—there is the tradition that he would decline invitations to beery bouts with the excuse that he was "in pain"—but it is doubtful whether he ate much either. There is gulosity in Ben Jonson's plays, but no slavering in Will's. Falstaff overeats, but only of capons—a healthy high-protein diet; pippins and cheese are mentioned approvingly in *The Merry Wives*; but banquets are never particularized. One gains the impression from many plays that Will was given more to nausea than to appetite at the thought of rich feeding. In *Troilus and Cressida* the associations of the word "candy" are sickening; in *Timon of Athens* there is a purgative feast of hot water; strong men like Antony have eaten meat that others did die to look on—like, perhaps, that ghastly pie in *Titus Andronicus*; Macbeth's *bon appétit* sounds like one of Mr. Woodhouse's: "Now good digestion wait on appetite, and health on both."

Even if he courted health by eating sparingly, Will did not necessarily enjoy a sound diet. Little was known in those days about a balanced regimen, and vitamins still lay in an-alphabetic sleep. Here is a typical recipe—from *The Good Hous-wives Treasurie*: it tells one how to make "Minst Pies":

> Take your Veale and perboyle it a little, or mutton, then set it a cooling: and when it is colde, take three pound of suit to a legge of mutton, or fower pound to a fillet of Veale, and then mince them small by themselues, or together whether you will, then take to season them halfe an once of Nutmegs, half an once of cloues and Mace, halfe an once of Sinamon, a little Pepper, as much Salt as you think will season them, either to the mutton or to the Veale, take viij yolkes of Egges when they be hard, halfe a pinte of rosewater full measure, halfe a pound of Suger, then straine the yolkes with the Rosewater and the Suger and mingle it with your meate, if ye haue any Orrenges or Lemmans you must take two of them, and take the pilles very thin and mince them very smalle, and put them in a pound of currans or dates, half a pound of prunes, lay Currans and Dates vpon the top of your meate, you must take two or three Pomewaters or Wardens and mince with your meate, you may make them woorsse if you will, if you will make a good crust put in three or foure yolkes of egges a little Rosewater, and a good deale of suger.

Very rich and nutritious—a little too much so. A banquet might have a great many such minglings of sweet and sour, and not a green leaf to be seen anywhere. Men and women got fat and had to be purged and bled. There was a lot of scurvy about, which argues a lack of Vitamin C.

It is doubtful whether Will's mouth would water greatly over the prospect of such a "minst pie," but it is equally doubtful whether he ate much more than spiced meat or fish, with bread (good roughage usually, but the bleached pappy travesty was coming in) and no vegetables. Potatoes had arrived, but they were very expensive. In winter especially, spices, to give a savor to salt flesh, irritated the bowels. Riding was good jolting exercise for the liver, and everybody sweated heartily (a moist palm was the usual proffer in greeting). The ale was excellent, but everybody was thirsty and drank too much. The skin was never exposed to sunlight. Washing and bathing were considered more hazardous than healthful, and fleas and lice were familiar friends. Teeth, with all that sugary eating, grew carious, and the dentist's, or stomatologist's, office of today was a sparetime activity of the barber's. But on the whole, on balance, the men and women of Shakespeare's time had as healthful a regimen as our own. They were not poisoned by chemical sprays and experimental fertilizers, and they ate nothing out of cans. They took plenty of exercise. We would be happy, I suppose, if we could, by time machine, impose the odd American-style salad on them. The secret of living in those days was simple: avoid dying in childhood.

If we worry at all about Shakespeare's regimen, it is because we envisage his being insufficiently concerned with refocillating wasted tissue—too much of the quick snack, then back to work. Work was what London was for, not nourishment and comfort. Nourishment and comfort, as well as rest, would come with retirement to New Place, Stratford. Shakespeare was determined to achieve monied retirement in his forties: he seems to have made it about the age of forty-six. But, before then, slaving away in London, he seems like one of those expatriate Britons living a single life in the colonies—a pennyworth of curry for dinner and, for dessert, a good gloat over money saved to take home.

Ill-nourished or not, Shakespeare's nerves were exquisitely raw when he came to write two tragedies which have much in common—*King Lear* and *Timon of Athens*. They are both near unactable in respect of their name parts: all that demented raving is hard to sustain without apoplexy. They are both profoundly pessimistic. They both, totally without pretext in the plot, scream against lechery. If Shakespeare was ill with something other than overwork, that something was venereal disease.

Here, in a speech made by Timon to two courtesans of Athens, is a fair description of some of the symptoms of syphilis:

> Consumptions sow
> In hollow bones of man; strike their sharp shins,
> And mar men's spurring. Crack the lawyer's voice,
> That he may never more false title plead,
> Nor sound his quillets shrilly. Hoar the flamen,
> That scolds against the quality of flesh
> And not believes himself. Down with the nose,
> Down with it flat, take the bridge quite away
> Of him that, his particular to foresee,
> Smells from the general weal. Make curl'd-pate ruffians bald,
> And let the unscarr'd braggarts of the war
> Derive some pain from you. Plague all,
> That your activity may defeat and quell
> The source of all erection.

Timon has not courted this disease. He has been shown solely in connection with the innocent pleasures of generosity to other men. A rich man, he has made himself poor through this generosity. The friends he had have melted away, and he has turned himself into a misanthropic hermit. Appalled by ingratitude, he calls down sexual diseases on the ingrates. Plagues and earthquakes would be enough, but he has to curse them in terms of syphilitic hoarseness, baldness, and the dropping off of noses. He has a gratuitous venereal obsession.

King Lear joins *Timon of Athens* in being an exhibition of rage against ingratitude. Lear, mad on the heath, find in sex a symbol of the hell he wishes on the whole world:

> The fitchew nor the soiled horse goes to't
> With a more riotous appetite.
> Down from the waist they are centaurs,
> Though women all above;
> But to the girdle do the gods inherit,
> Beneath is all the fiends'.

It is always dangerous to attribute to the author the sentiments of his characters, but both Lear and Timon go beyond simple

dramatic necessity in invoking woman as the source of degradation and disease. Shakespeare seems to have his own madness,
and though it can be seen as a sort of temporary psychosis, in
which the world is a hell of ingratitude, hypocrisy, corruption in
the social order ("A dog's obey'd in office"), the recurring and
abiding image is of rage and shame at the thraldom of sexual
passion with its degrading consequences. And man is powerless
to avoid concupiscence and evade its aftermath:

> All this the world well knows, yet none knows well
> To shun the heav'n that leads men to this hell.

That is the poet himself talking, not one of his characters. What
is confined in the fourteen lines of a sonnet erupts like pus or
lava in these two tragedies.

Occam's razor, which forbids the multiplication of entities
unless strictly necessary, is a good instrument for fiction, where
characters should be limited in number, but real life is grossly
hirsute with people and gets hairier all the time. What I mean is
that it is tempting to associate Shakespeare's pessimism and
obsession with sexual excess and disease with one particular
object—the Dark Lady—but, if we accept the powerful libido of
Will, it is probable that his fault was not a single fixation but
promiscuity. He loved not wisely but too frequently. And yet we
find, in the tragedies of this period, not only a very Dark Lady
but a Dark Man, as though Shakespeare were interested in the
emotions and behavior of a non-European, specifically a North
African, personality. Cleopatra is the final personification of
sexual allure, and the consequences of yielding to her are—so
the world would say—far worse than a dose of French pox (how
ironical, incidentally, Shakespeare must have found the fact that
Girolamo Fracastoro, who invented the name Syphilis—the
name of a stricken shepherd in a poetic discourse on the
disease—should have been a physician of the eternal lovers'
town, Verona). The consequences are multiple death and the
fall of an empire. But this time Shakespeare is on the side of
passion, and the hell is somewhat remote and abstract, not
expressed in chancres and fox-mange.

Othello, the Dark Man's tragedy, seems to be the earliest of the great post-*Hamlet* dark visions, and it is possible that it was composed while Elizabeth was still alive. The first recorded performance is in 1604, but there are odd extracts dumped into the corrupt quarto of *Hamlet* pirated in 1603. Again, Iago's name is Spanish (the Italian form would be Giacomo), implying dirty treachery attributable to a race that was still the enemy, and, moreover, the English equivalent is James. It would have been tactless, so early in the reign, to make a Machiavellian villain the namesake of the King. What is particularly, and shamefully, interesting to us now is the fact that a black man should be acceptable, to an audience inclined to xenophobia, as a great leader of men. Othello's color had no connotations of enslavable inferiority. There were great negroes about in those days (or Moors—Moor being a generic term for a dark-skinned man), like that Antonio Manoel de Vunth, who was the King of Congo's ambassador to the Holy See. A black Christian or even pagan was far preferable to a fair-skinned Muslim, and it is against Muslims of lighter skin than his own that Othello leads the Venetian army.

Othello is certainly the most sympathetic of the later tragic characters, and was far more sympathetic to his first audience than he can be today. That audience would see him as a man, endowed with the hot passions of his race, pushed to the limit of jealousy, and not only by Iago. Desdemona, so the Elizabethans and Jacobeans would think, was not altogether sweet innocence like Ophelia. She was a Venetian, and all Venetian women were regarded as courtesans; she was very forward in securing Othello as a husband, and her filial impiety would not be easy to excuse. Her behavior as a married woman would seem, though amiable, far too free. And the second verse of her "Willow Song" was certainly improper:

> I call'd my love false love; but what said he then?
>> Sing willow, willow, willow:
> If I court moe women, you'll couch with moe men—

But the excruciating hold that the play's action had on its auditors was the one we are perhaps too sophisticated to accept without a suspension of disbelief—the working of a spirit of pure evil on a nature essentially benevolent and noble.

This is at the root of *Macbeth*, though, in writing it, Shakespeare could depersonalize the evil and exploit one of the preoccupations of the King—witchcraft. For James was fascinated by the subject and had even written a little treatise on it—*Daemonologie*. In England he was perhaps more tolerant of old women who lived alone with black cats, or had warts which looked like supernumerary nipples for the feeding of familiars, than he had been as a Scottish king. England was civilized, and his throne looked safe. Scotland was half-savage, and he had often been in danger, and danger could lurk in the supernatural order as well as in the terrestrial. James's attitude to witches had, when he was merely James VI, been fearful, especially when he gained what looked like proof that the Earl of Bothwell, his mother's murderous third husband, had been using witchcraft with a regicidal purpose. A waxen image had been found with the label "This is King James the Sixth, ordained to be consumed at the instance of a nobleman, Francis, Earl of Bothwell." And there had been the occasion when James had been sailing to Denmark, and live cats tied to the severed joints of corpses had been cast into the sea to raise storms. The Devil had been after James, and his failure to prevail had only convinced the King the more that he was under God's protection as one of God's dearest own. *"Il est un homme de Dieu,"* a thwarted witch had cried in the Devil's name. If anybody could be believed on that point, surely it was the Devil.

In Scotland, James had sternly rebuked magistrates who failed to exact the full penalty from convicted witches. He had been a party to ghastly torture and excruciating deaths. But in England he merely conducted scholarly enquiries into the theological nature of witchcraft and, to this end, assisted in cross-examinations of suspects. Towards the end of his life, his belief in demons waned somewhat: he "grew first diffident of, and then flatly to deny, the workings of witches and devils, as but falsehoods and delusions"—so the historian Thomas Fuller recorded. But the fact of his earlier interest was enough to provoke mindless prosecution of eccentric innocents among small justices of the peace and bored villagers. The age throve on superstition. To Shakespeare, witchcraft was good dramatic material, apt for incorporation in a serious tragedy. To Ben Jonson it was good enough for a court entertainment like *The Masque of Witches*, but the purpose of a serious comedy like *The Alchemist* was to cast scorn on those credulous of any irrational marvel.

The supernatural element in *Macbeth* gave Shakespeare an opportunity to introduce a magical dumbshow showing King James's descent from the house of Banquo. And, while he was on the wonderful and miraculous, he added—at a point where the action could least use it—a little cadenza about the royal power to cure scrofula:

> How he solicits heaven,
> Himself best knows; but strangely-visited people,
> All swoln and ulcerous, pitiful to the eye,
> The mere despair of surgery, he cures,
> Hanging a golden stamp about their necks,
> Put on with holy prayers; and 'tis spoken,
> To the succeeding royalty he leaves
> The healing benediction.

Now one fact about James that Shakespeare, Groom of the Royal Bedchamber, probably knew, was that he did not believe in the power of the King's touch to cure the King's Evil. He said it was Romish superstition, but his aversion to the pretended miracle probably sprang from his squeamishness about touching the running ulcers of the common people. Still, so as not to offend, he sometimes went through the motions of believing in the healing gift. What was Shakespeare doing here? Trying to make his king feel uncomfortable at that simulation? Telling him to take it seriously? Using whatever device was available for a conventional interlude of flattery?

Will transferred himself to Scotland with the ease with which he had taken up temporary citizenship of Rome or Illyria. No better play with a Scottish setting has ever been written, and Macduff's sad cry "O Scotland, Scotland!" though the work of a Warwickshire man, can always bring tears to the eyes of a North

Briton. It is likely that King James was pleased with *Macbeth*, though at that probable court performance in the summer of 1606, when the King of Denmark was on a visit, there would be tactful excisions of scenes of conspiracy against Duncan: James was sensitive about that sort of thing, especially after the discovery of the Gunpowder Plot on November 5 in the previous year.

Ben Jonson, however much he secretly helped in that discovery, was certainly less of a Jacobean poet-pet than his friend Will. He had a knack of getting on badly with authority, owing to his personal pride and truculence as well as the excessively sharp references that got into his plays. He, Chapman, and Marston had collaborated on a comedy called *Eastward Ho,* and James took exception to certain sneers at the Scots that the ill-assorted three thought fit to garnish it withal. The colony of Virginia was described as populated "only by a few industrious Scots, perhaps, who indeed are dispersed over the face of the whole earth"—one of those wounding jibes at the Scot's eagerness to get out of his own country that the eighteenth-century Johnson was to revel in. The play also said that the Scots were good friends to England, but only when they were "out on't." Such witticisms went down badly. Still, long after the fist of authority struck, Ben was to pay a visit to Scotland, traveling from London on foot to the estate of William Drummond of Hawthornden. Drummond records what Ben told him about this affair:

He was delated by Sir James Murray to the King for writting some thing against the Scots in a play Eastward hoe & voluntarily Imprissonned himself with Chapman and Marston, who had written it amongst them. the report was that they should then have their ears cutt & noses. after their delivery he banqueted all his friends, there was Camden Selden and others. at the midst of the Feast his old Mother Dranke to him & shew him a paper which she had (if the Sentence had taken execution) to have mixed in the Prison among his drinke, which was full of Lustie strong poison & that she was no churle she told she minded first to have Drunk of it herself.

Somehow Ben's tale fails to convince. It is hard to imagine his telling the jailer to open up and admit him to damp stones and rats, I would fain be with my friends. He had shown what he thought of Marston in *The Poetaster*, and Chapman had too much talent and Greek for his liking. Their collaboration had been commercial, not amical. Still, it is a good story, one apt for a Falstaffian boaster like Ben, at his ease over flagons in Hawthornden, his host deferential and ready to take all down in his notebook. It is, so to speak, *Ben trovato*. One tale that he never seems to have told is how he went to supper with Catesby and his friends and learnt that the Gunpowder Plot was in the offing.

We know that the guy-burning and fireworks of British children on November 5 are an example of history overlaying some ancient folk ceremony, but it is significant that, out of all the countless attempts at assassinating a British monarch, this should have printed itself so indelibly on the popular mind. James, far more than Elizabeth, emphasized to his subjects the divine provenance of the crown: the monarch was a kind of god, and violence offered to his person was a blasphemy that (as Shakespeare was always ready to demonstrate on the stage) subverted the natural order. James's bishops were always ready, in ninety-minute sermons somewhat less entertaining, to crash out the doctrine of divine right. Now, with the Catesby plot, the people nearly came face to face with the ultimate apocalyptic vision of horror—their king, whom only holy oil had laved, blown skyhigh. His father had been blown skyhigh too, at Kirk-o'-Fields when his mother had gone to a ball.

This plot was the child of cruel disappointment. James, who had a Catholic queen, had promised toleration for Catholics. Then he had broken his promise and commanded rigorous persecution of the faith. Robert Catesby, along with other Catholic gentlemen and the brave soldier Fawkes, determined to blow up the Parliament building when the King, Queen, Prince Henry, bishops, nobles, judges, knights, and esquires were assembled for the opening of the new session. Guy Fawkes arranged for the lodging of twenty barrels of gunpowder in the cellar under the building, with readily inflammable faggots on top. It was a gesture of such immense foolishness that the heart still lifts at it: Marlowe, had he been alive, would have made a fine Machiavellian play out of the plot, deeming it the best plot ever. But Francis Tresham—the thirteenth member of the conspiracy—was worried about the injustice of Catholic peers being blown up with Protestant ones (the Catholic Queen did not, apparently, matter; she was a foreigner), and he sent a warning letter to his brother-in-law, Lord Monteagle. It said: "They shall receive a terrible blow this Parliament, and yet they shall not see who hurts them. The danger is past as soon as you have burned the letter." Monteagle did not burn it; he took it to Robert Cecil, Earl of Salisbury. Cecil, though big-headed and dwarf-bodied, had all his father's quickness. The King was shown the letter. He remembered what had happened to Lord Darnley, his own father. He ordered a search for gunpowder. The plot was thwarted. James, with the help of God, had saved not only himself but the entire realm. In 1606 a pamphlet appeared called A *Discourse of the Maner of the Discovery of the Late Intended Treason*. Though the writer was not James, it was James's version of what had happened.

Perhaps because the King had said all that had to be said, the dramatists were sluggish about putting on the stage fine rousing plays in which a noble ruler unmasked his would-be assassins. In *Macbeth*, Duncan's silver skin is duly laced with his golden blood. At Christmas 1606, the Court was regaled with *King Lear*. It is hardly festal entertainment, and one wonders what the pleasure-loving Queen Anne thought of it. Or James himself, for that matter, though he may have found that Shakespeare's demented fantasia on ingratitude struck a chord in himself. The theme of deference to a ruler by divine right is sounded loudly enough in the very first scene, but Lear is all too James-like in wanting fulsome flattery more than plain truth; his tragedy springs from a rejection of honesty. James would be unlikely to see any privy moral there: a mythical king of ancient Britain had nothing to teach a real king of modern Britain. Besides, the whole play was nothing more than a bizarre exercise in neotragedy, complete with pulling out of eyes on stage. Still, Gloucester's words about the decay of the state had a tang of immediacy: "We have seen the best of our time: machinations, hollowness, treachery, and all ruinous disorders, follow us disquietly to our graves." He meant more than the Gunpowder Plot. But his creator had only the Gunpowder Plot in mind when he made so much of his own plot hinge on the discovery of treachery through letters. The times gave him a dramatic device, but they could teach him nothing new about evil.

Indeed, except for the self-consciously sporraned and kilted *Macbeth*, Shakespeare's Jacobean tragedies look back more than they look around. Even in *Macbeth*, Essex is remembered: it is his execution we hear about, not Cawdor's:

> I have spoke
> With one that saw him die; who did report
> That very frankly he confess'd his treasons,
> Implor'd your Highness' pardon, and set forth
> A deep repentance. Nothing in his life
> Became him like the leaving it: he died
> As one that had been studied in his death
> To throw away the dearest thing he ow'd
> As 'twere a careless trifle.

The model for Cleopatra as sensual enchantress may still have been alive; but the queen in Cleopatra was dead, though in a sense her absence filled the new state more than the presence of the King. Cleopatra's Nile could be the Thames of thirty years before. Capricious, jealous, crafty, vindictive, majestic, adorable even though aging, Elizabeth seems to live on in the skin of a Moor or gypsy or brown doxy from a Clerkenwell brothel. And, purged of everything except patriotism, strength, and eloquence, she is Volumnia, mother of Coriolanus, hailed by the senators as "our patroness, the life of Rome." Meanwhile, James, nobody's model, a divinity but no myth, taught his realms to respect bishops and give up smoking.

Is there anything of the previous reign in *Timon of Athens*? Its hero begins as a nobleman like Southampton, wealthy and gracious, a patron of the arts. In the first scene, a poet is waiting to offer him lines that, perhaps inevitably, sound as if Shake-speare has written them:

> When we for recompense have prais'd the vile,
> It stains the glory in that happy verse
> Which aptly sings the good.

A painter, also seeking a patron, asks him if he is "rapt in some work, some dedication to the great lord." Shakespeare must have had those old days of *Venus and Adonis* vividly in mind. But then the poet melts out of the play, and we can have no doubt of where Shakespeare's real self-identification lies: he is Timon himself. It is an exaggerated, delirious, totally self-indulgent identification, but it may be seen as an act of catharsis necessary to prevent the author's falling into melancholy or dementia. This is not the old age but the new. The poet-actor-businessman has become a magnate to be preyed upon. Gener-osity breeds ingratitude; loan oft loses both itself and friend; the act of love is a door leading to disease. The mood of the tragedy is that of a man who has had enough of the great world, with its fawning, clawing, and biting. Timon turns his back on Athens forever. It was time for his creator to turn his back on London— not perhaps forever, but for longer and longer periods of rural peace which should imperceptibly merge into a sort of retire-ment. Sort of: no writer ever really retires.

18

New Place

❦❦❦❦❦❦❦❦❦❦❦❦❦❦❦❦❦❦

There are two routes from London to Stratford—one through
Aylesbury and Banbury, the other through High Wycombe and
Woodstock. Shakespeare seems to have preferred the latter road,
which enabled him to rest a night at Oxford.

"Mr. William Shakespeare," says John Aubrey, "was wont to
goe into Warwickshire once a yeare." He then tells of the boast
of Sir William Davenant, the man who did most to bring back
the drama to London after the Puritans had outlawed it for
nearly twenty years. Davenant held that he was the natural son
of Shakespeare, who was in the habit of staying at the Crown in
Oxford, an inn of which Mistress Davenant was the hostess.
She was, says Aubrey, "a very beautiful woman & of a very good
witt and of conversation extremely agreeable." As for Davenant's
often repeated story, this gave his mother "a very light report,
whereby she was called a whore." Well, perhaps it was worth-
while to have a mother who was a whore and to be a bastard
oneself if the cuckolder and bastardizer was called William
Shakespeare.

One route would bring Shakespeare into Stratford by way of
the Banbury Road, the other by way of the Shipston Road,
which meets the Banbury Road just before the Clopton Bridge.
Cross the bridge, turn left on to Waterside, then right on to
Chapel Lane. At the corner of Chapel Lane and Chapel Street
stood New Place. Here his wife Anne waited for him, with their
daughter Judith. Susanna had married Dr. John Hall, the
fashionable Stratford physician, in 1607.

New Place has long disappeared, but we have a fair notion of what it was like. It had been built in the 1490s by Sir Hugh Clopton, the Stratfordian who had become Lord Mayor of London, restored the Stratford Guild Chapel, and built the bridge which still bears his name. Clopton had done well and was not likely to stint himself on his "grete house," as he called it. It had a sixty-foot frontage and was seventy feet deep. There were ten fireplaces, which argues more than ten rooms. "A praty house of bricke and tymber," said a traveler in the middle of the sixteenth century. That was before it fell into the "great ruine and decay" from which William Underhill, Inner Temple lawyer and Warwickshire landowner, rescued it when he bought it three years after Shakespeare's birth. His son, another William, sold it to Shakespeare in May 1597—cheap at sixty pounds, for there were also two gardens and two barns. Two months after the sale, the second William Underhill was poisoned by his son Fulke, who was duly hanged in Warwick. The rude son shall strike the father dead. A bad omen? Ghosts? The new owner did not greatly worry.

He was an absentee owner till his retirement from acting, and he had to leave to his wife Anne the various tasks that fall on a householder—renovations and improvements, for instance. A good deal of stone was bought, too much in fact, for the borough took tenpennyworth off Anne's hands (naturally, it is "Mr. Shaxpere" whose name appears in the records). The two barns gave her, or him, an opportunity to hoard corn and malt during the time of shortage when citizens died of want on the London streets. In February 1597 it is recorded in Stratford that ten quarters of malt were in the possession of "Wm. Shackespere in Chapel Street ward." This, incidentally, indicates that the Shakespeares were in possession of New Place before the official date of purchase. The conveying of property was a slow process in those days. There had to be the ritual of a legal fiction, whereby the person to whom the property was to be conveyed sued the holder for wrongfully keeping him out of possession. The defendant acknowledged the plaintiff's right, and the particulars of the resultant compromise were set out in a document known as "the foot of the fine," the bottom portion of a tripartite indenture. An indenture was a "toothed" document, as the name implies. Tear a contract in half and you have two jagged edges which, brought back together, fit like upper and lower teeth—a proof of authenticity. With house purchase, there had to be jagged edges for vendor, purchaser, and court records. The court retained the lower third of the contract—hence the "foot of the fine." Shakespeare remembered all this in *Hamlet*— "a great buyer of land, with . . . his fines, his double vouchers, his recoveries." Recoveries had to do with entails of property.

Shakespeare presumably felt no shame at making a profit on cereals in a time of near famine. Business is business. But he was aware of what people thought about the high prices. The opening scene of *Coriolanus* shows a "company of mutinous citizens" who are ready to kill Caius Marcius (later to have "Coriolanus" added to his name to commemorate his victory over the Corioli) as the worst of those who "suffer us to famish, and their storehouses cramm'd with grain." There is a little of Coriolanus in Shakespeare—a gentleman who despises the mob.

Those of the mob that went to the playhouse were helping to swell Will's moneybags. In 1602 he was able to send three hundred and twenty pounds home from London to buy a hundred and twenty acres of land from the Coombe family. Gilbert acted as his brother's agent. In the same year a cottage suitable for a gardener was bought in Chapel Lane, near to New Place. The Shakespeare gardens needed full-time tending, along with the two orchards that Will had added to his personal property. His impersonal property was augmented in 1603 by a purchase of four hundred and forty pounds worth of tithes in Stratford, Old Stratford (agricultural land to the north of the town), Welcombe, and Bishopston. Meanwhile the dividends came in from the Globe, as they were later, additionally, to come in from the Blackfriars. But, wealthy as the Shakespeares were, they still took in a lodger. When Susanna left home to be married, there was room (one might suppose that there had been room before) for the Town Clerk, Thomas Greene, and his wife and two children to live at New Place. In a surviving document, Greene indicates that he may leave "newe place" in 1610, a convenient year to which to assign Will's shifting of his center from London to Stratford. He would still have his

London business, but this would be secondary to his Stratford life. He did not want a Greene around in his retirement (did that "upstart crow" still rankle?). He did not want another man's children shouting in his garden or gardens.

The year 1610 was busy for one group of men in London. This was when the final touches were being put to the King James translation of the Old and New Testaments. That great work had been started in 1604, three years after King James's eloquently expressed dissatisfaction with the biblical situation in England, where the people followed the Geneva Bible and the church used the Bishops' Bible, and the Geneva Bible was very bad because there was a lot of antimonarchical sentiment in its marginal notes—"very partial, untrue, seditious, and savoring too much of dangerous and traitorous conceits." The new unified Bible, said the King, was to be demotic—everything clear, no hard words. It was a good principle, and it yielded marvelous results.

There were fifty-four translators divided into six groups or companies—two at Westminster under Lancelot Andrewes, two at Oxford under John Harding, two at Cambridge under Edward Lively. When one company completed the translation of a chapter, it was scrutinized by the other two. Where there were special difficulties, learned men from the universities, not necessarily churchmen, were consulted. The poetical parts of the Old Testament—like the Psalms and the Song of Solomon— were vetted for euphony by men who knew all about the music of words. A short story by Rudyard Kipling—*Proofs of Holy Writ*—presents Shakespeare and Ben Jonson discussing a problem of language brought to them by one of the translators of the Bible. There is no reason, one feels, why this should not have happened. They were the greatest poets of their age; the Bible was to be a work of literature as well as piety.

It would be pleasant to think that Shakespeare was responsible, in part, for the majesty of the following:

God is our refuge and strength, a very present help in trouble.
Therefore will not we fear, though the earth be removed, and
    though the mountains be carried into the midst of the sea;

Though the waters thereof roar and be troubled, though the
mountains shake with the swelling thereof. Selah.

There is a river, the streams whereof shall make glad the city
of God, the holy place of the tabernacles of the Most High.

God is in the midst of her; she shall not be moved:

God shall help her, and that right early.

The heathen raged, the kingdoms were moved: he uttered his
voice, the earth melted.

The Lord of Hosts is with us; the God of Jacob is our refuge.
Selah.

Come, behold the works of the Lord, what desolations he hath
made in the earth.

He maketh wars to cease unto the end of the earth; he breaketh
the bow, and cutteth the spear in sunder; he burneth the
chariot in the fire.

Be still, and know that I am God: I will be exalted among the
heathen, I will be exalted in the earth.

The Lord of Hosts is with us; the God of Jacob is our refuge.
Selah.

Whether he had anything to do with it or not, he is in it. It is
the forty-sixth Psalm. The forty-sixth word from the beginning
is *shake*, and the forty-sixth word from the end, if we leave out
the cadential *Selah*, is *spear*. And in 1610 Shakespeare was
forty-six years old. If this is mere chance, fancy must allow us to
think that it is happy chance. The greatest prose work of all time
has the name of the greatest poet set cunningly in it. As for
Ben, Ben-oni, whom his father called Benjamin, he could
always boast that he was the favorite son of Jacob—James in
English. This was very nearly true. Ben's masques were doing
well while Will was packing his bags for Stratford. There were
twenty years to go before his final quarrel with Inigo Jones and
his loss of court favor.

In Stratford there was plenty for Shakespeare to do. He did
not, as his father had done, seek election to the borough
council, but he paid his contribution to "the charge of prose-
cutying the Bill in parliament for the better Repayr of the highe
waies." The roads of England were wretched, and Shakespeare

the traveler knew this better than most. There is no evidence that he dipped into his pocket in the cause of charity, though Stratford was, like any other town, often in need of "relief" when plague created widows and fires made families homeless. Fires especially devastated that town of timber, thatched roofs, and no fire brigade. Money indeed was raised to help the afflicted (two hundred Stratford buildings burnt down between 1594 and 1614), but all the evidence shows that the appointed collectors of donations took an overample percentage for their trouble.

Shakespeare, a great amateur of the law who had once, some of us think, been a near professional at it, had plenty of scope for litigation in his retirement. There was a long legal row about the enclosure of some of his land at Welcombe, and acrimony with the Coombe family over some details of that purchase of a hundred and twenty acres. There were debts to collect and defaulters to be harried. And, to keep the adrenalin flowing, there was the growing Puritan element in Stratford to provoke anger, especially since they had been responsible for the banning of dramatic performances in the town. Life in Stratford was not dull, and even the new hell-fire sermons, blaming the citizens' sins for visitations like fire and plague, would keep pewholders like Shakespeare angrily or scornfully attentive.

His married life, from 1610 on, would be a torpid business, occasionally shot by flashes of wifely recrimination. In that year Will was forty-six, but Anne was fifty-four. Their sexual life had long come to an end, but Anne must have known that her husband had fornicated, gaily or sadly, in London. Probably Dick Field had given her news on his frequent visits, and she could get hold of a copy of the Sonnets, in which—as an Aldous Huxley character coarsely puts it—Shakespeare unlocked his pants. She, who had been so hot for love in her late twenties, had lived chastely during her grass-widowhood: in a gossiping town like Stratford she could do little else. She might have, fulfilling Stephen Dedalus's theory, committed incestuous adultery with her brother-in-law Richard: there was opportunity for that, especially if, as some hold, Richard had for a time a room in New Place. But that, though sinful, was not indiscreet. Will's indiscretions had been erected into a poetic monument. Like many wives left on their own, she may have become pious, welcoming visits from Puritan divines, who would tell her how blasphemous was the career of player and leave her pamphlets to read—A *Comb for the Lousy Locks of the Ungodly* or A *Purge for the Atheistical Bowels and Bellies of Them that Scoff at the Word and Believe Not.*

Shakespeare certainly, if the last plays are any evidence, took pleasure in the company of his daughters. The charm and beauty of Perdita, Miranda, and Marina may be taken as a reflection of fatherly pride and love. Of the two, Susanna was certainly his favorite. Judith, as we shall see, let him down badly by making an unfortunate marriage. Susanna's marriage could, for a small borough like Stratford, hardly be better. At the age of twenty-four she had married Dr. John Hall, then thirty-two. Hall was a physician with a high-class practice: his patients included the Earl of Northampton, the Bishop of Worcester, and Sir Thomas Temple. He has left a casebook in which he describes his treatment of such diseases as dropsy, tertian fever, and the itch. Of his father-in-law's final illness he says nothing. Perhaps decency prevailed over clinical candor.

Physicians in those days had no minimal medical qualification, not even a Licentiate of the Society of Apothecaries. Hall had been to Queens' College, Cambridge, but he came away with no medical degree. This in no way invalidated his claim to be able to cure the sick, since the lore of the times was more magical than scientific. Hall purged and sweated and emeti- cized vigorously, but he was on the right modern lines with his treatment of scurvy—decoctions of flowers and herbs to restore Vitamin C. Here, from his casebook, is an account of how, in 1624 or 1625, he treated his own daughter Elizabeth for *tortura oris* or convulsion of the mouth:

In the beginning of April she went to London and returning homewards the 22nd of the said month she took cold and fell into the said distemper on the contrary side of the face, . . . and although grievously afflicted with it, yet by the blessing of God she was cured in sixteen days, as followeth: . . . the neck was fomented with *aqua vitae*, in which was infused nutmegs, cinnamon, cloves, pepper; she ate nutmegs often. In the same year, May the 24th, she was afflicted with an erratic fever: sometimes she was hot, by and by sweating, again cold, all in the space of half an hour, and thus she was vexed oft in a day... thus was she delivered from death and deadly disease, and was well for many years.

The tone of the entries seems to indicate relief at the efficacy of something that was not necessarily bound to be efficacious. The human body is tough and will withstand any amount of guesswork medication. Hall gained his reputation in spite of his fomentations and purges. He was right to give thanks to God.

Susanna, the doctor's wife, had the reputation of being a comforting caller on the sick, a woman of piety comparable to her husband's, and an inheritrix of her father's "wit" or intelligence. She was sociable and strong-minded, and she had at least one enemy. This was John Lane of Alveston Manor, two miles out of Stratford, who maliciously said that Mrs. Hall had "the running of the raynes and had bin naught with Rafe Smith." To have the running of the reins meant to wear the trousers at home; to be naught was to commit fornication. Smith was a haberdasher and hatter, like William Hart, Susanna's aunt's husband, of lower social standing than a doctor. Sexual defamation of this kind had to be dealt with by the church, and, in July 1613, Susanna slammed back at Lane with a writ for slander in the Ecclesiastical Court at Worcester (she had inherited that readiness to go to law). Lane entered no appearance, and his sullying of a matron's honor was punished with excommunication. Susanna's purity was vindicated: she had been prophetically named.

Susanna was bright, quick, literate, well thought of in the borough. Her sister Judith gives an impression of dullness, and also of ill luck—the worst of all curses at a christening. That she could not read or write seems certain: the crosses she scrawled on a couple of witnessed deeds in 1611 do not, with her, point to a mere impatience with name-signing. Susanna signed always with a confident flourish; why could not her younger sister—the daughter, after all, of a great literary man—do likewise? Only because she could not. The poor girl must have been sensitive enough to suspect that, to her parents, she would always carry sad associations and perhaps also be a vague object of resentment: her twin, Hamnet, had died; her survival was a cruel reminder. She may have had less than her reasonable endowment of beauty. Why, as the daughter of a well-off Stratford burgess, did she not marry till she was thirty? Young men ought to have licked their lips at the prospect of a fair dowry and a good slice of the personality and realty left by the bald old *rentier* who said he had written stage plays in London. But Judith sat on the shelf even longer than her scant-dowered mother.

The sad story of her marriage can be deferred till later, since it began only ten weeks before her father's death. So in all the full years of his retirement, Shakespeare would see Judith all day and every day and take her for granted. Susanna he would not take for granted. She paid visits to her parents only when she could, her time being taken up with her own daughter and the duties of a busy physician's wife. When she came for dinner or an hour's gossip she would be made much of, her new coiffure admired, her little girl dandled and cosseted. Judith, a superior serving wench (Bring the other wine, girl, the canary, not that muck from Quiney's), would inwardly resent her position and perhaps sometimes cry herself to sleep. It was no life for a young woman of marriageable age.

Will the grandfather would delight in little Elizabeth, born in 1608, but, as the years went on and Susanna produced no other children, and as the prospect of Judith's marrying grew remoter, he might wonder what curse had been laid on the Shakespeare name that it seemed destined to die out, and not only the name but—under whatever other name—the male Shakespeare blood. Fate would not whisper that he, Will, was claiming so large an immortality that the carrying of the genetic flag into the future was asking too much; fate, like literary London, did not yet realize how great Shakespeare was. To Will a man's blood was more important than a man's work. As for his work, it had done its work by enabling him to proclaim the greatness of his blood. The rest could very nearly be silence.

When we look at the Shakespeare family chronicle between 1607 and 1613, we can understand Will's probable twinge of superstition. Mary Shakespeare died in September 1608, thus outliving her husband by exactly seven years. But in the December of 1607, Edmund Shakespeare had died in London at the early age of twenty-seven. An actor like his brother, but not a member of the King's Men (he could have been, Will had enough influence), he was buried in the actors' quarter of the church that is now Southwark Cathedral. He had not married, but he seems to have had a bastard son. Gilbert died in February 1612—forty-five, unmarried; Richard in the February following—thirty-eight, again unmarried. The record is astonishing for those marrying days.

There was plenty to brood on as Will sat in the grounds of New Place, watching his mulberry tree grow. Things and people passed away, and one had to learn the great gift of resignation. Certain authors helped, so long as they did not philosophize too prosily or piously. Will, being a gentleman, had to have a library, but he was not inclined to fill it with Boethius and the meditations of divines. His copies of North's Plutarch and Holinshed's *Chronicles* were worn out: he wanted no more moral lessons from history. These brief essays of Michel Eyquem de Montaigne—in John Florio's translation, completed and published in that year of change, 1603—were the right length for an hour's reading, as were the even pithier jottings of Francis Bacon. There were the poets to reread—the great Edmund Spenser, for instance, but *The Faerie Queene* was somewhat tedious and seemed to deal with a world long dead. John Donne was interesting: he had passion and intellectual tortuousness, and this combination would go straight to Will's heart. He could only read him so far in manuscript copies; when was he going to publish? Some of the older poets, like Chaucer and Gower, wrote a strange English, but their stories were good. Gower's *Confessio Amantis* had a tale which might do well on the stage—"Apollonius of Tyre." "Apollonius" sounded too much like "Polonius": the name would have to be changed. Evidently, though he had retired to Stratford, he had not entirely left the theatre. Too many tales in his library were suggesting plays—that in Boccaccio's *Decameron* about Ginerva, and here was poor dead Greene's *Pandosto*. He forgave Greene now. He was ready to forgive everybody, or nearly everybody. But he would not rescind monetary debts—that was a different matter altogether.

19

Swansong

Meanwhile, back in the London playhouse—

With Shakespeare away, there should have been no question as to who ruled the stage. And, indeed, Ben Jonson flowered at last as the true heir of Marlowe. He had subdued his lyric gift in the early humors plays, reserving it—though modified to mere prettiness—for the court masques. Now, in *Volpone* in 1606, and in *The Alchemist* in 1610, he found a way of infusing a Marlovian magnificence into satires that look beyond contemporary London and represent, in a kind of jeweled exaltation, eternal rogues and eternal dupes. Volpone, the old fox of Venice, pretends to be both rich and dying. His wealth consists solely of the gifts he receives from men who expect to be his heirs. As for dying, this sort of speech is not for a deathbed:

> Why droops my Celia?
> Thou hast, in place of a base husband, found
> A worthy lover: use thy fortune well,
> With secrecy and pleasure. See, behold,
> What thou art queen of; not in expectation,
> As I feed others: but possess'd and crown'd.
> See here a rope of pearl; and each more orient
> Than that the brave Egyptian queen carous'd:
> Dissolve and drink them. See, a carbuncle
> May put out both the eyes of our St. Mark;
> A diamond, would have bought Lollia Paulina,
> When she came in like starlight, hid with jewels,
> That were the spoils of provinces; take these,

And wear, and lose them: yet remains an ear-ring
To purchase them again, and this whole state.

The circumstances are sordid, for Celia's husband has handed
over his wife as a temporary gift, but they are swallowed by the
poetry. This was Marlowe's way—the granting of lyrical splen-
dor to mouths that did not deserve it—but Marlowe's villains
were great sinners, heroes of evil, while Ben's are just men of
base appetite. Like Sir Epicure Mammon in *The Alchemist*,
who dreams of gold transmuted out of gross matter and a life of
baroque self-indulgence:

My foot-boy shall eat pheasants, calver'd salmons,
Knots, godwits, lampreys: I myself will have
The beards of barbels served, instead of salads;
Oil'd mushrooms; and the swelling unctuous paps
Of a fat pregnant sow, newly cut off,
Drest with an exquisite and poignant sauce;
For which I'll say unto my cook, *There's gold,*
Go forth and be a knight.

Our admiration of Jonson's mature art is always tempered by
a sense of the worthlessness of his characters—their moral
insufficiency, their inadequacy as subjects for serious literature.
Terms like that ought to apply even more to Marlowe's creations, but to talk of Tamburlaine or Barabas as worthless or
morally insufficient seems absurd: they inhabit a plane of evil
which invites the judgment of the theologian, not the secular
moralist. The great absolute terms—good and evil—are disappearing, it seems, from the English drama. Though Ben will
present hell in *The Devil is an Ass*, it is a mere property of
smoke-room anecdotage. The days of *Doctor Faustus* are gone.
There is evil enough in the tragedies of John Webster, whose
The White Devil (1608) and *The Duchess of Malfi* (1614)
approach—in language at least—the best tragedies of Shakespeare (from which, however, they proceed). Here is the guilty
Cardinal of the latter play; he enters reading a book:

I am puzzled in a question about hell:
He says, in hell there's one material fire,

And yet it shall not burn all men alike.
Lay him by. How tedious is a guilty conscience!
When I look into the fish-ponds in my garden,
Methinks I see a thing arm'd with a rake,
That seems to strike at me.

Here is the dying villain Flamineo in *The White Devil*:

My life was a black charnel. I have caught
An everlasting cold; I have lost my voice
Most irrecoverably. Farewell, glorious villains.

Here is the murderous brother of *The Duchess of Malfi*, looking on the corpse of his sister:

Cover her face; mine eyes dazzle: she died young.

These samplings are enough to show how large is Webster's poetic talent, but if we proceed beyond samples to grope through the labyrinths of intrigue which make up the plays, then we find we are back in the old *Spanish Tragedy* epoch of Italianate Senecanism. The evil is not huge and theological, as in Marlowe; the motives which corrupt great men are not, as in Shakespeare, closely examined. The intrigues, with their resultant torturings, murders, and madness, are there to intrigue. There is titillation, the deliberate employment of flesh-creeping devices in the service of a somewhat corrupt kind of entertainment. Evil is *out there*—a Machiavellian property with all the Italian garnishings. In Shakespeare it is *in here*—an aspect of ourselves.

The plays of Cyril Tourneur—*The Revenger's Tragedy* (1607) and *The Atheist's Tragedy* (1611)—are a more blatant example of the employment of highly sophisticated language, and horrors that Kyd never dreamed of, to feed a public appetite that seems not unlike that of the Romans under Caligula and Nero. *Titus Andronicus* has more cruel ingenuities than either of Tourneur's plays, but the language of early Shakespeare breathes a comparative innocence, the crude boisterousness of schoolboys playing a game of villainy. The Jacobeans had learnt every possible chilling nuance of tone and rhythm. When we read the synopsis of *The Revenger's Tragedy* we can stand outside the concept and laugh off the horror. The Duke poisoned Vindice's betrothed for refusing to yield to him, and Vindice contrives that the Duke shall kiss the poisoned mouth of her skull. Then, while the Duke is screaming in agony, Vindice stamps on him. The Duke cries, reasonably, "Is there a hell besides this, villains?" That sounds improbably melodramatic enough, but not when it is clothed in Tourneur's words and rhythms. This is how the last major speech in *The Revenger's Tragedy* ends:

> And now, my lord, since we are in for ever,
> This work was ours, which else might have been slipp'd!
> And if we list, we could have nobles clipp'd,
> And go for less than beggars; but we hate
> To bleed so cowardly, we have enough,
> I'faith, we're well, our mother turned, our sister true,
> We die after a nest of dukes. Adieu!

It is the final shaft of wit before death that, in Webster and Tourneur alike, we find so chilling.

George Chapman, too, brought his immense vocabulary and individual music to the Jacobean redaction of the tragedy of revenge: the two Bussy D'Ambois plays—1608 and 1613—are remarkable. But was not all this, despite the verbal sophistication and the fashionable psychological quirks, really a return to the days of *Gorboduc* and *Locrine*? Thomas Heywood may have thought so, for he attempted a tragedy without bloodshed in *A Woman Killed with Kindness*. In a contemporary English setting, a husband discovers his wife's infidelity but, instead of drawing the conventional Italian dagger, sends her to live in comfort but alone, far from himself and their children, so that at leisure she may contemplate her folly. She wastes away with remorse. There is a touching deathbed scene where there is forgiveness without sentimentality. And there are two lines which, says T. S. Eliot, "surely no men or women past their youth can read without a twinge of personal feeling":

> O God! O God! that it were possible
> To undo things done; to call back yesterday...

The most popular dramatist of the late Shakespeare period was not one man but two. These were Francis Beaumont—just twenty years younger than Shakespeare—and John Fletcher, fifteen years younger, who worked in collaboration with other men but chiefly with each other. They were commercial playwrights, learned, intelligent, determined to make money by giving the public what it wanted. They were popular because they recognized that the public, and chiefly the female public, loved dreams better than real life. They did their best to avoid representing reality, of which, to cite Eliot again, mankind cannot bear very much. The citizens' wives wanted dreams that ended nicely, and these they got. Not that Beaumont and Fletcher had any qualms about disclosing their opinion of this bourgeois taste for romance and prettiness. In their very charming comedy *The Knight of the Burning Pestle*, a London grocer and his wife, especially his wife, comment incessantly, from their seats on the stage, on the play they have come to see. They want chivalric romance, crossed love, dragons, marvels, villainy foiled, and, by God, they have the money to pay for it. The authors submit and, submitting, are crowned kings of the theatre. Ben, Tourneur, and Webster were too good for the middle class; Beaumont and Fletcher were just good enough.

They churned out their romances, singly, together, or in collaboration with others, and the style is homogeneous enough to be regarded as a kind of impersonal plastic:

> Be you my witness, earth,
> Need I to brag? Doth not this captive prince
> Speak me sufficiently, and all the acts
> That I have wrought upon this suffering land?
> Should I then boast? Where lies that foot of ground,
> Within this whole realm, that I have not past,
> Fighting and conquering: Far then from me
> Be ostentation.

The rhythms are supple enough—they have studied their Shakespeare—but there is no dangerous subtlety. Nobody in the audience ever need knot his brows at hard words or complex syntax. The story is plain, the morality of the simplest. And where they take up a theme which demands a complex moral attitude, they skirt the dangers by trickery. Thus, in A *King and*

No King, a brother and sister appear to commit incest. At the end it is disclosed that they were not really brother and sister. A play like John Ford's *'Tis Pity She's a Whore*, which was written in Charles I's reign, will face this incest issue squarely, without tricks. Incest really does take place, and all its implications are worked out to the bitter end. Beaumont and Fletcher do not dig. Their flowers are without roots; it is all specious appearance. But they are superb confectioners.

William Shakespeare could never resist the challenge of new fashions. His *King Lear* was an attempt to show that he could work in the new mode of sophisticated horror as well as any. But, being a genius, he could not help transcending mere fashion, and his concern with the human psyche was such that his characters tended to burst the bonds of form: the Prince of Denmark becomes too big for *Hamlet*. Now, perhaps to his shame, he began to write plays of the Beaumont and Fletcher type, and the first of these—*Pericles, Prince of Tyre*—is one of the worst plays he ever wrote. It is not to be found in the 1623 Folio, and very few Shakespeare lovers have ever complained about that. It is a mess of a play.

Why did he, well off and out of the theatre, trouble to engage in such mean competition? It is probable that he told Burbage, on one of his visits to London, or when the King's Men were on tour in Warwickshire, that there was a very reasonable story in Gower's *Confessio Amantis* and that somebody ought to be commissioned to dramatize it. Somebody was—probably a hack called George Wilkins—and the result was so bad that Will was undoubtedly called in to do what he could to redeem it. We cannot believe that the speeches of Gower as chorus were Will's work:

> To sing a song that old was sung,
> From ashes ancient Gower is come,
> Assuming man's infirmities,
> To glad your ear and please your eyes.
> It hath been sung at festivals,
> On ember-eves and holy-ales;

And lords and ladies in their lives
Have read it for restoratives.

The plot is a creaking engine, with incest, shipwreck, pirates, a
dead wife who is not really dead, attempted murder, miracles,
and there is no room for character development. We can see
Shakespeare's hand in the fishermen's dialogue and in the
brothel scene ("We were never so much out of creatures," says
the madam. "We have but poor three, and they can do no more
than they can do; and they with continual action are even as
good as rotten") and, most of all, in the beauty of Marina, the
lost child born at sea:

My dearest wife was like this maid, and such a one
My daughter might have been: my queen's square brows;
Her stature to an inch; as wand-like straight;
As silver-voic'd; her eyes as jewel-like,
And cas'd as richly; in pace another Juno;
Who starves the ears she feeds, and makes them hungry
The more she gives them speech.

But, in general, *Pericles* is a play to read dutifully, as part of the
Shakespeare canon, and then—after a couple of drinks to clear
depression—to forget.

The Winter's Tale is a much more heartening confection. It is
formally clumsy—we have to have Time as chorus to cover the
gap of sixteen years between the first and second parts of the
action: Ben Jonson must have groaned (would Will never
learn?)—but it has lines like the following:

And many a man there is, even at this present,
Now while I speak this, holds his wife by th' arm
That little thinks she has been sluic'd in's absence,
And his pond fish'd by his next neighbor, by
Sir Smile, his neighbor.

That is Leontes, irrationally convinced that his best friend is
conducting an affair with his wife Hermione. Three words are
enough to convey authenticity: the weak preposition at the end
of a line (who would have dreamed of so ending a line fifteen

years before?) and the brilliant "Sir Smile." And there are the fine Autolycus scenes, which come far too late, and the bewitching Perdita. If, as seems likely, Perdita's part was doubled by the boy actor who took Leontes's son Mamillius, who dies early in the play, then we have a resurrection of deep significance for the man Shakespeare. Hamnet died, but a loved daughter takes his place, and their lineaments are the same.

There is a dirge for a dead boy in *Cymbeline*, and a very lovely one:

> Fear no more the heat o' the sun
>   Nor the furious winter's rages;
> Thou thy worldly task hast done,
>   Home art gone, and ta'en thy wages.
> Golden lads and girls all must,
> As chimney-sweepers, come to dust.

But the boy is only sleeping, and he awakens as another lost daughter—Imogen. The play itself is the most curious of all Shakespeare's mixtures. We have ancient Britain, with the Romans invading, but Rome itself is the capital of a Renaissance Italy. There is a Posthumus, but there is also an Iachimo, with a Philario to bridge the time gap. The main plot is typical Beaumont and Fletcher, with a husband betting on his wife's virtue and—seeming to lose the bet when the challenger cheats— punishing the wife most cruelly. Figures from Holinshed and a tale of Boccaccio's make bizarre bedfellows. Here again, as with *Pericles*, Shakespeare appears to be collaborating. Why? Had he nothing better to do in his semiretirement?

The Tempest, though in this new romantic fairy-story vein, is very much all Shakespeare and, though another play was to follow, it begs to be taken as the Swan of Avon's swansong. The old magician Prospero is also an old bore, and he sometimes seems to realize it, but Miranda is the most delightful of all the final heroines. The dangerous device of personifying the id in Caliban and the poetic imagination in Ariel comes off, and even Caliban is touched by the lyrical magic of Shakespeare's last rich phase:

> Be not afeard. The isle is full of noises,
> Sounds, and sweet airs, that give delight, and hurt not.
> Sometimes a thousand twangling instruments
> Will hum about mine ears; and sometimes voices,
> That, if I then had wak'd after long sleep,
> Will make me sleep again; and then, in dreaming,
> The clouds methought would open and show riches
> Ready to drop upon me, that, when I wak'd,
> I cried to dream again.

In this, as in the other romances, Shakespeare shows himself willing not only to give the people dreams, but to hint at what he might have done if he had really liked the masque form. The brief masque put on by Prospero is charming, and it has its place in a fairy story which is strengthened by a kind of philosophy of resignation. This world, says Prospero, is Maya, a show that will shift and melt and fade as though engineered by some divine Inigo Jones. The notion is Montaigne's: "*La vie est un songe... nous veillons dormants et veillants dormons.*" (So, incidentally, is that discussion between the shipwrecked notables about a Utopian island.) It is an enervating philosophy, and it seems contradicted by an energy of language that Shakespeare, even in his more boisterous years, never excelled. Stephano and Trinculo, the drunkards, smite the air "for breathing in their faces; beat the ground for kissing of their feet." Lumpish Caliban does not talk of mere fresh water but of "quick freshes" —the passive must become active. The whole earth is feverishly alive; even the blind moles in it are listening for human feet. If Shakespeare is making a poetic farewell, he is determined to show that it is volitional, not imposed by the failure of his powers. The abjuration of rough magic is made while the magic is still most potent. Then the magician, having seen his daughter comfortably married, will

> ... thence retire me to my Milan, where
> Every third thought shall be my grave.

For Milan read Stratford. How typical, by the way, that this valediction should have such a roaring title.

The Tempest was not quite Shakespeare's last word. He may have said, talking over the past with his friends at a fish dinner in the Mermaid, that he regretted not having completed his great saga of English history. He had brought the story up to the accession of the first Tudor. To go further might have been indiscreet in the old Queen's time; besides, there had been a long interdict on historical representations. And, again, the reign of Henry VII had never seemed to afford big dramatic opportunities: the Lambert Simnel and Perkin Warbeck adventures were small stuff, the character of the king himself was not attractive. But his son was different. His daughter, whom many now said openly had been a bastard, was dead and could not be offended. It was a pity that the public taste no longer favored true history, as opposed to the fairy-tale kings and queens that Beaumont and Fletcher spawned so readily. A pity, too, that he, Will, lacked the energy and time to read up Henry VIII's reign and make a play of it. Well, Burbage might say, there was no need for Will to do all the work. Collaborate. Why not see how you get on with one of the young men—John Fletcher, for instance? A play of Henry VIII, perhaps only going as far as the birth of Elizabeth, would do well for the Globe. Pageantry, guns, fanfares—a real open-air piece. We have been doing too much of this intimate stuff at the Blackfriars: it is time we opened up our lungs again.

And so the play was written. It did not romanticize: it presented King Henry as the fathers of some of the older auditors might remember him. It showed him affable but capable of manic rage. It did not involve itself in argument about the validity of the divorce, the legitimacy of Anne Boleyn's daughter, or the legality of the break with Rome. It gave the facts and left the conclusions open. The title of the play, as it was first presented at the Globe, was *All Is True*. But, at that performance, very little of the truth could be told. The final scene of the first act is set in the Presence Chamber of York Place. Anne Boleyn enters with "divers other Ladies and Gentlemen." Sir Henry Guildford bids them welcome on behalf of His Grace the Cardinal. The Lord Chamberlain comes in, along with Lord Sandys and Sir Thomas Lovell. Then, to the accompaniment of hautboys or oboes, Cardinal Wolsey enters, richly attended. The feast begins. Offstage, King Henry "and Others, as maskers, habited like shepherds" prepare to give the Cardinal a surprise, coming to the feast uninvited. Henry will see Anne and fall heavily for her. But, at that first performance, the action got no further than the sounding of drum and trumpet and the discharging of chambers to herald the royal party's arrival. The linstock for firing the cannon fired the thatch of the theatre as well. The blaze was uncontrollable.

So, in that summer of 1613, the prophecy of Prospero came true. "The great Globe itself" dissolved. The timber burned speedily, and a noble edifice became a charred nothing. "See the world's ruins," said Ben. Nobody was injured, though one man's breeches were set on fire and quickly doused with "pottle ale." But the material loss to the King's Men must have been heartbreaking. Besides the fair structure itself there were all those costumes and properties, all those play scripts. Who knows what plays of Shakespeare himself, unpublished in quarto, failed to enter the 1623 Folio because they perished with the Globe?

Another Globe was to be built, but it would not concern the living Shakespeare. The fire of 1613 marked the end of his career. He had put so much of himself into the life of that playhouse that its destruction was like the destruction of a faculty or a limb. It was time to go home in earnest.

20

Will

The old actor had nearly three years to wait for his final call. Meanwhile it was a choice between something like the justice, in fair round belly with good capon lined, and the lean and slippered pantaloon. Somehow we cannot see him as a Shallow. He was closer to linen-filching Autolycus than a country gentleman ought to be. And we cannot see him following the sports of the rural *rentier*—hare-hunting and deer-slaying. He was always on the side of the hunted and slain. Gentleman was, to him, less a rank than a role. No artist of any stature can ever be wholly a gentleman. The demon comes out at the parish council meeting; there are stories of drunkenness in the public bar.

But Shakespeare was a countryman by birth, and his knowledge of flowers and trees and the habits of small creatures could be refreshed in this time of leisure. There was nothing more to be gained from books; perhaps even the gods and goddesses and classical heroes lived only for him now on the painted and embroidered hangings that covered the walls of New Place. I feel that in the last years he took music more seriously than he had been able to in his working days. He had known musicians like Thomas Morley, who had set some of his play lyrics and, indeed, been his near neighbor in Bishopsgate, but that craft so close to his own had been something of a mystery. Now was the time to learn more about it.

He had, in *Love's Labor's Lost*, composed a musical theme of six notes and given it to Holofernes. Curiously, no musician has ever taken that theme up and developed it. C D G A E F—it is suitable for a ground bass; it can be extended into a fugal subject. If we repeat it a tritone higher or lower, we have a perfect twelve-tone *Grundstimmung* for a serial composition. We are still waiting for Variations on a Theme by William Shakespeare.

I see, or rather hear, the Shakespeare family sitting around the table in the drawing room of New Place, with one of those madrigal scores open before them. These were printed in such a way that a part was readable from any one of four angles. Susanna, I think, was a clear soprano, a clever sight-reader. Judith had not much of a voice and was so slow at picking up a part that she became a dumb listener. Hall, the son-in-law, was a bass. Anne was a grave contralto. Will was certainly a tenor.

If he wanted to talk about literature, he would welcome visits from Michael Drayton. Over the Avon, in the village of Clifford Chambers, there was the house of Sir Henry and Lady Rainsford, and Drayton stayed with them frequently. Indeed, Dr. Hall had cured him of a tertian fever there, giving him an emetic mixture whose fetid components were inadequately sweetened with syrup of violets. Both Sir Henry and his wife were good scholars, and Lady Rainsford had been the "Idea" of Drayton's early sonnets. Drayton was a year older than Will, but was not to die till 1631. At present he was working on a long topographical poem called *Polyolbion*, a celebration of the beauties of England, systematically set forth in the form of journeys up and down rivers, with references to historical events associated with the various places. Perhaps it had been Will's own *Henry V* that had inspired him to write his Agincourt poem, beginning "Fair stood the wind for France." And this ode to the Virginian colonizers had—and still has—the power to send a shiver of pleasure down the spine:

And in regions far,
  Such heroes bring ye forth
    As those from whom we came;
    And plant our name
Under that star
  Not known unto our North.

Shakespeare was well aware that the world was opening up. There was a flavor of new lands in *The Tempest*. While writing

Hamlet he probably remembered William Parry's *A New and Large Discourse of the Travels of Sir Anthony Shirley*, with its account of the true wonders to be seen on voyages, not the lies of inland sailors about men with three heads and talking fishes that climbed trees. Parry talked of "the resplendent and crystalline heavens over-canopying the earth," and Hamlet "of this most excellent canopy the air." To Parry the wonders beneath that air, so many still to be discovered, were a substitute for the heaven that men still sought. Hamlet knew that, however much this new curious enquiring breed, Renaissance man, became the paragon of animals, he would still have bad dreams.

Did Shakespeare concern himself much with the afterlife that, so the divines told him every Sunday, might be, unless God's infinite mercy interposed, all fire and blackness for men like players and playwrights who had followed the wrong path? To judge by his writings, he had none of Marlowe's vestigial fascination with religion. An eighteenth-century tradition tells us that he "died a Papist." It is as possible as that he died a lukewarm Anglican. But however he died, one cannot believe that in his last leisure he began to examine the claims of either faith with any seriousness. His works are the product of a Christian culture, but that culture, through its fixation on ancient Rome, had its pagan elements. The Catullan poems of Ben Jonson and the "tribe" of poets that he begot, enjoy dwelling on the endless night to come, the brief sunlit span which it is a present duty to enjoy. Shakespeare had had his span and, when the bright day was done, he was ready for the dark.

It was a gentleman's duty to make a will, and Will took the duty seriously. We cannot know whether he had a presentiment of his coming death, but it was in January 1616—two months before that event—that he made his first draft. He had written his plays straight off, without drafts, but this was more important than a play. And between the first and final forms of his will certain things happened which impelled him to violent changes in it. The things that happened had to do with his daughter Judith.

The Stratford parish register has this entry: "1616, Feb. 10, M. Tho. Queeny tow Judith Shakspere." So, then, at the age of nearly thirty-one, Judith at last married. Her bridegroom was twenty-seven. His name was usually spelt Quiney; it was a name well known to Stratford and the Shakespeares. Richard Quiney, Thomas's father, had been a neighbor and friend—a decent sober man, not too well off. He had been a vintner and twice mayor of the borough—in 1592 and in 1601. In 1598 he was in London, staying at the Bell Inn in Carter Lane, E.C.4, and there he wrote the only surviving begging letter to his more successful fellow citizen. He wanted a loan of thirty pounds to help him "out of all the debettes which I owe in London." He got the money but, Will being Will, must certainly have had to pay it back. He died in 1602, leaving his wine business in the hands of his widow, who was helped by her son Thomas. Thomas took the lease of a tavern, a useful outlet for the wine that came all that way from London or Bristol, and, as a publican, considered it was time he had a wife. He chose Judith Shakespeare.

Marriage to a tavern-keeper was scarcely what Will would have chosen for his younger daughter, especially as it was—like his own—a marriage conducted in suspicious haste. The haste is attested by the fact that February 10 came within the period for special licenses. The special license that had been obtained for Will and Anne, all those years before, had been obtained in a regular manner and from the proper authority—the Bishop of Worcester. But Thomas Quiney got his license from the Stratford vicar, and apparently this was so irregular that he (and not, as would have been just, the vicar) was summoned to the consistory court at Worcester. He refused to go, or forgot, and was fined and excommunicated. This was not a very good start to the state of holy matrimony.

The hasty wedding was not the result of what Will, remembering the reason for his own, had most cause to suspect. Judith was not pregnant. But a certain Margaret Wheelar had yielded to the incontinent Quiney some nine months before, and this—a month or so after the wedding—came sordidly into the open. Mistress Wheelar and her newborn child had died and were buried on March 15, 1616. On March 26, with the lawyer Greene, Will's former lodger, as prosecuting counsel, Quiney confessed in court that he had had "carnal intercourse with the said Wheelar" and was conventionally sorry about it. He had good reason for being genuinely sorry for, the day before the trial, his father-in-law had altered his will drastically, much reducing poor Judith's expectation. She was to be punished for her unwise match. But the unwise match was to prove punishment enough.

Thomas was ordered to make public penance. He was to appear in the parish church on three successive Sundays, wearing a white sheet, so that the preacher could denounce him in such terms as "See how the sin of the fornicator is rebuked by the hue of holy purity that he weareth." The fornicator got out of this by paying a very reasonable fine of five shillings, and the Stratfordians—except for the Shakespeares, the Halls, and the wretched six-weeks bride—were disappointed of three delicious spasms of *Schadenfreude*. Thomas was evidently not a good man. He had married into the Shakespeare family under false pretenses. He had failed to produce his share of the marriage settlement—one hundred pounds in land. Later, he was to be fined for swearing and for allowing drunkenness on his premises. There is a tradition that he deserted his wife, but there is no evidence of it. His date and place of death are not known. His tavern was called, appropriately for Judith, the Cage. The site now houses a hamburger bar. No dignity for either of them, even three hundred years after the death, in 1662, of Judith, a tough woman who had survived much degradation.

It was to her elder sister that Shakespeare willed all his personal property, New Place, two houses on Henley Street, a house in Blackfriars, London, and "all my other landes and tenementes and hereditamentes whatsoever." These were entailed on Susanna's eldest son—Will was still hoping—or, failing a son, her male heir, this being Dr. John Hall if he survived her. (He did not: he died in 1635, and Susanna lived on till 1649.) Thereafter there was an entail on the sons of Judith, but she herself did badly. She was bequeathed a dowry of one hundred pounds and, if she forwent her claim to the

Chapel Lane cottage, she would be entitled to another fifty. If she or any child of hers should be living three years after the signing of the will, then another hundred and fifty pounds would be forthcoming. But she would not be entitled to touch this as capital; she must be satisfied with the interest on it. Her husband was to have no right to handle any of this money unless he settled land of the same value on his wife or their children.

Shakespeare's longing for a grandson was not to be satisfied in his lifetime. Judith gave birth to a son in November 1616, but he died in infancy. He was named Shaxper. Another son, Richard, was born in February 1618, and he died at the age of twenty-one, leaving no issue. The third son, and last child, was Thomas, born in January 1620; he was dead at nineteen. Elizabeth, Susanna's daughter and only child, was to marry twice but bear no children. Only Joan Hart, Will's sister, was able to pump male Shakespeare blood to posterity. Her grandson George begot a Joan, a Susanna, and a Shakespeare. But Will himself was almost supernaturally unlucky in the male seed that sprang ultimately from his own loins.

Elizabeth Hall had, as second husband, a knight—Sir John Barnard. At last something better than minimal gentility entered the family, but far too late for Will to know of it. Lady Elizabeth, as last lineal descendant, took over the Shakespeare property and bequeathed it, in equal portions, to the Harts and the Hathaways. This seems fair. Shakespeare Hart was thus to gain more than a name from his namesake, though how much we do not know. For that matter, we have no knowledge of the value of Will's personalty—whether it was hundreds or thousands. John Ward, who became vicar of Stratford in the year of Judith's death, heard that Shakespeare "spent at the rate of a thousand pounds a year"—a great deal of money. Whatever he spent, it would not be on expendables, and we can be quite sure he did not overspend.

With the name Hathaway chiming in our ears, we come to the mystery of Will's bequest to his widow. He left her "the second-best bed" and nothing else. Whatever the significance of that solitary item, his provisions for her were less harsh than they seem. She had her widow's dower at common law, and her dowager's place in the great house that Susanna and her husband took over. She was content to live with Susanna and she got on well enough with her son-in-law. The second-best bed was installed in a particular chamber, and this chamber was to be inalienably hers. The best bed was in the master bed-chamber, and the inheritrix took that by right. It was thus a means of clarifying accommodation. To show Will in an un-pleasant light, we can prefer to believe that the second-best bed was the double bed she brought from Shottery, and all he did was to give her what was already hers. This implies a failure of love, an absence of love, a detestation long hidden from the world, a desire to humiliate from the grave. Let us try to keep Will likable.

The end came in April 1616. The Rev. John Ward's note-books tell of a "merrie meeting" with Michael Drayton and Ben Jonson. Shakespeare ate too many pickled herrings and drank too much Rhenish wine. He sweated, took cold, and died. If the cause of death was really overindulgence, then Dr. Hall was showing proper discretion in making no entry about it in his casebook. Will may have been weak already—from venereal disease, from a seasonal cold, from Bürger's arterial blockage or anything we wish to wish upon him. He was tired with a life's overwork, depressed about his daughter's marriage: the life-urge may not have been too strong in that last spring. He was, perhaps, not overdisposed to take care of himself. He may have drunk with abandon, encouraged by Ben, then sweated in a hot room, walked out hatless and cloakless to speed his guests on their way, pooh-poohed warnings of the danger of a chill April night. A quick attack of pneumonia, which his son-in-law's emetics and electuaries would do nothing to relieve, was enough to effect his quietus. That Drayton and Ben assisted at a vinous session of nostalgia I am ready to accept. Drayton was often in the district. Ben may not have felt disposed to ride north from London solely to see an old friend, but he walked to Scotland in 1618 and may have started a walk in 1616. Stratford would be a natural calling-place. Discouraged by Will's death, he may have ridden back to London and postponed his weight-reducing feat. The death took place on April 23. If that, as we are taught, was also Will's birthday, then he had lived just fifty-two years. The parish record gives the date of his burial as April 25, 1616, and refers to him as "Will. Shakespere, gent."

He was buried, as was his right, in Holy Trinity Church. His bust is a travesty, but the sculptor must have believed that Shakespeare looked plump, complacent, and faintly imbecilic. The inscription, of anonymous composition, runs:

GOOD FREND FOR IESVS SAKE FORBEARE,
TO DIGG THE DVST ENCLOASED HEARE.
BLESTE BE YE MAN YT SPARES THES STONES,
AND CVRST BE HE YT MOVES MY BONES.

This is a doggerel of the order of Gower's chorus speeches in *Pericles, Prince of Tyre*. It is, nevertheless, moving in a way that an appropriate quotation from one of the great plays would not be. The curse is rather frightening. It is good to know that we are all blessed. Except, perhaps, biographers, whose curse is to find that the bones, once moved, refuse to live. If Shakespeare himself wrote the lines, which is more than doubtful, then they are the only ones of his that contain—undistorted, and in a context of piety—the name Jesus.

Anne's last office was to place pennies on his eyes. Then she settled quietly into widowhood. In 1623 she died, at the age of sixty-seven. In the same year, but just too late for Anne to see it (she may not, of course, have been particularly interested), the First Folio appeared. This was the work of John Heminge (or Heming or Hemings or Heminges) and Henry Condell, those friends and colleagues of Will's, to whom, following the custom of the time, he had left money for the purchase of mourning rings. It contains all the plays of which Shakespeare was the sole, or main, author, but it omits *Pericles* and does not include *Troilus and Cressida* in the "Catalogue" or list of contents. This latter omission may have been because there was some difficulty in wresting the right to reprint from the quarto publisher, a difficulty resolved only when the folio was already in the press. *Troilus* appears as the first of the tragedies, though it was meant for a comedy.

The great work was an act of posthumous devotion, and the world can never be grateful enough. King James was the luckiest of monarchs: the two most important books in the English language both appeared in his reign, with only twelve years between them. The First Folio is the compilation of theatre men, not scholarly editors, and in it we have the texts—though often botched and disfigured—which the King's Men themselves used. The book is dedicated to the Earl of Pembroke and the Earl of Montgomery, but the "Great Variety of Readers" are not forgotten. In a charming and witty address to these, "Iohn Heminge" and "Henrie Condell" tell of their old companion's fluency in writing: "His mind and hand went together: And what he thought, he vttered with that easinesse, that wee haue scarse receiued from him a blot in his papers." Ben Jonson, in a later reminiscence, wished that Will had gone in for blots more than he did. He was too ready, too much a river of words: *sufflaminandus erat*—he needed to be curbed, slowed down, cooled, quenched.

But the friend rather than the critic appears in the memorial ode which is Ben's contribution to the preliminaries of the First Folio. Here he is noble, brilliant, affectionate, magnanimous, laudatory with neither reserve nor fulsomeness. He knew the worth of the man he called "my beloved"; not many had yet properly assessed it. To many, Shakespeare was as good as Fletcher or Chapman, certainly better than Dekker, a fine enough playwright but no eternal glory blazing in the firmament. To Ben, he was "not of an age, but for all time," a dramaturge to be compared with Euripides and Sophocles for tragedy and Aristophanes and Terence for comedy. And yet, for all his stage-shaking thunder and the lance of his wit, the "Sweet Swan of Auon" remains "gentle Shakespeare"—reserved, amiable, *generosus*.

Shakespeare is still "gentle" in the caption to Martin Droeshout's engraving, which appears as frontispiece. The picture has never been greatly liked. Lord Brain, the scientist, says that it has two right eyes. *The Tailor and Cutter* observed that the coat has two left sides. The face is the face of a commercial traveler growing bald in the service of an ungrateful firm. If it ever appeared, the back hair suitably cropped, with a decent subfusc suit below it, in the saloon bar of a Stratford pub, it would hardly be noticed.

We need not repine at the lack of a satisfactory Shakespeare portrait. To see his face we need only look in a mirror. He is ourselves, ordinary suffering humanity, fired by moderate ambitions, concerned with money, the victim of desire, all too mortal. To his back, like a hump, was strapped a miraculous but somehow irrelevant talent. It is a talent which, more than any other that the world has seen, reconciles us to being human beings, unsatisfactory hybrids, not good enough for gods and not good enough for animals. We are all Will. Shakespeare is the name of one of our redeemers.

Index

Anthony Burgess

A Dead Man
In Deptford

The whole world of Elizabethan England is brilliantly recreated in Anthony Burgess's novel, a joyous celebration of the life of Christopher Marlowe, murdered in highly suspicious circumstances in a tavern brawl in Deptford four hundred years ago.

'Burgess's life-long love affair with the English language finds its consummation here in a rich and moving piece of art'
John Banville, *Observer*

'Burgess...still blazes as some sort of comet entire to himself, spinning through galactic dictionaries and returning again and again to give us sighting. Long may he continue to fly'
Melvyn Bragg, *Evening Standard*

'This is not just a very good novel; it may well be Mr Burgess's masterpiece'
Robert Carver, *New Statesman*

V

VINTAGE

BY ANTHONY BURGESS
AVAILABLE IN VINTAGE

☐ BYRNE	£5.99
☐ A DEAD MAN IN DEPTFORD	£5.99
☐ ANY OLD IRON	£6.99
☐ THE DEVIL'S MODE	£5.99
☐ FUTURE IMPERFECT	£6.99
☐ MOZART AND THE WOLF GANG	£5.99
☐ NOTHING LIKE THE SUN	£5.99
☐ A MOUTHFUL OF AIR	£7.99

---

* All Vintage books are available through mail order or from your local bookshop.
* Please send cheque/eurocheque/postal order (sterling only), Access, Visa or Mastercard:

☐☐☐☐☐☐☐☐☐☐☐☐☐☐☐☐

Expiry Date:_____ Signature:_____

Please allow 75 pence per book for post and packing U.K.
Overseas customers please allow £1.00 per copy for post and packing.

ALL ORDERS TO:
Vintage Books, Book Service by Post, P.O.Box 29, Douglas, Isle of Man, IM99 1BQ.
Tel: 01624 675137 • Fax: 01624 670923

NAME:_____

ADDRESS:_____

_____

_____

Please allow 28 days for delivery. Please tick box if you do not
wish to receive any additional information
Prices and availability subject to change without notice.